DOCUMENTS DEPARTMENT

CALIFORNIA LEGISLATURE

Ninth Report of the Senate Fact-Finding Committee on Un-American Activities

1957

MEMBERS OF THE COMMITTEE

SENATOR NATHAN F. COOMBS, *Vice Chairman* SENATOR JOHN F. McCARTHY
SENATOR EARL D. DESMOND SENATOR JOHN F. THOMPSON
SENATOR HUGH M. BURNS, *Chairman*
R. E. COMBS, *Counsel*

MARY E. HOPE, *Executive Secretary*
ELIZABETH W. NIELSEN, *Secretary*

Published by the
SENATE
OF THE STATE OF CALIFORNIA

LIEUTENANT GOVERNOR HAROLD J. POWERS
President of the Senate

HUGH M. BURNS   JOSEPH A. BEEK
President pro Tempore   *Secretary*

LETTER OF TRANSMITTAL

SENATE CHAMBER, STATE CAPITOL
SACRAMENTO, May 30, 1957

HON. HAROLD J. POWERS
President of the Senate, and Gentlemen of the Senate;
Senate Chamber, Sacramento, California

MR. PRESIDENT AND GENTLEMEN OF THE SENATE: Pursuant to Senate Resolution No. 121, which appears at page 4324 of the Senate Journal for June 8, 1955, the Senate Fact-Finding Committee on Un-American Activities was created and the following Members of the Senate were appointed to said committee by the Senate Committee on Rules: Senator Nathan F. Coombs, Senator Earl D. Desmond, Senator John F. McCarthy, Senator John F. Thompson, Senator Hugh M. Burns.

The committee herewith submits a report of its investigation, findings, and recommendations.

Respectfully submitted,

HUGH M. BURNS, Chairman
NATHAN F. COOMBS, Vice Chairman
EARL D. DESMOND
JOHN F. MCCARTHY
JOHN F. THOMPSON

TABLE OF CONTENTS

FOREWORD

With the issuance of this report, the Committee on Un-American Activities completes 17 years of activity. During that time it has endeavored to change its methods of operation to match the changing techniques of the Communist Party. To those who may be unfamiliar with some of the subversive problems we have faced, it should be made clear that while Communism is by far our greatest subversive danger, we have by no means neglected the Fascists and myriads of lesser subversive movements.

In earliest reports we have described investigations of the German-American Bund, the Italian Fascists, the Japanese subversive organizations, the Ku Klux Klan, Friends of Progress, Mankind United, and many others. We shall continue to investigate and expose subversion, Communist or otherwise, wherever we can find it and to the fullest extent our jurisdiction will permit. In this connection, it is appropriate to point out that legislative committees on un-American activities do not exist for the sole purpose of recommending legislation. They, like other interim committees, are established primarily to keep the Legislature accurately informed of current conditions by holding investigations, developing facts and making reports. Our mandate authorizes us to report both to the Legislature and to the people. We have also recommended the enactment of much legislation, but this is only one of the functions of a legislative committee.

Fifteen years ago, the public apathy towards subversive activities in general, and Communism in particular, was our greatest problem. The Communists of that era, flushed with success, were acting defiantly, openly, and with brazen impertinence. The uninterested public almost took the Communists for granted as a part of the American way of life. Many departments of our State Government, our educational institutions, our trade unions, our basic industries, and the entertainment and cultural fields were literally becoming saturated with fanatic Communists, dedicated to subverting and destroying us from within.

So effective was their propaganda that many intellectuals were actually afraid to be anything but "progressive"; and a conservative college professor was regarded with suspicion and contempt by his "liberal" colleagues.

Operating in that atmosphere was quite different from the operation of our committee today. In that era, we had fist fights and disturbances deliberately staged to disrupt our hearings. We were picketed, booed, intimidated, insulted, and threatened. Frequently, there was no choice but to eject the trouble-makers by force or suffer them to completely take over our public hearings. We elected to eject them, of course. Then would come the inevitable propaganda barrage, accusing the committee of crude sensationalism, strong-arm tactics, and of destroying civil rights.

Naturally, the more sensational aspects of such hearings received the enthusiastic attention of the press. Most of the papers printed objective accounts, but as any informed reporter of that day was aware, the Communists had infiltrated the press to some degree, and a few of the accounts were anything but factual.

As the exposures continued, the press began to clean house. Throughout the committee's entire existence the newspapers of California have been overwhelmingly fair, objective and sympathetic to our work. In fact, the Hearst press, during the early era described above, became such a constant source of irritation to the Communist movement, that it became the target of a special front organization. This front, called The National People's Committee Against Hearst, operated from Room 701, 268 Fourth Avenue, New York City. Some of its more active sponsors included Clarence Hathaway, Carol Weiss King, Freda Kirchwey, Robert Morss Lovett, Vito Marcantonio, and Maxwell S. Stewart.

In this report we devote considerable space to the Abrams case at U. C. L. A. The alert, vigorous, and intelligent coverage of this hearing in Los Angeles by every paper (except the *Daily People's World*) and the wire services amply demonstrates the interest and ability of the press in this field.

During recent years, the Communist Party, after being harried, investigated, and exposed by various state and federal agencies, retreated to underground positions. A part of the organization was left to operate above ground—directing the front groups, running the three book stores in this State, manning the picket lines, and handling the propaganda. It became increasingly difficult to flush the more important Communists from the dark recesses of their underground sanctuaries. No party membership cards have been issued since 1947, and the infiltration of non-Communist institutions has recently been conducted with the greatest of care.

But investigative techniques can also be changed to meet new conditions. Hitherto untapped sources of information are now being utilized and the party is realizing that it must accelerate its propaganda and recruiting to save itself from the stagnation of inactivity. This, in turn, has resulted in a resumption of open action and a consequent vulnerability to exposure. As we have remarked before, there can be no such thing as a really inactive Communist. Even the "sleepers" lie dormant, but strictly according to plan, ready to spring into action at the proper time.

Since the Khrushchev speech of February 14, 1956; the downgrading of Stalin; the slaughters in Poland and Hungary; the dissolution of the Cominform, and the widely publicized defections of many party members in this country, we are tending toward a lapse into the easy apathy of 15 years ago. But parents of at least two former U. C. L. A. students, whose bodies were found near that university, cannot be expected to be apathetic toward the Communist menace. Nor are the officials of the Los Angeles City Board of Education. Nor is the Board of Directors of the San Francisco Public Library. Nor are the heads of public utilities in this State. All have recently come into rude, awakening contact with the Communist apparatus. Each of these experiences is detailed in the pages of this report. These experiences are merely examples of many, and should serve as eloquent warnings that the Communist menace is more dedicated now than ever before.

Our greatest danger now is our tendency to relax vigilance and sink back into the old apathy.

There is no more sincere, conscientious, accurate source of information in this field than J. Edgar Hoover, Director of the Federal Bureau of Investigation. This is what he said on March 12, 1957, to the Senate Judiciary Subcommittee on Internal Security:

> "The Communist Party before and after its 1957 convention is part and parcel of the worldwide Communist conspiracy. It is still responsive to the will of Moscow; it still works for the destruction of the American way of life; and it still is dedicated to the building of a Soviet United States patterned after the basic concepts of Marxism-Leninism.
>
> "The changes in the party's constitution, organization, and announced public objectives are designed to bring to an end a period of isolation from the American public caused by the disclosures of their tactics and objectives. Should it succeed in further hoodwinking certain people, as it has with some success since the convention, then it will emerge stronger than it ever was and more dangerous to the peace and security of the United States.
>
> "Contrary to statements issued by its spokesmen, the Communist Party in the United States has not severed its ties from the Soviet Union but, on the other hand, has consolidated its position consistent with the Soviet Union's 'New Look.'
>
> "The Communist Party's 1957 convention was designed to hoodwink the public with a 'New Look.' Its program is designed to enable them to develop a militant assault to accomplish their 'historic mission' of wrecking and infiltrating this Nation.
>
> "It is the Communist technique to lull a peaceful people into a sense of false complacency with 'The New Look' and 'The Big Smile.' That is an old Communist trick which is being demonstrated almost daily by Communists the world over. Even the gullible were sickened by the savagery of the Soviet Communists' attack on Hungary and the realization that Khrushchev and nine of his associates in highest offices in Russia were executioners for Stalin. In the United States it is the same old story. Foster, Dennis, and their gang of Soviet-directed puppets still control the American Communist Party and still hop to the old Leninist refrains which require—
>
> > 'The strictest loyalty to the ideas of Communism must be combined with the ability to make all the necessary practical compromises, to tack, to make agreements, zigzags, retreats, and so on— * * *'
>
> "We should judge the Communist Party for what it is, not what it says it is, but by its deeds."

THE ABRAMS CASE

HISTORY OF COMMUNIST INFILTRATION AT U. C. L. A.

The Communist Party of the United States was created as the result of a meeting which was held at Chicago, Illinois, in September, 1919. Shortly thereafter, the communist high command in this country divided the entire United States into 20 Communist districts, of which California, Arizona, and Nevada comprised District 13. Headquarters for this district was situated in San Francisco on Grove Street, later moved to 121 Haight Street in that city, and is now designated by a sign which reads, "CP of Calif.," which is displayed on the wall in the foyer of a building at 942 Market Street in San Francisco. The main office of the *Daily People's World*, Communist Newspaper for District 13, has always been situated in San Francisco; so has the principal source of its printed propaganda, which is disseminated up and down the Pacific coast through the medium of the International Book Store in the 1400 block on Market Street, and which also supplies subsidiary outlets such as the Twentieth Century Book Shop in Berkeley and the Progressive Book Shop at 1806 W. Seventh Street in Los Angeles.

It would appear only natural that since the Communist Party must have a continuous supply of intellectual leaders it should draw this type of personnel from the universities of the country. District 13 headquarters, being situated in close proximity to one of the world's greatest universities, lost little time in establishing its faculty and student units on the campus of the University of California in Berkeley. Recruiting activities among both faculty and students were simultaneously being conducted at other educational institutions at the university level throughout the State, but for several years the party concentrated most of its attention in that regard on the university at Berkeley.

The committee, in previous reports, has described how an organization known as the International Federation of Architects, Engineers, Chemists and Technicians established a chapter of its organization in Alameda County and proceeded to infiltrate its Communist members into positions of exceedingly important and secret scientific research; how Steve Nelson was sent to California from the east coast and immediately set about to build an espionage apparatus for the purpose of endeavoring to get our atomic bomb secrets; the committee has also described the activities of the Soviet vice consulate in San Francisco, as the headquarters for the espionage apparatus operating in the Bay area, and has done its best to alert university administrators throughout the State to the constant menace of Communist recruiting and infiltration among both faculty and students.

For a period of about 10 years, commencing in the early thirties and ending in the early forties, the Communist Party was most interested in conducting its overt activities at the university in Berkeley. There were demonstrations off the university campus in front of Sather Gate, there were strong *Young Communist League* units planted throughout the student body, there was a constant barrage of propaganda, both in mimeographed form and through the columns of *The Daily Californian*, student newspaper, and the names of professors who should have had more loyalty and better sense adorned list after list of the sponsors of Communist front organizations. In 1941 and 1942, however, it became necessary for the Communist espionage apparatus to go to work in deadly earnest for the purpose of trying to steal our atomic bomb secrets. Since a great deal of the pioneer work in that direction was being conducted by scientists at the University of California at Berkeley, and since the ubiquitous Mr. Steve Nelson and his followers had gone to great pains to perfect an espionage underground, it became necessary to soft-pedal the open activities of the party so far as recruiting and agitation were concerned, for the purpose of keeping public attention away from the more important business of infiltrating our secret laboratories and research projects.

Consequently, the open activities of the party and its mass recruiting techniques were suddenly switched to the University of California at Los Angeles. Almost overnight there was a peculiar quiet and serenity at Berkeley and a simultaneous opening of agitation and activity on the campus of the university in Los Angeles.

There are certain infallible evidences of Communist activity in any college or university. It is obviously impossible for the small group of student Communists and their adult advisers to exert very much propaganda effect on the great mass of students if they are compelled to use the direct contact technique. Consequently, the Communist minority always endeavors to get its members elected to positions of control on student newspapers. Thus, one or two dedicated, hardworking young Communists can capture the editorial control of a medium for propagandizing that reaches every student in the university and most of the faculty members. If, at the same time, the faculty members who are also Communists, do everything in their power to foster the free-wheeling radical flavor of the student publication and to protect the young Communists who control it, an entire university can be gradually saturated in an atmosphere of radicalism and tolerance toward Communist front organizations and propaganda in general. This is precisely what happened at U. C. L. A., as we will see during the development of the circumstances surrounding the peculiar death of Sheldon Abrams, a graduate student at that institution.

The committee had previously investigated the circumstances concerning an even more mysterious death which occurred to an undergraduate student, Everitt Hudson. This case was described in detail by the committee in its 1951 report, and since many of its aspects are also applicable to the death of Sheldon Abrams, a brief resume of the Hudson case is appropriate here.

DEATH OF EVERITT HUDSON

Everitt Hudson, the only son of Mr. and Mrs. W. A. Hudson of Beverly Hills, got his first infusion of Marxian propaganda while he was a student at the University High School. Thereafter, he enrolled as an undergraduate student at Stanford University and while at that institution was induced to become a member of the Communist Party.

Young Hudson had an amazing aptitude for languages, being fluent in Italian, Spanish, and French, and having mastered Chinese, Japanese, and Russian while attending the Military Intelligence Language School at Monterey, California. Previously, young Hudson, when inducted into the Army and compelled to disrupt his university career, had been sent to Fort Knox, Kentucky. From there he wrote gloomy letters to his parents, sprinkled with pessimistic observations about the American way of life which were couched in the peculiar phraseology of one fairly steeped in Marxism. After returning to Stanford, young Hudson was groomed for an important Communist position abroad, due to his unusual aptitude for languages and his apparently thorough indoctrination as a Communist. He moved in important circles both on the Stanford University campus and also in the immediate vicinity, where he attended evening meetings graced by the presence of high ranking Communist party members who were eager to develop young Hudson to a point where he would be ready to operate as a Communist agent. They were too eager, as it turned out, and tried to develop the boy far too rapidly. He became apprehensive and disillusioned, disobeyed the party's order to remain at Stanford and transferred to U. C. L. A.

Shortly before he left Stanford he wrote a letter to his parents which was a normal, chatty letter that could have been written by any university student to his parents. In it Hudson stated that he intended to go horseback riding over the coming weekend. He did not mail the letter until the following Monday, and added a postscript in which he said he was somewhat sore as a result of his horseback riding experience, and then added that in the event of his death he wanted his body examined immediately to ascertain the cause. He said that this was not because he was particularly apprehensive, but something he insisted be done in the event "anything happens." It is a general rule in Communist circles that if one member of a family is converted to Communism, he must either convert the other members of the family or move out of the home. The Communist theory is that none of its members should be permitted to live in a bourgeois environment because it is utterly incompatible with their new Communist way of life. Accordingly, young Hudson tried to indoctrinate his parents. He even brought a Communist functionary to see them in an endeavor to interest them in the movement. Failing this, Hudson moved out of the family home and took up his residence in Robison Hall, a cooperative dormitory located off the U. C. L. A. campus.

No sooner had Hudson enrolled as a student at U. C. L. A. than he immediately identified himself with known Communists at that institution, among them Joseph Price, Lola Whang, and Helen Edelman. Miss Edelman was one of the editors of the student newspaper, and an admitted member of the Communist Party. After leaving college she became a writer for the Communist newspaper in San Francisco, and thereafter contributed some pieces to the *Daily Worker* in New York.

One evening young Hudson took Price and the two girls in his automobile to a Communist meeting in Los Angeles. This affair was addressed by Elizabeth Gurley Flynn, then a member of the National Committee of the Communist Party of the United States and in charge of all of its women's activities throughout the country. Miss Flynn now stands convicted under the Smith Act for having been a leader in an organization advocating the unlawful overthrow of the Government of the United States.

On the following morning the body of young Hudson was found in a basement near the lounge of the dormitory, and an autopsy by the Los Angeles County Coroner's office failed to disclose any cause of death. The committee managed to obtain possession of copies of letters Hudson had written to some of his Communist contacts, and also obtained several original letters, including a death threat, which he had received from a Communist named Bipan Chandra, an Indian exchange student at Stanford with whom Hudson had roomed for a time. There were many other papers and documents relating to Communism found among the decedent's effects, all of which showed the extent of Communist activity at U. C. L. A., and the committee later discovered that Hudson had committed the fatal mistake of telling a friend that he had become apprehensive because he had gotten so far in the Communist movement, and intended to get out as soon as possible. There was also an indication that he had a feeling he should tell the authorities about his experiences, particularly those that developed after he had ceased being an ordinary rank and file Communist Party member, and had progressed through the upper echelons toward his ultimate destiny of becoming a Communist agent.

With the cooperation of university authorities, the committee held a hearing on the Hudson case in 1950, and for further details concerning it, the reader's attention is directed to the committee's 1951 report.

At this point, it may be well to indicate that not only can the extent of Communist infiltration among students and faculty members be gauged with a fair degree of accuracy by an analysis of the type of propaganda that appears in the student newspaper, but also the extent of such activities may be gauged by ascertaining the extent to which faculty members are actively collaborating with the Communist organizations on the campus. It is a relatively simple matter to ferret out the prominent members of the young Communist organizations; but it is a much more difficult problem to get accurate information about the Communist affiliations and activities of faculty members. No teacher or faculty member is permitted by the Communist Party to praise Communism in the classroom or to criticize the institutions of the Government of the United States. Such activities would bring immediate suspicion against the individual involved, and lead to his removal, something that would be extremely costly to the Communist organization. Consequently, he is given an extremely thorough and clever course of instruction by Communist experts in this field, as a result of which he learns how to inject the Communist Party line into his lectures without attracting undue suspicion to himself. By subtly guiding student discussion along the proper lines, the carefully-trained instructor can mold his course along lines that will nudge his students farther and farther toward the left and into a more and more critical attitude toward the American way of life and a more tolerant attitude toward a world government led by the Soviet Union.

But student radicals are notoriously as careless as their adult Communist instructors are careful. It is a relatively simple matter, we repeat, to find out who the young Communists are at any educational institution. These young students are far too busy with their Communist activities to pay much attention to the matter of maintaining a sufficiently high academic standard to keep them in the institution. Consequently, they are told to take certain courses from designated instructors. Thus, one may secure the curriculum of a given student from the recorder's office of his university and will find that in the courses where he makes the best grades and does the least work, there is a common faculty denominator. These common faculty demoninators are also present in the courses taken by all the other young Communist leaders who are majoring in the same general field. Hence, by a simple process of elimination, one is led to a system of collaboration between adult and student Communists at the same institution.

Commencing about 1942, and continuing on a scale of steadily increasing virulence, the Communist infiltration at U. C. L. A. reached its climax during the school year 1949-1950. As will be seen from excerpts taken from the testimony of Dean Milton Hahn, Dean of Students at U. C. L. A., this intensification of the problem was accurately reflected in the columns of the student newspaper, *The Daily Bruin*. The testimony of Chancellor Raymond Allen also discloses the fact that while he was president of the University of Washington, the same increasing incidence of Communist infiltration and activity at that institution was reflected through the columns of the student newspaper there, although, because the paper was somewhat unique in its operation and editorial policy, it did not provide as active a barometer as does a paper wholly operated by the students and therefore more susceptible to infiltration and control by a handful of hardworking young Communists who are carefully guided by adults and who succeed in molding the editorial policy of the publication and bending it to their own subversive purposes. At U. C. L. A., the editorial policy of the paper had been taken over by such a group of radical young Communists, and they became so firmly entrenched that their clique became self-perpetuating, through a system of electing successive editors and assistant editors.

In preparing the Abrams hearing, the committee obtained files of *The Daily Bruin* extending back to the early '40's, and has carefully analyzed the propaganda content thereof. In complete corroboration of the testimony given by Dean of Students Milton E. Hahn, the committee found that there was a steadily increasing incidence of subversive propaganda that appeared in the columns of the newspaper beginning in the early '40's and increasing until 1951, when there was a decrease in this type of material that has continued until the present time. Until 1951, the columns of the student paper were freely used by avowed members of young Communist organizations, such as American Youth for Democracy and the Labor Youth League, together with representatives of a wide variety of Communist youth front organizations. The atmosphere of radicalism had so permeated the campus by 1948 that U. C. L. A. was being sarcastically referred to as "the Little Red Schoolhouse at Westwood," and people became accustomed to seeing parades of student pickets marching back and forth near the university campus bearing placards and signs that were worded in precisely the same language as those carried by their adult comrades in picket lines elsewhere. Every effort on the part of university administrators to control this condition was met by a tirade of abuse and criticism by the highly articulate liberals—both student and faculty—accompanied by accusations of witch-hunting, thought-control, fascism and reactionism.

When the body of Everitt Hudson was discovered and the committee had completed its analysis of the documents found in his possession, it was decided that a hearing was mandatory. For more than a year the committee refrained from making any public disclosure concerning this case in order that the material which it turned over to Federal authorities could be thoroughly pursued without hindrance or embarrassment of any kind. In 1950, the committee opened its public hearings in Los Angeles, and in establishing the circumstances surrounding the recruitment of young Hudson into the Communist Party at Stanford, and his subsequent activities in the young Communist organization at U. C. L. A., the revelations caused a reaction on the part of university administrators and the public in general that quickly brought the matter to a climax. Thenceforth there was a noticeable decrease in Communist activities both at U. C. L. A. and at other universities throughout the State. We attribute this, in part, to public exposure of the grim consequences of Communist recruiting and indoctrination at educational institutions, and also to a realization on the part of university administrators that the anti-Communist policy established by the board of regents was not enough, but that it had to be implemented by firm and courageous action. President Sproul has since extended this committee every possible cooperation, and, as will be seen from the testimony of Chancellor Allen, designated every chancellor and every provost on the various campuses of the university as his representatives to maintain liaison with this committee in order that the university and the committee could exchange information and cooperate for the common purpose of eliminating subversive infiltration of the state university by a program of constant vigilance. This does not mean that the various campuses are now, or ever have been, subjected to snooping, stool pigeons, or any other operation on the part of either the committee or the university that would in any way stifle academic freedom—in the true sense of that term—or violate civil liberties.

Space does not permit the committee to set forth in this report copies of the various propaganda articles that appeared in *The Daily Bruin* during the 1940's. The articles have been copied and preserved and are now on file at the committee's office for the inspection of any properly qualified individual who may be interested in seeing the evidence. It is enough to point out that the paper was replete with articles defying university administrators, undermining and smearing anyone who presumed to oppose the editorial policy of the paper, in articles written by students who proudly proclaimed themselves as young Communists and leaders of Communist front groups, and a constant barrage of Communist and party line propaganda that appeared year after year, as the clique of young radicals perpetuated itself in control of the newspaper from one academic term to another.

SHELDON JOSEPH ABRAMS

Sheldon Joseph Abrams registered at U. C. L. A. on November 23, 1955, as a graduate student majoring in sociology. His application, filed with the university under No. 145450, set forth certain statistical facts, to wit: That he was born in Minneapolis, Minnesota, on December 25, 1930; that he was unmarried, then resided at 1429 Ocean Front, Santa Monica, California, and came to California in October, 1954; that he had attended high school at Chicago, Illinois, went to the University of Illinois for a short time during 1950, and completed his undergraduate work at Roosevelt College, Chicago, receiving a Bachelor of Arts degree from that institution as a sociology major in February of that year. His undergraduate studies included accounting, sociology, and psychology, and he maintained a uniformly high academic standard. Records at U. C. L. A. show that although he enrolled as a graduate student at that institution, he attended no classes and, as he expressed it in a letter, he had lost all interest in pursuing his academic career and was devoting himself exclusively to "politics."

In February, 1956, young Abrams rented a small apartment at 133 Wadsworth Street, Santa Monica, California, and on the morning of April 20, 1956, his dead body was found at that address in a room literally jammed with hundreds of Communist, Marxist, Socialist, and Trotskyite literature—comprising bound volumes, minutes of meetings, original letters received by the decedent and copies of letters sent by him to various contacts throughout the United States. These documents were scattered throughout the room in a state of complete confusion and disorder when the Santa Monica police arrived at the premises pursuant to a telephone call at approximately 8 o'clock a.m.

The details of the circumstances surrounding the death of Abrams are set forth at some length at the hearing which occurred in Los Angeles on December 10 and 11, 1956, excerpts from which are set forth below.

The evidence shows that while Abrams was an undergraduate student at Roosevelt College in Illinois, he interested himself in Marxism and Socialism to such an extent that he became extremely active as a member and functionary in the Young Socialist League. We wish to emphasize at this point that no official agency, so far as the committee is aware, has ever listed the Young Socialist League as subversive, and we found no evidence to indicate that young Abrams was a member of the Communist Party or any other subversive organization. As will be seen, the committee's prime interest was in meetings which Abrams was attending with top members of the Communist Party organization in Southern California, in an analysis of the documents found in his possession, and in the fact that he was sufficiently trusted by members of the Trotskyite movement, the Socialist Party, and the Communist Party, that he had been invited to participate at meetings which, according to his own records, were also attended by members of all of these movements.

Almost simultaneously with the arrival of Abrams at U. C. L. A. an obvious effort was being made to circumvent the university administration's attitude of opposition toward Communist infiltration of the paper and the university in general, an effort to conduct propaganda operations through Communist fronts, and to recapture the position that the Communist Party and other radical student groups had lost since the committee exposed the circumstances surrounding the death of Everitt Hudson in 1950.

The committee is also in possession of letters written to various people at U. C. L. A. castigating both Dean Hahn and Chancellor Raymond Allen because of their steadfast and firm attitude against Communist infiltration. Chancellor Allen, indeed, was one of the first university administrators in the United States to meet such a problem. While he was president of the University of Washington at Seattle a similar situation arose, three members of the university faculty were dismissed from the university, and President Allen wrote a book—the first of its kind—entitled "Communism and Academic Freedom." This book is a classic in its field, and the committee enthusiastically recommends it to all educational administrators.

THE ABRAMS HEARING

As a result of its investigation of the Abrams case, the committee opened a public hearing in Los Angeles at the State Building on December 10, 1956. Senator Hugh M. Burns, chairman of the committee, called the hearing to order with the following statement:

"Chairman Burns: The committee will come to order. This is the Senate Fact-finding Committee on Un-American Activities meeting today primarily for the purpose of going into a review of the events surrounding the death of a graduate student of the University of California at Los Angeles, chiefly to determine the progress of Communists and other subversive groups infiltrating into the field of higher education. We are conducting this hearing with the full cooperation of the university officials. We appreciate very much the fact that they have agreed to cooperate with the committee in going into all of the facts surrounding the death of Mr. Abrams.

"The committee is made up of the following: John F. McCarthy of Marin County; I represent Fresno County and the State Senate. We will open the hearing as a subcommittee.

"General counsel for the committee, Mr. R. E. Combs, is in attendance today. He will make a preliminary statement which may be enlightening to you and to the members of the press.

"Mr. Combs: Mr. Chairman and Senator McCarthy, the attention of the committee was directed to documents that were found in the premises occupied by the decedent, Sheldon Abrams. An examination of those documents discloses a change in the Communist Party line not only in California but also throughout the United States. That is the primary object of this hearing. All of those documents have been correlated, analyzed, and compared with documents that came into the possession of the committee at least six months prior to the death of Abrams, which occurred on the twentieth of last April.

"Tomorrow, the committee will introduce copies of the Cominform Bulletin from Bucharest, copies of the monthly ideological publication of the Communist Party of the United States entitled *Political Affairs,* also copies of the *Daily Worker* and the *People's World,* so that they may be compared with the documents found in the possession of Mr. Abrams. Those documents will establish a fact which should not be obscured by the dramatic circumstances which may be disclosed concerning Abrams' death. So far as we have been able to discover, and we have been as diligent as we could possibly be, these documents found in the possession of young Abrams will show the first active implementation of a new international Communist Party line that has occurred in the United States. The records should also show that the committee has no evidence that Abrams was in any way a member of or was associated with the Communist Party or any other subversive organizations, except in those few cases that will be described later on. He was not a member of the Communist Party so far as we know.

"Subordinate to that main objective, the committee has asked Chancellor Allen and Dean Hanan to testify for the purpose of getting into our record from authoritative sources actual information concerning the exact situation at U. C. L. A. as far as rumors and charges are concerned, largely irresponsible, of an extremely critical subversive infiltration at that institution.

"Chairman Burns: Who is your first witness?

"Mr. Combs: With that preliminary statement, Mr. Chairman, the first witness I would like to call is Chancellor Allen.

"Question (By Mr. Combs): Your name is Raymond B. Allen?

"A. Yes, sir.

"Q. You are at present the Chancellor at the University of California at Los Angeles?

"A. Correct.

"Q. Dr. Allen, by way of foundation I would like to go into your academic qualifications and background, if you don't mind.

"A. Go right ahead, sir.

"Q. Where did you take your undergraduate work?

"A. University of Minnesota. I graduated in 1924, bachelor's degree, and in 1928, medical degree.

"Q. What is your specialty? What is your field?

"A. My specialty is surgery and medical education and administration.

"Q. Did you later become President of the University of Washington at Seattle?

"A. I did, in 1946.

"Q. That presidency continued until when?

"A. Until January, 1952.

"Q. What did you do at that time?

"A. I went into the government service for about nine months.

"Q. What was that service?

"A. I was appointed by the President as Director of the Psychological Strategy Board, which was planning for the government. It was the strategical planning board of the government.

"Q. Did you go to Washington?

"A. I did.

"Q. For the purpose of carrying out that duty?

"A. That is correct.

"Q. When did you become Chancellor at U. C. L. A.?

"A. November 15, 1952.

"Q. You have been Chancellor at that institution continuously since that time?

"A. That is correct.

"Q. While you were President of the University of Washington, there was a legislative committee in 1948, I believe, is that right?

"A. That is correct—yes.

"Q. It undertook to investigate the allegations of Communist infiltration at that institution. Isn't that true?

"A. In general throughout the State, and it included the University of Washington.

"Q. Senator Burns and I happened to be in Seattle at the time and attended the meeting which I think was in June, 1948, and as a result of that hearing, certain action was taken by you as president regarding some members of the faculty at that university. Is that correct?

"A. That is correct, but it requires some explanation and amplification.

"Q. Would you amplify, please?

"A. If I may.

"Q. Certainly.

"A. You may interrupt me if I am not responsive to what you want.

"Q. All right.

"A. The Un-American Activities Committee of the State of Washington conducted this searching investigation state-wide, including all free institutions where it was thought there might be some penetration of the Communist Party or other subversive organizations. It turned up some information which seemed to indicate there was some activity at the University of Washington that might be of a subversive nature. They did nothing more than to simply put it on record and then turned it over to the University of Washington. At that point, I directed that the Special Committee on Tenure and Academic Privilege of the University Senate conduct an investigation. This was a committee appointed by the senate and not by me. The committee conducted very lengthly hearings, during which time it was developed, in fact, at the first session, that two individuals of a number who were suspected of activities of this nature admitted for the first time that they were members of the Communist Party.

"Q. Those individuals were Joseph Butterworth of the English Department and Herbert Phillips of the Department of Philosophy?

"A. That is correct. When that occurred, the university dropped all charges against them except that they were members of the Communist Party and this, alone, was enough to disqualify them from membership. They then proceeded to develop at these hearings the fact that membership in the party constituted a conspiracy against the Government of the United States and the people, and that an individual committed to this doctrine of conspiracy of the forceful overthrow of the Government of the United States was not a free man, and therefore could not really speak the truth and teach the truth, and for this reason was disqualified from membership. The hearings were lengthy. I think it was the first time that an academic community had examined such questions.

"Q. At any place in the United States?

"A. At any place in the United States, and for all I know in the world. We took it very seriously. We felt that all pertinent facts should be brought forth about the Communist Party and the nature of the conspiracy. The university leaned over backward to see that it was a fair trial, an actual fair hearing, and actually paid the traveling expenses of persons that the defense counsel wanted to have testify on behalf of the accused. The result of these prolonged hearings was that I made recommendations to the Board of Regents to the effect that the admitted members of the Communist Party be dismissed, and that one other person in an unequivocal position also be dismissed.

"Q. Was that Dr. Ralph Gundlach?

"A. That is right. There were other reasons which applied in his case which need not be gone into here. The regents accepted that recommendation and the dismissals were made. I believe it was the first time that occurred in the history of American higher education.

"Q. As a matter of fact, Dr. Allen, is it true that some time after this occurrence you wrote a book called *Communism and Academic Freedom?*

"A. That is correct.

"Q. It is now out of print?

"A. Yes.

"Q. May I say that it is an excellent book. So far as I know, it is the first treatise of its kind on the subject. It went into the situation that you have described in quite elaborate detail, didn't it?

"A. Yes.

"Q. At this time, I wish to call your attention—and this is one of the reasons I went into this seemingly ancient history—to the publication I hold in my hand, which is entitled *Political Affairs*, May, 1956, issue, a publication of the National Committee of the Communist Party of the United States which appears monthly, and is published in New York. On page 39 is an article entitled "The Question of Academic Freedom," by Herbert Apthecker. I will only read the first paragraph which mentions you in not too complimentary terms in connection with the episode you have just described. It reads as follows:

"'In 1948, the University of Washington in Seattle fired two of its faculty members, Joseph Butterworth, a member of the English Department, and Herbert Phillips of the Philosophy Department. Both men had been on the faculty for many years and *both declared themselves to be members of the Communist Party* (committee's italics). On the grounds of that membership, they were dismissed by the Board of Regents, at the recommendation of President Raymond Allen. This action was taken despite the fact that a majority of the university Faculty Committee on Tenure and Academic Freedom had found that Professors Butterworth and Phillips were fully competent and had not used their positions for purposes of indoctrinating propaganda and, therefore, recommended that the men not be fired.'

"The article continues along the same vein to and including page 51. Is that an accurate description of the occurrence?

"A. I would have to study this carefully. I think one point made there is that these men had openly declared themselves as members of the party. They never did anything of the kind until the charges were brought against them.

"Q. And they had been teaching at the university for many years, as the article states?

"A. That is correct. They were covert members of the party. The case would have been quite different if all of these years they had openly declared themselves, and therefore were not really conspirators.

"Q. A matter which you point out in the book that you wrote?

"A. Yes, sir. To be attacked in a publication like that is a great credit to an individual.

"Q. You take it as a compliment?

"A. I do.

"Q. Would you like to read the entire article?

"A. If you don't need it.

"Q. I would like to have it back later.

"Now, Dr. Allen, immediately prior to the investigation so far as the University of Washington at Seattle was concerned, in 1948, was there any indication to you of a condition that would indicate that there was a problem of subversive infiltration at that university?

"A. Yes.

"Q. At that time, did the student body of the University of Washington publish a paper?

"A. It did.

"Q. Were you able to detect at any time immediately prior to 1948 through the columns of that paper any indication of subversive propaganda?

"A. It was to be suspected at times that some of the reportorial material was slanted; however, at that university the student paper was a laboratory journal of the School of Journalism. For this reason, it is edited probably more carefully than papers which are run exclusively by the students.

"Q. The paper at U. C .L. A., *The Daily Bruin,* is one of the latter category?

"A. That is correct.

"Q. Run exclusively by students themselves?

"A. That is correct, with faculty advice.

"Q. What were the other matters indicated by you which led you to believe there might be a series of problems of infiltration at the University of Washington immediately prior to 1948?

"A. I would rather not try to develop all of the reasons. I will merely say that the pattern of activity of covert operators—which this hearing will bring out, I take it—is not difficult to detect unless one is just not used to looking for it. It follows the usual tactic of a small, inner, dedicated group waiting out the larger groups that assemble for committee, faculty, and other meetings, constantly driving them toward what they think is the goal to be reached. This reflects itself in actions presumably representative of the large group, but is actually taken by a relatively few. This was not an uncommon occurrence.

"Q. Have you noticed any similar condition at the University of California at Los Angeles at any time during your tenure as Chancellor?

"A. Yes.

"Q. Comparable conditions?

"A. Yes. I have been concerned a number of times during this period about activities and among students which indicated that there was some sort of a pattern emerging which made it appear that a few people were controlling or endeavoring to control the organs of communication, of publication—the *Daily*. This, however, I could never satisfy myself was actually a covert activity. This is not so this year, may I say. I have not observed it this year at all.

"Q. When did you—when did it appear to be most serious?

"A. I think for dates and details——

"Q. I mean offhand.

"A. —You had better address these questions to Dean Hahn because he is more familiar with the paper angle.

- "Q. The university, through its Board of Regents, has adopted a policy toward Communism in general and Communist infiltration of the campuses?

"A. That is correct, Mr. Combs. I would like to put this policy into the records. It was adopted by the regents of the university as early as 1940, which, I may say, is an action taken by this highly responsible body, the first of its kind among the great universities of this country.

"Q. It has been in effect ever since?

"A. Every since. Yes.

"Q. Since the date of its adoption?

"A. That is correct.

"Q. And still is?

"A. That is correct.

"Q. You may read it into the record.

"A. It states:

> 'The regents believe that the Communist Party gives its first loyalty to a foreign government; that, by taking advantage of the idealism and the inexperience of youth, and by exploiting the distress of underprivileged groups, it breeds suspicion and discord and this divides the democratic forces upon which the welfare of our country depends. They believe, therefore, that membership in the Communist Party is not compatible with membership in the faculty of a state university. Tolerance must not mean indifference to practices which contradict the spirit and purposes of the way of life to which the University of California, as an instrument of democracy, is committed.'

"The above appears in the minutes of the regent's meeting of October 11, 1940. I might add that this policy was reaffirmed by the regents in 1949, and has been concurred in by the Academic Senate. The regent's resolution of June 24, 1949, directed that no member of the Communist Party shall be employed by the University. The Academic Senate, northern section, adopted the following resolution in 1950. Let me say at this point, the State of California, by constitutional provision and by provision of law, requires that all persons receiving salaries from the State, before entering upon the duties of their employment, shall subscribe by affirmation or oath nonmembership in any organization advocating the overthrow of the Government by unlawful means.

"This is the resolution adopted in 1950:

'That no person whose commitments or obligations to any organization, Communist or other, prejudice impartial scholarship and
free pursuit of truth will be employed by the University. Proved
members of the Communist Party, by reason of such commitments
to that party, are not acceptable as members of the faculty.'

"The faculty, 100 percent of them, the regents and I believe the
student body, 99 percent perhaps, fully subscribed to the doctrines and
the philosophy which the regents have so wisely laid down. This is one
of the great universities of the world and I am proud to be a member
of it. I consider our job one of creating such a healthy environment
for American youth in all of its phases, a good, broad, educational program which includes the teaching about Communism so that they will
know what the nature of the evil is, thus, to create such a healthy
environment, and an environment of awareness, that the students, the
youth especially, will benefit because the older people know or should
know about it, but the youth especially, should realize the danger that
exists in this international conspiracy. One such means is what this
committee is doing and in which the public appears to be interested.
There will be some publicity about it. You are describing the methods
by which penetration and infiltration are carried out so that the public
will know how to recognize it when it is going on. This, I think, is good
education.

"Q. It would be virtually impossible to combat such a movement—
such a disciplined conspiracy, unless we knew the techniques by which
it functions. Is that correct?

"A. Exactly.

"Q. Bearing in mind the difference between objective teaching and
advocacy?

"A. Exactly.

"Q. Such courses are being taught at the university?

"A. It comes in under political science, history, and a variety of
courses, but I think our study body itself, the *Daily* under its management now, the student legislative council and its president in producing
this statement, which I did not see myself until it appeared in the press,
so I called for a copy of it and I have it in my hand—some reference
was made to it in the daily press yesterday and today—in my opinion,
it is one of the finest statements about the nature of the conspiracy and
the steps necessary to combat it that I have seen.

"Q. How did that emanate?

"A. This was wholly voluntary on their part.

"Q. On the part of the students?

"A. On the part of the students. They heard that such an investigation as the committee is conducting was to take place. They heard that
it concerned activities in the student body. They conferred amongst
themselves. I just asked Dean Hahn if the students produced this
themselves and he said absolutely yes. To me, this is a wonderful
recognition of the fact that the University of California at Los Angeles
and its fine student body are alert to the dangers and are fighting them.
Of course, all of us know in a student body of 16,000 students where
the only entrance requirement that must be met is a scholastic require-

ment, it may well include a few—a half dozen or a dozen or maybe two dozen, I don't know—people who are conspirators of the left or of the right, the extreme left or extreme right. These people get involved, or involve organizations which are quite innocent, I believe, in knowing what is going on, manage to gain enough influence and control so that the honest and real purpose of the organization can be subverted to these conspiratorial ends. This is what I have fought all of my adult life and I shall continue to fight it. The best way to fight it in the university is to have freedom, to have alertness and awareness of these dangers and then these youngsters will grow up mature. They have to know what evil is in order to combat it. They should know what ideas and ideals make up the body of our doctrines of true America. Altogether, I am satisfied that the steps that are being taken here and throughout the country, and particularly with the exposure of the ugly face of Communism, the Russians, international bandits, their actions in Hungary, that there can be no one who can read or think who does not know at this time the nature of the beast we are fighting.

"Q. Has it been your experience, Dr. Allen, both at the University of Washington and here, that small, conspiratorial, covert groups of students at a great university, although almost microscopic by comparison with the body under which they operate, are individuals so highly disciplined and so thoroughly indoctrinated that the noise they generate and the activities in which they engage seem out of all proportion to their actual numerical strength?

"A. Exactly. And thereby, they produce a public feeling that everybody in such an institution, or most people, are people who are not loyal to the American system and the American way. That is the unfortunate part about it. U. C. L. A. I have heard referred to as "The Little Red Schoolhouse." This is nonsense; there isn't a more loyal or able group of faculty people as well as students with great creative ability—and I have worked in a number of campuses in this country—but they have inspired me and to me this is the greatest.

"Q. About three or three and a half years ago, the president of the university, Dr. Sproul, designated each chancellor and each provost on each of the eight campuses of the University of California for the purpose of maintaining a liaison with this committee. Is that right?

"A. Yes, indeed.

"Q. That liaison has been maintained so far as your office is concerned, has it not?

"A. That is correct. I think that liaison occurred before I arrived. It was in May, 1952.

"Q. Yes.

"A. It preceded me; I picked it up since.

"Q. Pursuant to that directive on the part of the president, contact has been made and maintained between the committee and your office, is that right?

"A. That is right, but I want to underline this: not in any sense to mean that this committee which is established by the Legislature, the Senate and the Assembly, has intruded one iota into the affairs under my jurisdiction; in terms of management, responsibility and internal organization, we function on our own.

"Q. May I add that the committee will continue to follow that policy.

"A. I know that is the case. You wouldn't want it any differently and I wouldn't want it any differently. In view of the fact that the committee, the State Legislature, the regents, and myself, and as far as U. C. L. A. is concerned, we are working toward exactly the same end, that there should always be a free America, that conspirators will be uncovered. It only makes good sense that I, as top administrator acting under President Sproul's approval and under the direction of the regents, shall exchange any information which is of interest and help in achieving the objectives that every honorable American is seeking.

"Mr. Combs: I believe that is all, Mr. Chairman.

"Chairman Burns: Thank you, Dr. Allen. Any questions, gentlemen?

"Let the record show that Senator John Thompson of Santa Clara County is sitting here on the committee as a member.

"You may be excused, Dr. Allen.

TESTIMONY OF DEAN MILTON E. HAHN

"Q. Your name is Milton E. Hahn?

"A. That is correct.

"Q. You are Dean of Students at the University of California at Los Angeles?

"A. Yes, sir.

"Q. How long have you held that position?

"A. Since February, 1948.

"Q. And you occupy it at the present time?

"A. Yes, sir.

"Q. Dean Hahn, by way of background I would like to get into the record your academic and biographical history, if you don't mind. I have some background before me which I will read and if I make a mistake would you interrupt me, please. You received your B.A. degree in economics at the Hamline University, St. Paul, Minnesota; your master's degree in psychology at the University of Minnesota. You are a doctor of philosophy and received your degree in educational psychology at the same university. In 1935 and 1936, you were Director of Guidance at the St. Paul Central High School and for two years thereafter you directed the guidance program for the St. Paul Public School System. Then you went back to the University of Minnesota. This was in 1938, and remained there until 1942 as coordinator of vocational orientation and as director of men's activities. Then, in 1942, you received a commission as an officer in the United States Marine Corps, and were made Chief of the Measurement and Evaluation Section, Classification Division, in Washington, D. C. My record is incomplete here. How long did you hold that position?

"A. That and others until late in 1944, sir.

"Q. Then you went to Syracuse University as Director of Psychological and Services Center and Professor of Educational Psychology. You were a guidance consultant in counseling, both to the State Department of Education in New York and the United States Office of Education. In 1948, as you have testified, you became the Dean of

Students at the University of California at Los Angeles, and also Professor of Psychology there. Do you hold that position, Professor of Psychology?

"A. Yes, sir.

"Q. You have published technical works in your field?

"A. That is correct, sir.

"Q. Have you acted as consultant to private business concerns?

"A. Yes, sir, to General Electric, Revere Copper and Brass, Prudential Insurance Company and others.

"Q. You are affiliated with the American Psychological Association?

"A. That is correct.

"Q. You have been a member of its Board of Representatives?

"A. Of a division of it, sir.

"Q. Of Division 17?

"A. That is correct.

"Q. From 1948 to 1951?

"A. That is right, sir.

"Q. A member of the National Board of Representatives of the American Personnel and Guidance Association, Diplomate of the American Board of Examiners in Professional Psychology, you hold a New York State diploma in clinical psychology, President of the Division of Counseling and Guidance of the American Psychological Association. I think that is ample qualification, Dean Hahn. Now, would you please explain in general terms for the benefit of the committee just what the duties of a Dean of Students comprise?

"A. Without being facetious, sir, I am not quite sure; but in general, it means supervision of a staff of 70 to 80 people covering loans, scholarships, housing, psychological services which are nonmedical, foreign students, general student activities and teaching.

"Q. Can you give us an idea, approximately, of the proportion of your daily time which is devoted, on the average, to carrying out the duties of your office as Dean of Students as compared to your duties and obligations as professor of psychology?

"A. These mathematics don't make sense. I am 100 percent administrative. Teaching is an avocation. I carry about 50 percent of the normal teaching load.

"Q. Do you receive extra compensation for your work as dean?

"A. I believe the administrators at the university in a dean's position are paid on an academic scale of 11 months; therefore, you are paid as a professor on an 11-month appointment. This is general practice.

"Q. You came directly to U. C. L. A. as Dean of Students?

"A. Yes, sir.

"Q. At the time you commenced your tenure there, was there a student newspaper called *The Daily Bruin?*

"A. Yes, sir.

"Q. That newspaper has been published continuously ever since you have been at the institution?

"A. That is correct, sir.

"Q. As a part of your duties as Dean of Students, have you concerned yourself with the problem of Communist and subversive infiltration at the university?

"A. That is not part of the job or the function of any administrator at the university other than Dr. Allen. If you concern yourself, you concern yourself as a citizen and not as part of your job.

"Q. Have you concerned yourself with that problem?

"A. Yes, sir.

"Q. During all of the period you have been at the university?

"A. Yes, sir.

"Q. In your opinion, what part has the student paper, *The Daily Bruin*, played in the dissemination of subversive propaganda among the students at the university?

"A. It has been a very prominent aspect of the paper, in my opinion, for all but a few semesters.

"Q. You say for all but a few semesters?

"A. That is correct.

"Q. Are you referring to semesters at the beginning of your tenure at the university or at the present time?

"A. Dr. Allen made the statement that this semester's *Bruin* has been almost, or has been completely free, in his opinion, and in mine. There have been semesters in between where the writings by alleged or admitted Communists and a clearly distinguishable party line have been less than in others. Let me point out, if I may volunteer a statement there, beginning with the year 1949 and 1950, there were 1,969 column inches of space written by people who claimed to be Communists or who followed the Communist line very completely.

"Q. How many column inches?

"A. One thousand, nine hundred sixty-nine, and this is a conservative estimate.

"Q. Do you have similar statistical data for other periods of time?

"A. It would be quite simple, sir, for someone to figure it out if we had an adding machine. I have the column inches, but they are not totalled. This is the worst year since I have been there.

"Q. 1949?

"A. The year 1949-50.

"Q. You have made available to the committee, through me, these compilations?

"A. Yes, sir.

"Q. I have copies of them here?

"A. That is correct.

"Q. For the purpose of identification, I wish to show them to you at the present time and have you identify and authenticate them so that we can incorporate them into our records.

"A. Those are true copies.

"Q. Thank you. For the record, the documents are as follows: spring of 1948—these are the semesters, Dean Hahn?

"A. Yes.

"Q. Spring of 1948 issue of *The Daily Bruin*, beginning February 23d and ending July 15th. Spring of 1950, commencing with the issue of February 7th and ending with the issue of July 18th. For the fall semester of 1950, the issue of *The Daily Bruin*, beginning September 13th and ending on October 25th. The spring semester of 1951, beginning with the issue of February 14th and ending with the issue of July 13th. For the fall semester of 1951, the issue beginning December 28th and ending with the issue for January 7th. Spring of 1952, the issue beginning February 21st and ending May 14th. The fall of 1952, beginning with the issue for September 24th and ending with the issue for January 9th. Spring of 1953, issue beginning February 9th and ending with the issue for May 29th. Fall of 1953, the issue beginning September 14th and ending with the issue for January 8th. Spring of 1955, the issue beginning on February 18th and ending with the issue for June 3d. Spring of 1956, which would be a partial coverage, beginning with the issue for April 9th and ending with the issue for May 14th.

"Now, Dean Hahn, would you explain how these documents were compiled? I mean by what process.

"A. Page by page review for the entire year.

"Q. A page by page review was taken and this is the result of the analysis?

"A. Yes, sir.

"Q. During your testimony, Dean Hahn, in conformance with the policy of the committee, we would like you to refrain from using names of either students, faculty members or anyone else in your testimony unless they are asked for by me or by the committee. This is not only to protect the individuals, but it also affords us an opportunity for checking and investigation and it also serves to avoid any inference as to the subversive record or activity of any person you might mention.

"In 1948, there was an occurrence at Robison Hall at the University in Los Angeles involving a boy named Hudson.

"A. Was this 1948 or 1949?

"Q. I think it was 1948—it is really immaterial for the purpose of this question. Do you recall the case?

"A. Yes, sir.

"Q. At that time, what was Robison Hall; what was it during that general period of time?

"A. It was the first major unit of cooperative housing, which, by the way, has been an excellent move at U. C. L. A. It was sold to the students by the owner. It was either a Neutra, or one of the architects who did it. It was called Robison Hall. It was sold to the students on a long-term basis by the owner. Through doing their own cooking, their own maintenance, and their own housework, they were then and are still able to permit a much lower board and room charge than is true of other types of houses.

"Q. Is that building, Robison Hall, located on or off the U. C. L. A. campus?

"A. It is off the campus.

"Q. In 1948 and 1949, was it or was it not under the jurisdiction of the university administration?

"A. Jurisdiction is probably not the completely correct word. In other words, student groups, even that house off of the campus, if they use the university name and use the facilities of the university, must comply with the rules of the university. This was their status; but actually, the living quarters was not a university function.

"Q. That was under the students themselves?

"A. Yes, sir, and the corporation which held the mortgage.

"Q. Is that still the practice with reference to Robison Hall?

"A. It is the practice regarding all groups, including various women's and men's groups, fraternities and sororities.

"Q. What was the situation at Robison Hall, if you know, with regard to subversive activities and propaganda in 1948 and 1949?

"A. This is hearsay, but the reputation was extremely bad.

"Q. Has it since improved?

"A. I think the students living there have done a remarkable job in that respect.

"Q. Since 1949?

"A. I think a tremendous improvement has come about since 1953-1954. They should be commended for what they have been able to do.

"Q. You are familiar, in a general way, with the so-called Hudson case?

"A. Yes, sir.

"Q. That involved an undergraduate student of the university whose body was found in the basement of Robison Hall. This committee held a hearing concerning documents found in his possession and the manner in which he died in 1950; isn't that true?

"A. Yes, sir.

"Q. Now, Dean Hahn, would you mind giving the committee the benefit of your opinion and experience as Dean of Students, commencing with your arrival at the university in 1948 and throughout the entire period of your tenure up to the present time, with relation to the problem of subversive infiltration and propaganda at the university? I don't expect you to be specific because it is a matter of memory and because it is an enormously broad subject. Before doing so, I wish to call your attention to some names of students, all and each of whom have been formerly identified by this committee, some of whom have appeared before this committee and are in the committee's reports. Do you recall a student by the name of Helen Edelman?

"A. I knew Miss Edelman quite well.

"Q. What was the period of her activity at U. C. L. A.?

"A. As a student, or over-all?

"Q. As a student, first.

"A. I would place it from approximately 1950 into the last of 1952-53.

"Q. Did she write for the student newspaper?

"A. Yes, sir.

"Q. *The Daily Bruin?*

"A. Yes, sir, and held an editorial board position.

"Q. On that paper?

"A. Yes, sir.

"Q. Did she exert considerable influence, in your opinion, so far as the editorial policy of the paper was concerned?

"A. Yes, sir.

"Q. She was a member of the Communist by her own admission, was she not?

"A. She so stated in print.

"Q. After leaving the university, she became a reporter for the Communist newspaper, the *Daily People's World?*

"A. I have heard this.

"Q. Have you seen any articles under her name in that paper?

"A. Not in the *People's World*, Mr. Combs, but in a Communist newspaper which she and another former university student at U. C. L. A. had issued.

"Q. A Communist publication?

"A. I believe it was so designated.

"Q. Were you acquainted with a student at the university by the name of Joe Price?

"A. Slightly.

"Q. Did you know a student at the university by the name of Lola Whang?

"A. By sight, I don't think I ever met Miss Whang.

"Q. Do you have any information concerning the activities of either or both of those students?

"A. It would be hearsay, sir; by direct observation, no.

"Q. Can you tell us first on what you base your hearsay information?

"A. Comments by students and people in the community and some students who knew all of these people quite well, who were identified with these and others and who were disgusted with what was going on and wanted to do something about it.

"Q. What was that concensus of opinion that came to you?

"A. That all three were either members of the Communist Party or were closely identified with it so that they might as well have been.

"Q. Did you ever hear of an organization called American Youth for Democracy?

"A. Yes, sir.

"Q. Were any units of that organization operating on the campus of the university, to your knowledge, at any time?

"A. Officially, never; but unofficially, quite active just before I came. By the time I arrived at U. C. L. A. the AYD changed their name, I believe, to Labor Youth League. They still used AYD to cover some activities, but generally speaking, it was the Labor Youth League.

"Q. What was American Youth for Democracy?

"A. That was a lineal descendent of the Young Communist League, I believe.

"Q. And the Labor Youth League?

"A. That was a lineal descendent of the AYD.

"Q. So the Young Communist League changed its name being American Youth for Democracy, and later changed it to Labor Youth League?

"A. Correct.

"Q. Is the Labor Youth League operating at U. C. L. A. at the present time?

"A. Never, officially; unofficially, the name is still used for cover-up operations, but I don't think as such it has been real active since they had a purge there for chauvinism and threw out the chairman and brought in a new one from Nashville, Tennessee.

"Q. How long ago was this, approximately?

"A. 1952.

"Q. I am now looking at a document which has been compiled for the spring of 1950, an analysis of the material in *The Daily Bruin*. I note on February 15th, there was an article by Helen Edelman; on March 1st, there was another article by Helen Edelman; on March 3d, there were two by Helen Edelman; on March 29th, there was another, and so on. Dr. Hahn, in each instance, the number of column inches devoted to that type of material can be ascertained and can be computed from the documents which you have submitted to us?

"A. That is correct.

"Q. So that the committee can compare that type of material in the student newspaper with other types of material which have been evaluated by your office as carrying a pary line content?

"A. It would be an underestimate, sir; there is one semester missing here in which she wrote that you could get a quite accurate count.

"Q. Before we go into a general description of conditions at the university, there are some other documents which I think we had better identify. I hand you now a file of papers in a manila folder entitled *The Observer*, 1955, and ask you if you will examine that file, please, and tell me of what it consists.

"A. This is a file of a paper published off campus. It was a weekly. It was staffed by individuals who had been members of *The Daily Bruin* staff. I think one comment needs to be made, if I may make it, Mr. Combs.

"Q. Surely.

"A. Prior to 1950, I think it is proper to talk about Communism and Stalinism in regard to our campus and other campuses—a better term is collectivism—in that year the Stalinist groups began working with many of the Socialist groups and even some of the Trotskyites. They *appeared* to be cooperating. So what happened prior to 1953 was pretty well in the control, as far as one could tell, of the Labor Youth League, the Communist Party; but what happened since 1953 has been influenced by the Socialist and Trotskyite groups.

"Q. That has been very marked in certain groups?

"A. Those, I would classify as collectivist groups and not Stalinist groups.

"Q. This is 1955?

"A. Yes, that is 1955; it was after 1953.

"Q. The second document in this file which you have just identified is entitled '*Student Division, Labor Youth League.*' That is the young Communist organization which you have just finished talking about. Is that right?

"A. Either that, sir, or a group using the name. Does that bear the union printer's stamp?

"Q. It bears no union printer's stamp. '*Issued by Student Division, Labor Youth League, Box 163.*'

"A. That was probably mimeographed downtown by the Communist Party.

"Q. Were these issued in connection with the issues of *The Observer*?

"A. No, sir. These were passed out off campus by various groups, probably not by U. C. L. A. students but City College students; passed out illegally at U. C. L. A. by City College students and by U. C. L. A. students at City College.

"Q. Off campus?

"A. This was to avoid certain disciplinary measures.

"Q. By acting off campus and getting as near to the campus as possible, they would evade the jurisdictional control of the administration at the university?

"A. And by changing names with other members of the university, they avoided identification.

"Q. What is the policy of the university officially concerning such groups as Socialist groups, Labor Youth League, and so on, functioning on campus?

"A. No political or religious groups may use the university's name. That is covered both in the State Constitution and, I think, in a law passed in the Legislature in 1947.

"Q. No political or religious groups of any kind?

"A. That is correct.

"Q. Is that regulation of the university rigidly enforced?

"A. To the best of my knowledge.

"Q. Are there any institutions near the university campus at which admitted members of the Communist Party and of the Labor Youth League are permitted to speak?

"A. By institutions, do you mean organizations?

"Q. Yes.

"A. Owning property?

"Q. Yes.

"A. The Y. M. C. A., which is not connected with the university in any way, does have a policy which permits anyone to speak on any topic.

"Q. Do Communists and members of the Labor Youth League speak there from time to time?

"A. Advertisements and folders giving it as a place of meeting would so indicate.

"Q. Does the Y. M. C. A. use the university name in any way?

"A. It may not and does not.

"Q. It does not?

"A. The word 'university' is in the public domain. They may not use U. C. L. A., the University of California, U. C. L. A. N., or anything like that.

"Q. It designates itself as the University Y. M. C. A.?

"A. In the same way the University High School uses the name.

"Q. How close is the building of that organization to the U. C. L. A. campus?

"A. The width of the street.

"Q. Right across the street?

"A. Yes, sir.

"Q. These pamphlets by the Labor Youth League that we have just talked about and similar written material, where is that material passed out to the students?

"A. This has not occurred for about a year now, but in the past, it has been on the city streets of Los Angeles adjacent to the entrances to the campus.

"Q. Has that steadily decreased since about 1949, that is, the practice of passing out this type of literature?

"A. The big drop came following 1953.

"Q. For the purpose of identification of this file, it commences with a letter dated February 14, 1955, and the last document is a copy of *The Observer*, No. 15, June 1, 1955. Just what was *The Observer*, Dean Hahn? How did it originate, if you know, and what was the extent of its circulation?

"A. This may take an hour or five minutes; which do you prefer?

"Q. Any length of time which, in your view, is adequate for the purpose of covering the question.

"A. Going back into *Bruin* history, up until 1950—I have to count on my fingers—up until four semesters ago, the *Bruin* was controlled by a self-perpetuating group, theoretically responsible to student government, but actually, able most of the time to completely force student government to do as it wished. It is a publication of the regents. Any publication bearing the name University of California is published by the regents. The publisher and owner by privity is the student council on each of the campuses at the University of California which has a paper. The key people on the *Bruin* are paid university journalists. They do not buy yachts, but they are paid enough for car fare, and so on. Four semesters ago, because of things that were happening, it was deemed necessary to change the system.

"Q. What do you mean by things that were happening?

"A. Oh, complaints of alumni, complaints of former members on the *Bruin* staff who had been squeezed out, complaints by the faculty, the administration, and students.

"Q. What complaints were made? What were they mostly concerned with?

"A. They varied all over the lot. Many students came in over the years complaining that they wanted to work on the student paper, but apparently their viewpoints were wrong and they were squeezed out. In the years I mentioned, with the tremendous output, 1949 and 1950, they had developed some interesting methods of election. The *Bruin* staff, reportedly, by majority vote, recommended their successors; but in that year, a practice was introduced of taking written ballots for the editor and the managing editors, removing them from the room and announcing the results, but nobody ever saw the ballots. If the staff was split, as it frequently was, they would wait until someone walked out and broke the quorum; or at midnight, they would hold their meetings and the members would object to going out that late. They even threatened to strike if the student council wouldn't let them do as they wished. This happened several times. It was a closely controlled organization, spending from 60 to 100 thousand dollars a year of someone else's money. As I said, that system was changed four semesters ago, so that any person having the qualifications to be editor could run for that position. The one who received a majority of the votes became editor and had a very strong voice in selecting his own staff. Since that time, the personnel and journalistic aspect has changed markedly. In other words, by introducing more democracy, we obtained a different result.

"Q. How does that situation connect itself with *The Observer*?

"A. *The Observer* staff were people who lost out in the election and decided to publish the paper. The financing of it probably cost about a thousand dollars. Some of it came from subscriptions, where the rest of it came is a direct mystery, we don't know.

"Q. Was any effort made to obtain university permission to circulate on the campus?

"A. This is against the regulations of the university to distribute more than one university paper and that franchise was held by the *Bruin*.

"Q. But an effort was made by *The Observer*?

"A. Yes.

"Q. When that was denied by the then administration, was *The Observer* circulated off campus?

"A. Yes, sir. It reached a number of people.

"Q. Is it still being printed?

"A. No, sir. One of the key people went to Mexico City, I believe, shortly after that last issue. The others—some stayed in school.

"Q. Do the names of the staff members and editors, and so on, appear in the various issues of the papers?

"A. Yes, but, in fairness, let me point out that a number of these are fine young men and women who believe that they were fighting a legitimate, liberal cause. I don't think there should be any implications made.

"Q. That is the reason we prefer not to introduce names publicly at this time. That is a general technique with subversive groups, isn't it, particularly front organizations, to attract sincere liberals, nonsubversive personnel for the purpose of recruiting and propagandizing?

"A. That is correct, sir.

"Q. Now, going back to the general question I asked you earlier concerning the development of the situation from the time of your tenure as dean until the present time, are you prepared, or can you give us any general statement as to the situation and status at the present time at the university, so far as the problem of subversive infiltration is concerned?

"A. I think, Mr. Combs, it could never be truthfully said that student groups on our campus, however small or however large they may have been, were directed by students. I think the events, from the very beginning, had their activities set up and financed and directed by people other than students. I think that should be made clear.

"Q. Both within the university and outside?

"A. Yes, sir. I could give you one very clear example of how it worked.

"Q. Will you, please?

"A. Let me take one from 1948, the Taylor rally. The rally was set up.

"Q. Do you mean Senator Taylor?

"A. The IPP meeting was during the election year where every regulation in the university was fractured wide open; where a telephone call came in a couple of days ahead of the meeting, held with proper permission in the streets just off the campus, saying that the fraternities were going to use violence to break up the meeting; where airplanes distributed literature across the campus concerning the meeting; where, after the group putting on the meeting held its meeting, all of a sudden professionally-prepared signs and placards appeared at the meeting, and where a photographer, later identified as a member of the Communist Party, appeared with a 16-millimeter camera and made movies. We took the campus police at the university out of uniform. We had a fine meeting with the metropolitan police, explaining in advance what was supposed to happen; there was a nice meeting; there was no violence; the photographer did not get a good place from which to take pictures, etc. This was not financed on the campus. Some rather important functionaries of the Communist Party were in evidence at the meeting. I come now to a later operation which falls within the purview of this committee. An excellent national organization, the National Association for the Advancement of Colored People, applied for recognition at the university a year ago this fall. The university does not, by policy of the regents, involve itself in community disputes. If a partisan issue is involved, the university stays out for obvious reasons. The request for recognition was made. It was endorsed by five faculty members, none of whom made any attempt to find out what the rule book said on it. It was explained to the students who brought it in what the policy of the university was and a statement was issued for publication in the *Bruin* and published. The matter was automatically referred to President Sproul's Advisory Committee to see that there was no error. If you read the *Bruin* for that semester, you will see what happened. This parallels one other occasion when one of our finest organizations, the Carver Club, was organized by Negro students for cultural purposes. Professor Kuntz was adviser. Suddenly, they voted to admit white members. This is a fine example of how a good organization can be knocked out of existence, because that January, without observing any of the policies which are usually observed by student groups, letters were written to prominent Negro professionals and people in the entertainment world. Then, when the thing was all set up, when you are suddenly hit with the fact that a program was arranged with no sanction, having invited speakers of some prominence and excellent reputation, it was necessary to refuse permission to speak at the university.

"Q. When did this occur?

"A. I can find it in the file. Dr. Kuntz died early in 1952 or 1953, the preceding semester. The NAACP has a fine membership, some excellent, earnest and brilliant students in it. They did the same thing the Carver Club did; they were loaded with white students, some of whom it is alleged have interesting records. If you will follow the *Bruin* through, you will see how it works on issues deliberately created, and it has caused one of our fine groups of students a lot of headaches and heartaches over the last year.

"Q. The National Association for the Advancement of Colored People, which started out as you have described as a fine and sincere organization, the instant they threw the doors open to white membership, did the infiltration begin?

"A. No, sir, here is what happened. I think chiefly, the members of the white group who are eligible—any of us may belong to the National Association for the Advancement of Colored People—but most of the white group were very clear that they could not get recognition for a social, political group under the ruling of the regents. They made an attempt to create an incident and to cause trouble and to cause disunity and a fight between the students, the faculty, and the administration.

"Q. What is the status of the NAACP at the present time?

"A. It is not recognized, falling into the category to which it does.

"Q. Is there an off-campus unit functioning, to your knowledge?

"A. Yes, and there are some very fine people in it. They are in charge of it this year. This is the type of operation I am speaking of.

"Q. So, it is your opinion, Dean Hahn, that the student activities, and by that I mean that portion of the student activities, that portion that is carried on by the Labor Youth League, a subversive organization, communist, and so on, functions because of adult direction?

"A. I have a very strong feeling that is the truth.

"Q. Has that been your opinion throughout your tenure as Dean of Students?

"A. Yes.

"Q. I think you said in your experience and in your view, the height of infiltration and subversive activity was about 1949?

"A. That was the height of the Stalinists, yes, sir.

"Q. Then, as you described, about 1953, a so-called collectivist operation occurred. Now, what, in your view, is the present situation at the university?

"A. Pretty much as Dr. Allen described it. In my opinion, there is unquestionably a group operating. I have some documents here which bear on this. Unquestionably, a group is operating which cuts across these lines prior to 1953, the Socialist Labor Party, some people who were formerly identified as Trotskyites.

"Q. That is the Socialist Workers Party, is it not?

"A. There seems to be a distinction, perhaps not a real one, between the militant Trotskyite group and the group which formerly had another name and the Socialist group which moved toward the Socialist Workers Party. I may be wrong in my terminology, but it is a working together of a number of organizations that previously were inimical or did not work together. Here is what happened. It is a far less militant movement than the earlier one. I think in all probability, the reason they have been able to bring this about is a playing down of the physical violence aspect in the revolution tomorrow, and, on the surface at least, an agreement between the former Stalinists that this is a long-term process which can be brought about by peaceable means. I think this is a bait which is used. Whether anyone can work with the former groups on that basis, I doubt.

"Q. Would you mind referring to the documents which you have with you, Dean Hahn, and continue with your general testimony and explain them.

"A. Certainly, sir. I am giving you here documents that are of some general interest; I think they identify themselves. This may be the property of the committee.

"Q. Thank you.

"A. The big blow-up on the campus, if I may backtrack a moment —I think that the most activity for control, from the standpoint of the students and adult directors of these movements, were directed toward *The Daily Bruin*. There is no use creating incidents and fight-

ing causes if you can't get publicity. In the semester because of strong
presidents of the student body and strong editors of the *Bruin,* I
think you can follow a very clear drop-off. It is impossible to get
publicity, so why waste time. If you get a weak student body president
or a council that is confused and a *Bruin* staff that is willing to be used
—it doesn't have to be strong, but the activity steps up markedly.
That is quite a clear trend as you look back on it. I don't know whether
you want me to read something into the record, but Mr. Charles Fran-
cis, who is one of the finest college newspaper men that it has ever
been my privilege to meet and one of the most courageous, in 1948
and 1949, when things were rough and there was physical danger apparently, said in his 'Gideon's Dirty Linen,' a five-part editorial that
ran for a week in which is included Mr. Frank McNitt's *Westwood
Hills Press* editorial: 'All of the evidence in this series, however, is a
matter of record and it forms a meaningful and alarming pattern for
me. After dealing with this group for two years, I can arrive at none
but the following conclusions.'

"Q. To whom is he referring?

"A. The Labor Youth League, who put on the Carver rally.

"Q. All right.

"A. (Continuing) 'That their activities are planned to harrass and
harm the reputation of the University of California at Los Angeles.
Their methods in dealing with the university and student organizations
are dishonest, sub rosa, and insincere. That as long as the rest of the
students continue their present unwillingness to contribute articles representing their own viewpoints and convictions, *The Daily Bruin*
feature page will be dominated by ideas of a militant minority. Lastly,
I have learned that to do business with the Students for Wallace is to
be double-crossed, smeared, and misguided.' I would substitute the
LYL there. Then, there was a second editorial written by Peter Braber.
He closed out what was the number two editorial written in the *Bruin*
on this subject; it is entitled 'Kiss of Death.' He writes:

" 'Discrimination, faculty loyalty oaths, clamp-downs on the student
press and the prohibition of political speakers on the campus all are
problems which liberal students are endeavoring to rectify. Yet, as soon
as these students launch programs designed to correct such evils, the
first- and second-string Communists and their red squads, the LYL,
YPA, et al., come forward with outstretched arms. A conservative reaction which curtails any progress. In many instances, the liberals
are unaware that they are being used by the reds; in other cases, they
welcome any and all support they can get, not fully realizing the implications involved. Thus, it is often the liberal's own naivete which
plays into the Communist hands though liberal leaders recently seem
to have become more aware of the red infiltration.' Mr. Graber was an
excellent, sincere and sound liberal.

"Q. What was the date of that?

"A. That was written May 7, 1952. Coming down to the present
situation, I don't think we are in any better or worse condition than
most state institutions. The public is unaware of some of the differences.
In a private institution, the student can be asked to leave, his money
refunded, because he attends as a privilege. In a state institution, as
Dr. Allen pointed out, he attends as a right. This is as it should be,

unless there is a civil action or criminal action where guilt is proved in court, regardless of what the individual does he remains in the institution. We don't run courts; we are not an adjudicating or a legal body, so we work under completely different sets of circumstances. The system that seems to be working at the present time with this collectivist approach, has been a constant attempt to create disunity beween the students, the faculty, and the administration. This is done by a series of created events, and if you had control of the *Bruin* you would be able to get publicity. In the larger picture, they seek control of some university employees as well as the student body and if they can't make it in one jump, they will make it in 10. It is important to them to control the university and also, if possible, control the smaller campuses, such as, Santa Barbara and Riverside and the smaller campus south of here. You are seeing a small number of very hard-working, determined people who are doing everything in their power, No. 1, to control the university, No. 2, wherever possible, to make it lose public confidence. This is a standard operating procedure.

"Q. It is a standard technique, is it not?

"A. Yes, sir.

"Q. There have been widely circulated rumors in this part of the State, have there not, Dean Hahn, largely irresponsible, concerning the extent of subversive activities at the university?

"A. Unquestionable.

"Q. Is it not also a fact in any educational institution, particularly a state institution, the Communist Party would naturally be desirous of infiltrating, recruiting and developing leadership; has that been your experience?

"A. Yes. The recruiting aspect has been played down, cut out in 1952, but it has been resumed in the last year and a half or two years.

"Q. There is a problem of infiltration at the university at the present time, is there not?

"A. Being a university and a state institution, I don't see how it could be otherwise.

"Q. Has there been an infiltration at the university by Communists ever since your tenure as Dean?

"A. Yes, sir.

"Q. But, as you have testified, it has been on a decreasing scale since about 1949 or '50?

"A. Decreasing from the former Stalinist line, in my opinion. I could not make an accurate estimate of what the numbers are for the collectivist group; for example, student sympathizers and members of various organizations, in 1949, probably numbered some place between 200 and 400. The number is not that large at the present time, certainly. At one time, for a number of reasons which I would rather not go into, in 1950 and '53, that number was well below 75 of any hard core group. It is much more difficult to estimate now what I will call the collectivist approach in numbers. I don't know.

"Q. As you define the term collectivist, as a matter of fact, it would have a broadening influence.

"A. Yes, sir.

"Q. Reaching out and including a sort of popular front activity?

"A. Definitely, that is what it is.

"Q. With non-Communist liberal groups?

"A. Yes, sir.

"Q. Neither Joe Price, Helen Edelman, nor Lola Whang are at the university at the present time?

"A. To the best of my knowledge, no.

"Q. Do you have any other documents to submit, Dean Hahn?

"A. Yes, sir. These types of documents are self explanatory, I would rather not comment on them. I am giving you my outline notes which will carry some information explanatory to that. Here is something in writing which you may have.

"Q. Do you have anything to add to your testimony, Dean Hahn?

"A. No, sir, except I agree with Dr. Allen that it is a privilege to have a chance to work with a governmental agency which may be called hysterical or witch-hunting, but completely undeservedly. I think the university owes you a debt of gratitude for what you, gentlemen, are doing.

"Mr. Combs: Thank you, very much, Dean Hahn. We certainly wish to reciprocate for the cooperation which you and Dr. Allen have shown to the committee."

It should be emphasized at this point that when Dean Hahn testified about the collectivist nature of subversive groups of students working on the U. C. L. A. campus after 1950, and particularly since 1953, he stated that in his opinion even some of the Trotskyites were cooperating with the Communists. Dean Hahn later testified that "there seems to be a distinction, perhaps not a real one, between the militant Trotskyite group and a group which formerly had another name in the Socialist group which moved toward the Socialist Workers Party. I may be wrong in my terminology, but it is a working together of a number of organizations that previously were inimical or did not work together."

HOSTILITY BETWEEN STALINISTS AND TROTSKYISTS

As will be seen later, and particularly in connection with the testimony of Professor Robert G. Neumann, the collectivist group referred to by Dr. Hahn did not include members of the militant Trotskyite organization. On the contrary, the implacable hostility between the Stalinist group and the Trotskyite group persisted until after the speech of Nikita Khruschev to the Twentieth Congress of the Communist Party of the Soviet Union, which he delivered on February 14, 1956. The collectivist groups on the campus, according to the committee's investigation, did indeed include a great many groups that were theretofore inimical. Thus, we saw, after 1953, collaboration in many instances between the Stalinists and the members of the Young Socialist League, Students for Wallace, Young Progressives of America, and a heterogeneous array of Socialist student fronts with which the Communists theretofore had very little or nothing to do—regarding them as undiciplined and impotent organizations upon which the Communist movement could not afford to waste time. As a matter of fact, the *only* group with which the Communist organization steadfastly refused to do business was the Trotskyite group. Those who have a working knowledge of the development of Communism will realize that when Stalin, with the assistance of Kamenev and Zinoviev, undermined the political prestige of Trotsky and banished him from Russia, there was unleashed throughout the world a campaign of constant abuse and vilification against Trotsky and his followers which seeped down to the very lowest levels of the Stalinist organization in all countries where a Communist Party existed. In a short time, all Stalinists came to hate members of the Trotskyite movement with a fanatical bitterness. No greater insult could be hurled at a Communist than to call him a Trotskyite. So great was the influence of Stalin, that even after his death this bitter enmity between Stalinists and Trotskyites persisted, and was ended only with the historic speech by Khrushchev in which he downgraded Stalin, and in which he declared that pursuant to a new united front movement throughout the world, Communists could thenceforth do business with Socialist groups and all other liberal and progressive organizations.

As will be seen, documents found in the possession of Abrams indicate the hostility even between the Young Socialist League and the Trotskyites up to the time of the Khrushchev speech; it is a grim fact that Russian propaganda has been so diabolically effective that the unrelenting anti-Trotskyite campaign flowed down through the Communist ranks, through the fellow-travelers, and even affected great masses of so-called liberals and progressives, who exhibited no hesitancy about doing business with the Stalinists, and permitted their names to adorn the sponsor lists of Communist front organizations, but who, unconsciously or otherwise, were so affected by the anti-Trotskyite propaganda that they scrupulously avoided doing business with members of the Socialist Workers Party—another name for the Trotskyite organization. It should also be pointed out here that even after the assassination of Leon Trotsky in Mexico during the summer of 1940, the propaganda campaign continued—in fact, it was even accelerated and continued full blast until the Khrushchev speech of February 14, 1956.

Dr. Allen testified briefly concerning some Communist techniques and provided infallible evidence of subversive infiltration at the university. We have already mentioned the incidence of propaganda in the columns of student newspapers, and Dr. Allen alluded to small groups who unfailingly attended all university meetings, persisted in throwing proceedings into as much confusion as possible, remaining until most of the opposition had gone home exhausted, and then jammed through resolutions that were in consonance with their subversive motives. In that connection, we deem it proper to set forth here a recent statement by a former member of the Communist Party who specialized in subtly injecting the party line in his classrooms. It indicates the utter impossibility of any disciplined Communist teacher using his classroom for the purpose of indoctrinating students with obvious propaganda. On the other hand, as we have already pointed out, he is very careful to conceal his real motives. The following excerpt is taken from *The New England Teacher*, February, 1956, by John M. Barry. In part, he said: "The first principles were dinned into our minds; 'never mention Communism in the classroom. Never praise Communism or the Communists. Never criticize openly and adversely the American form of government.'

"A Communist teacher is one of the most valued members of the party. Nothing must be said or done to arouse suspicion that a teacher is a member.

"The reason for such a teacher's value is obvious. A high school teacher meets about 180 pupils every day—perhaps more. He is in an excellent position to direct and guide the thinking of these pupils. Truly, one equals 180 and if there are 10 such teachers in the community they have a controlling power over more than 1,800 pupils who go home every day to 1,800 homes. They can by slow, careful methods introduce slanted opinions into those homes. And if persons are inclined to scoff at that statement, then they are guilty of a common American weakness of underestimating the cleverness and thoroughness of the Communist reasoning power.

"I mentioned that a well-drilled teacher never violates the rules laid down. This is an example. A short time ago a teacher was called before a group investigating infiltration into the schools. In an indignant voice he declared that his honor had been impugned, that as a matter of principle and ideals he would invoke the protection of the Fifth Amendment on every question other than his name and address. He declared that he had never even mentioned Communism in his classes and that he could prove it by the pupils he had had in school.

"In the days following, the newspapers were filled with angry letters from pupils he had had in class throughout the years. All voiced the same thought—the teacher had never mentioned Communism in any class.

"What the investigating committee did not know was that they were questioning a teacher who had been thoroughly and expertly grounded in the classroom methodology. He had been taught and drilled *never* to mention Communism or to praise it.

"The pupils were telling the truth. They had sat before him during the school year, had had their views on current events deftly twisted toward the party line and never realized it.

"That was the instruction we were given—how to sway a class into thinking along the proper lines without being obvious. Every step was laid out carefully. The aim was not to force upon them a blanket belief, but to introduce a slanted thought in such a way that the pupil might think it had been his own. It was the touch of the rapier, not the blow of a broadsword. The teacher might spend a few minutes for several days in general conservation just to induce a pupil to make a statement. At a meeting one night we were told to introduce a line of directed thought into our classes. The war with Japan was over and it was imperative that American soldiers be returned to this country from the Pacific area. There had been considerable agitation among the general public that this be done, and we were ordered to work among the high school students so that they, in turn, would influence their parents."

Dr. Allen also advocated that accurate information concerning the real nature of the Communist movement in the United States, its long-range objectives, its duplicity and deceit, its organizational structure and operation—all pertinent facts concerning the Communist movement both in the United States and throughout the world, be taught in colleges and universities. The committee is in complete accord with this assertion, and is happy to report to the Legislature and to the people of this State that in the University of California, both at Berkeley and in Los Angeles, excellent courses along this line are currently being taught in the Political Science Department by persons who are not only 100 percent loyal, but who are among the greatest experts in the world concerning the real nature of Communism. It should not be necessary to add, also, that these courses are being taught with complete objectivity, are carefully documented, presented in an interesting manner, and provide accurate information concerning the world Communist movement, the Russian Revolution of 1917, the foreign policy of the Soviet Union, Communist propaganda techniques, the operation of front organizations, and the current Communist Party line. These classes are becoming increasingly popular and are already well attended.

TESTIMONY OF WILLARD JOHNSON

"Q. (By Mr. Combs): Will you state your name and address for the record, Mr. Johnson?

"A. Willard Johnson, 10954 Ophir, Los Angeles 24.

"Q. You are a student at U. C. L. A.?

"A. Yes.

"Q. Do you have any official position as a student body officer?

"A. I am student body president.

"Q. When were you elected to that position?

"A. Last spring.

"Q. You have indicated to the committee that you have a document which you wish to read into the record at this time?

"A. Yes, sir.

"Q. You have just handed copies of it to the committee. Would you explain the document, please, together with the circumstances that gave rise to its origination?

"A. Yes. This document was prepared by the Student Legislative Council, which is the official legislative body for the Associated Students at U. C. L. A. It was prepared at a special meeting called last Friday, December 7th, and distributed to this group and to the press and to various university officials. I would like to read it into the record at this time, if the committee will so permit.

"Q. By way of preliminaries, Mr. Johnson, was there any conference between you or any member of the Student Legislative Council and this committee antedating the preparation of this document?

"A. Not that I know of.

"Q. There was no solicitation of it on our part, was there, to your knowledge?

"A. Not to my knowledge.

"Q. There was none so far as the committee is concerned. It was passed, as you say, on December 7th of this year?

"A. That is right, sir.

"Q. Would you read it, please.

"A. 'This statement of principles is prepared by the Student Legislative Council of the University of California at Los Angeles in order that at this time, while the possibility of subversive activities on university campuses is being studied by our California Government representatives, the public might know our firm stand against Communist aggression and infiltration and in support of full and fair investigation of such activities by the representatives of a free people.

"'1. We affirm that the peoples of the United States must keep alert and informed in the face of subversion in the free nations.

"'2. We oppose the following principle of action set forth in 1920 by Lenin, in the *Infantile Leftism in Communism*—a principle which has governed Communist thinking in all nations including the United States to the present day—namely, that any ruse, any cunning, unlawful method, evasion, concealment of truth is justified to bring about total Communist world control.

"'3. We assert, in answer to this Leninist principle, the necessity for absolute moral standards and the absence of moral compromise in the conduct of personal life and in relationships between nations in order that subversion, confusion, and diversion shall not lead the world into utter chaos or totalitarian enslavement.

"'4. We realize that we, as students, have often failed to live by the highest and best that we know to be right in human conduct. But we also know that the setting right of wrong and not accepting our failures as the standard of future conduct, is the way to become and remain free citizens of a free nation. We accept for ourselves and our university life the precept of Rear Admiral Richard E. Byrd, that the greatest need of the hour is that we become "a nation strong, clean and united."

"'5. We believe in a fair and open investigation of subversion on this campus or any other campus by the representatives of the people, state or federal, in order to bring subversion into the light of day where subversion cannot continue to exist. There is every reason to carry on such investigations, openly and fairly, if such investigations are believed to be needful by our elected representatives. The people of this State have created this institution of higher learning, and through their representatives they have every right and duty to keep it free.

"'6. We know that American universities serve as the training ground for our Nation's future leaders and are therefore prime targets of the Communist conspiracy. Because U. C. L. A. is one of our Nation's leading universities, it is obvious to us that attempts will be made to exploit and misdirect us and to create confusion and doubt about our fellow Americans, our government and our way of life.

"'Our American system of government provides for investigation as a tried and sound method for discovery of truth and the elimination of error and evil. This procedure provides for and serves as a protection for the people. The Communist ideology is directly opposed to our American concept of liberty, morality, justice, and human rights. We, therefore, welcome this investigation.'

"That is the end of our statement.

"Q. Is there any other comment you care to make?

"A. No, sir, I think the statement speaks for itself.

"Mr. Combs: Thank you, very much, Mr. Johnson. It is an excellent statement. The committee appreciates it very much, indeed; particularly because of the spontaneous manner in which it was formulated and presented to us. Thank you, very, very much. I might add that I don't know of any similar resolution that the committee has ever received since its inception. I don't know of any such statement ever having been received by any other committee in this field."

TESTIMONY OF MAURICE KAPLAN

The next witness, Maurice Kaplan, was the only witness who appeared before the committee with an attorney, being represented by Mr. A. L. Wirin, Los Angeles, California. Mr. Kaplan testified as follows:

"Q. (By Mr. Combs): Your name is Maurice Kaplan?

"A. Yes, sir.

"Q. You reside at 133 Wadsworth Avenue, Santa Monica?

"A. That is right, sir.

"Q. About how long have you lived there?

"A. Well, it will be in January 10 years.

"Q. How long have you lived in Southern California?

"A. About 10 years it will be in January.

"Q. There is a little building behind your place of residence?

"A. Yes, sir.

"Q. A one-room building in back?

"A. That is right.

"Q. From time to time you have rented that out?

"A. That is right.

"Q. * * * Were you acquainted with Sheldon Abrams?

"A. Well, as long as he used to live with us.

"Q. He rented the little building from you, did he not?

"A. Yes.

"Q. Did you know him before he came to see about renting the building?

"A. No, sir.

"Q. You did not know him at all.

"A. Well, we usually give an ad in the Santa Monica *Evening Outlook* when we have that empty, and that is the way the people come.

"Q. You put ads in the Santa Monica *Evening Outlook*?

"A. That is right.

"Q. He came in response to the ad?

"A. That is right.

"Q. About when did you rent it to him; do you remember?

"A. I think it was in February, because that was the third month when this happened.

"Q. February of this year?

"A. Yes.

"Q. Early in the month?

"A. I couldn't remember when it was, but I think it was about early in the month. I didn't look up the receipt, otherwise I could give it to you exactly.

"Q. Did he move in after he made arrangements to rent the place?

"A. Yes.

"Q. It was just one room?

"A. That is right.

"Q. Did it have any windows in it?

"A. It had three windows.

"Q. One on each side of the door?

"A. Yes.

"Q. And one on the left side of the building?

"A. That is right.

"Q. What is the building constructed of, wood or plaster?

"A. It is plaster.

"Q. Do you recall how large it is?

"A. I wouldn't say exactly.

"Q. You are not quite sure. It wasn't very big, was it?

"A. It wasn't too big; it is just for one person.

"Q. When you rented the room to Mr. Abrams, was there a refrigerator in the room?

"A. That is right.

"Q. What kind of a refrigerator was it?

"A. We had a gas refrigerator.

"Q. A Servel refrigerator?

"A. Servel refrigerator.

"Q. Was there a portable gas heater in the room?

"A. Yes. It was a little one.

"Q. There was a gas plate in the room, wasn't there?

"A. That is right.

"Q. With two burners?

"A. Yes.

"Q How did the gas get to the two appliances, the heater and the burner?

"A. It was a connection.

"Q. A flexible hose?

"A. Well, it was this hose—I don't know how to explain it, though.

"Q. Go right ahead.

"A. It was a kind of hose which connects it with a rope on top.

"Q. It fitted over a little pipe?

"A. That is right.

"Q. Was there a place on the hose where the end of the hose fitted onto the pipe?

"A. That is right.

"Q. That came in from the outside of the building?

"A. That is right

"Q Was there a place where the gas could be turned off?

"A. Yes.

"Q. On both appliances, both the heater and the plate?

"A. Yes. It could be turned off on the heater and it could be turned off on the wall.

"Q. In other words, each one could be turned off.

"A. Separately.

"Q. At both places?

"A. That is right.

"Q. At the appliance itself and at the place where the gas came in through the side of the building. Is that right?

"A. Yes.

"Q. How far from the rear of your residence was that little building situated?

"A. It is pretty far.

"Q. Fifty feet?

"A. I don't know the exact measurements, but I would say maybe more than 20 feet, 20 to 25 feet, something like that.

"Q. Something like 25 feet, you think?

"A. Yes, I guess that is what it should be.

"Q. Was there an entrance to the little building other than the one door in front?

"A. No.

"Q. That was the only method of entry?

"A. Yes.

"Q. That was the only means of entrance?

"A. Yes.

"Q. Was it equipped with a telephone?

"A. No.

"Q. Did he ever use your telephone?

"A. Well, he never used to come into our house except paying the rent, that is all.

"Q. How often did he pay the rent?

"A. Every month.

"Q. He was only there two months?

"A. Yes, that was his third month.

"Q. In April?

"A. Yes.

"Q. Did you have occasion to go into the room from time to time?

"A. No.

"Q. You never went into it at all?

"A. I never had to go. I realize if somebody rents it I don't have to go behind him and look after him.

"Q. I understand. So you never went in there at all?

"A. No, sir.

"Q. Did Mr. Abrams receive his mail at that address?

"A. Yes, sir.

"Q. How did he get his mail when it came to him?

"A. Well, we have a letter box on the outside of our house, on the front of the house, and all of the mail comes there.

"Q. He would go out there and pick it up from time to time?

"A. That is right.

"Q. Were you usually gone from your residence during the daytime?

"A. Yes, sir, I am going every day to work here in Los Angeles.

"Q. What time do you usually leave in the morning?

"A. I usually leave about 25 to 6 or 20 to 6 in the morning.

"Q. Before 6 o'clock?

"A. That is right.

"Q. Do you come home for lunch?

"A. No, I come back about 5.30 or a quarter to six.

"Q. You come home about 5.30?

"A. That is right.

"Q. Were you usually there in the evenings?

"A. In the evenings, I am usually home, more or less.

"Q. Was Mr. Abrams a university student? Did he go to U. C. L. A., do you know?

"A. I knew after. When he came to rent he said he was a U. C. L. A. student.

"Q. He told you he was a student?

"A. That is right.

"Q. Did he have very many visitors?

"A. This, I never noticed.

"Q. You never noticed?

"A. Because I was gone.

"Q. Did you ever notice a light burning in the house at night in the place occupied by him?

"A. I usually go very early to sleep. I usually go at the latest about 10 o'clock.

"Q. So you did not pay much attention to that?

"A. Well, I couldn't pay much attention at night. What could have been happening?

"Q. Is the telephone at that place EX brook 6-2351?

"A. That is right.

"Q. Going back to the morning of April 20th of this year, did you have occasion to go out to the room occupied by Mr. Abrams for any reason?

"A. Do you mean that day?

"Q. Yes.

"A. Yes, sir.

"Q. How did you happen to go out on the morning of that day; was that on Friday?

"A. Friday morning, it just happened that day I didn't work.

"Q. Why didn't you work on that particular day?

"A. It was very slow and we used to work four days a week, so it happened that Friday I didn't work.

"Q. It happened to be your day off?

"A. Yes, but I noticed all day Thursday, when I came home, I noticed his mail in the letter box.

"Q. Mr. Abrams' mail?

"A. That is right. Then Friday, I was up early. It just happened —I don't know what the occasion was, but I was up early and I saw the mail still lying around there. I said there must be something wrong. Maybe that fellow was either sick or something. So I went over, and he had one side of the window, it was open a little bit that you could be noticing.

"Q. Just a minute, now, what time of day was this?

"A. Oh, I think it was about 6.30 or later than that, I don't recall what time because I called the police and they marked the time down.

"Q. You called the police?

"A. After that, I called the police.

"Q. On the previous day, Thursday, which would be the 19th of April—is that correct?

"A. Well, I noticed the mail, I guess that is correct.

"Q. You noticed an accumulation of mail for Mr. Abrams in the mailbox?

"A. That is right.

"Q. He didn't pick it up, so you concluded something was the matter with him?

"A. Maybe he was sick, or something.

"Q. Pardon me?

"A. I thought maybe he is sick, lying around, or something.

"Q. So you picked up his mail?

"A. No, sir, I didn't pick up any mail, I just went over to see whether he is home or not.

"Q. This was on the following morning?

"A. That is right.

"Q. Early Friday morning?

"A. That is right.

"Q. Did you go out of the back door of your house?

"A. Yes, sir.

"Q. You walked to the front of the placed occupied by Mr. Abrams?

"A. That is right.

"Q. Did you look through the window first?

"A. That is right, sir.

"Q. Which window did you look through?

"A. I looked through the—how would you call it? Well, both windows are facing the doorway; there was one window towards the west side; it was open a little bit, because the other window I would notice right away what happened, but the other way I could just notice through the corner his feet, just like that, on the end of the bed (indicating), that is why I knew he was dead. Otherwise, I wouldn't even know it.

"Q. You looked through the window on the left side of the house?

"A. That is right.

"Q. It was open?

"A. It was open not completely.

"Q. How high was that window, about?

"A. The window, I would say, would reach me up until here, from here on (indicating), I don't know what it would be. I would say about—

"Chairman Burns: Four feet?

"A. Four or five feet. Well, five feet it couldn't be, because I am five-five.

"Q. More nearly four feet, do you think?

"A. Yes, because it would reach me up here (indicating).

"Q. It doesn't have to be exact. We want your best estimate. Of course, it can be measured. About how wide would you say that window was?

"A. The window is pretty wide. I would say that the window would be about almost a yard in width.

"Q. About three feet?

"A. Something like that.

"Q. Did the window raise up and down vertically, or did the whole window swing open on hinges.

"A. It swings open on the side.

"Q. The whole window?

"A. Yes.

"Q. So when it opened there was a space at the top and bottom?

"A. That is right.

"Q. And the side?

"A. That is right.

"Q. You went around and looked through that window and you saw Mr. Abrams on the bed?

"A. Just the feet laying on the bed.

"Q. What did you do then?

"A. Well, I just—I knocked right away on the window, calling him. There was no answer. I knocked on the door harder, I thought maybe he was sleeping hard, and no answer. So I jumped in the house and took the keys and opened the door and went over to touch him. I noticed his hands were as cold as ice. I jumped back, because this is the first time anything like that happened. I never seen such a thing.

"Q. Why did you go back into the house to get the keys?

"A. Because the door was locked; I couldn't open it.

"Q. Did you try to open it?

"A. That is right.

"Q. It was locked?

"A. It was locked.

"Q. So you went back in the house and got a key?

"A. I got a key.

"Q. What kind of a lock was on the door?

"A. It is a Yale lock.

"Q. You had a key and he had a key?

"A. Oh, yes, we always have a key in case of emergency.

"Q. When you opened the door and went in, did you notice any odor of gas?

"A. No, sir.

"Q. None. Did the air from the window ventilate the place?

"A. I guess it would. *Quite a bit was open, because I could notice his feet from the corner. It was quite a bit open; I guess that would ventilate it.* (Committee's italics.)

"Q. Did you make any examination to see whether or not the gas on those two appliances was turned on or off?

"A. Sir, I didn't examine anything because I was so shocked that I couldn't talk.

"Q. Did you leave right away?

"A. I left right away, and I locked the door and left.

"Q. You locked the door?

"A. That is right, and I called the police.

"Q. How long, would you say, you were in the room?

"A. Oh, I was there just a second. As soon as I touched him, I jumped back.

"Q. Then you left immediately?

"A. That is right.

"Q. Where did you go to put your call in to the police department?

"A. In the house.

"Q. What police department did you call?

"A. The Santa Monica Police Department.

"Q. How long after you called the Santa Monica Police Department was it before the police officers arrived at your home?

"A. It didn't take long. I would say about five minutes.

"Q. About five minutes?

"A. I would say more or less.

"Q. How far is your residence from the police department?

"A. It isn't too far.

"Q. It only took about five minutes to get there?

"A. We have a couple of stations. We have one station right at the beach near Pier Avenue, if you know that section.

"Q. Your house faces the ocean, doesn't it?

"A. That is right. It is between Nelson on the new way and the old speedway.

"Q. When the officers arrived, you showed them where to go?

"A. That is right, I gave them the keys.

"Q. Did you go with them into the premises again?

"A. That is right.

"Q. How long did you remain there at that time?

"A. Until they made the whole statement written out and I told them everything the way I found it and what happened.

"Q. They questioned you?

"A. That is right.

"Q. They gave you a statement?

"A. That is right.

"Q. You signed it?

"A. Yes.

"Q. Did your wife sign it?

"A. No. My wife wouldn't go in.

"Q. Only you signed it?

"A. I didn't even let her know about it because she is a very weak person and I would have more trouble with her than anything else.

"Q. After the police were there inspecting the premises, what did you do?

"A. They told me that is all what they have for me to do and they told me to go to the house.

"Q. Did you go back into the room again after that?

"A. No, sir.

"Q. Let me ask you this question: Is that structure, that one-room building occupied by Mr. Abrams in the same condition now that it was when he occupied it in April of this year?

"A. Everything is in the same condition except they made us take out the little stove and the refrigerator. That was orders from the health department that there shouldn't be any more gas there.

"Q. No gas at all?

"A. That is right.

"Q. You took those out?

"A. Yes.

"Q. What about the refrigerator?

"A. The refrigerator and everything was taken out.

"Q. Have you rented the premises to anyone since then?

"A. Yes, sir.

"Q. Somebody occupies the premises now?

"A. Yes.

"Q. But there is no eating facility in there now of any kind?

"A. We have an electric refrigerator and an electric two-burner there.

"Q. Did you notice anyone come to visit Mr. Abrams while he was there?

"A. No, sir.

"Q. You don't know how frequently he occupied the premises during the day, do you?

"A. I wouldn't know that because I am all day out.

"Q. You are gone most of the time?

"A. I am out all day myself.

"Q. You were on the premises on two occasions, when you first went in with the key——

"A. That is right.

"Q. And the second time when you went in after the police officers got there?

"A. After the police officers.

"Q. Those were the only two times you went in there?

"A. They had it sealed up right after they took out the body.

"Q. On either of those occasions, did you notice any books, papers or documents scattered about the room?

"A. It was after the police came. They looked into it. I mean, I wasn't there.

"Q. You were not there?

"A. No. They told me that was all they have in common with me and whatever they did I don't know. They told me about these books and all kind of things, but I didn't know, I never searched him. I never had anything in common with him so I didn't know anything about it. I was surprised myself when they told me what it was.

"Q. Why were you surprised?

"A. Because I didn't know. I thought he looked to be such a nice, quiet fellow. It really surprised me.

"Q. What did they tell you was there that surprised you so much?

"A. They said they found such books there, Communist books or Socialist books and I didn't know he would be doing those things.

"Q. They told you they found Communist books?

"A. That is right.

"Q. The police told you that?

"A. That is right.

"Q. Did Mr. Abrams receive very much mail?

"A. Occasionally. I wouldn't know how much he would receive.

"Q. Mostly letters or packages? Did he get packages of any kind?

"A. He used to get from home or his mother, or I don't know who it was.

"Q. You didn't pay much attention to that, I presume?

"A. No, it is not my business."

TESTIMONY OF DETECTIVE RALPH FELIX, SANTA MONICA
POLICE DEPARTMENT

"Q. (By Mr. Combs) : Will you state your full name for the record, please?

"A. Ralph Felix.

"Q. Where do you live, Mr. Felix?

"A. In the City of Santa Monica.

"Q. What is your occupation?

"A. Police officer attached to the detective bureau.

"Q. Mr. Felix, how long have you been a member of the Santa Monica Police Department?

"A. Approximately a little over 12 years.

"Q. How long have you been attached to the detective bureau?

"A. Since 1951.

"Q. Continuously?

"A. Yes, sir.

"Q. Were you so occupied on the morning of April 20, 1956?

"A. I was.

"Q. On that date, did you have occasion in the course of your official duties, to go to the premises known as 133 Wadsworth Avenue or Street in Santa Monica?

"A. I did.

"Q. Would you explain the circumstances under which you went to that address?

"A. I was in the bureau at approximately 8 o'clock that morning of April 20th, when the call came in to investigate a dead body.

"Q. From whom did the call come?

"A. It came from our desk sergeant downstairs. They had already detailed a uniformed crew out there. I arrived at approximately 8.20 or 8.25.

"Q. Will you describe what you found after arriving at the premises.

"A. If I may look at these notes.

"Q. Surely. Were those notes made in connection with the investigation of this particular case?

"A. They were.

"Q. By whom were they made?

"A. By myself.

"Q. You may proceed.

"A. On arrival at this address, 133 Wadsworth, I was directed to a small bungalow in the rear of the property. This bungalow was located on the northeast corner of 133 Wadsworth. Upon entering the bungalow, my attention was directed to numerous books and literature referring to Lenin, Marx, Trotsky and Stalin, Communism and Socialism and also to a large quantity of small newspapers with different or numerous titles referring to *Labor Action* with the head of 'Dear Comrade' and stuff like that. The body was located in the northeast part of the building there on the bed, in pajamas, fully clothed in pajamas.

"Q. Mr. Felix, was this the only room in the building?

"A. Yes, it was.

"Q. At the time you got there, did you notice a window on either side of the door?

"A. As you entered, there was a window on the left-hand side of the building and one right around it.

"Q. Were any of those windows open when you got there?

"A. I didn't notice right away. Our uniformed officers, Wilkerson and Ortega, were there at that time. They had looked through the room pretty well before I arrived.

"Q. Where was this literature and these books located in that room. What I am getting at is this: were all these papers and these documents and the things you have described—I am not speaking of bound books now, but the papers—were they in orderly arrangement, or were they scattered around the place?

"A. Well, they were scattered pretty well.

"Q. How about the books? Were they scattered?

"A. The books were in apple crates or in apple boxes.

"Q. Stacked up?

"A. Some were out of the box laying in various locations of the room.

"Q. Were any of them open, lying open?

"A. No, sir.

"Q. Were papers scattered around the room?

"A. They were on a small table and off to the side of the bed. The exact location I can't give you.

"Q. Were there a great number of them or just a few?

"A. There was a great number of them, I would say.

"Q. When you first went into the premises did you notice any odor of gas?

"A. No. As I said, the uniformed officers had been there; the door was wide open and so was the window at that time.

"Q. Will you continue and tell us what you did, please?

"A. I immediately contacted our I. D. bureau and had the identification technician come to the room and take pictures. I contacted the coroner's office. I looked about the premises for any evidence of foul play and made the general investigation regarding a dead body.

"Q. Were you there when a representative from the coroner's office arrived?

"A. I was.

"Q. Did he advise you as to the cause of death?

"A. He did after examining the body approximately two days later.

"Q. What did he advise you caused the death?

"A. Excessive carbon monoxide in the body, approximately *35 to 50 percent* (committee's italics).

"Q. If you don't mind telling us, are you reading from the police report?

"A. Yes, I am.

"Q. Would you re-examine that report. Wasn't it *71 percent* (committee's italics).

"A. He mentioned that at first.

"Q. Didn't he add something?

"A. But it wasn't correct at the time. The report finally read a possibility of 35 to 50 percent.

"Q. May I see the document from which you are reading? Would you read that portion I have indicated into the record, please?

"A. 'The doctor advised us that the deceased has expired from carbon monoxide poisoning. He stated the blood of the deceased had been checked twice and was found to have a high carbon monoxide level, *71 percent.*' (Committee's italics.)

"Q. Read the next sentence, please.

"A. 'He further added, death *could* result from a 35 to 50 percent carbon monoxide level.' (Committee's italics.) I am sorry, I didn't see that the first time.

"Q. It is difficult to read. Your copy is blurred and difficult to read, but mine is typed. If I make a mistake, will you correct me. I will read another paragraph into the record.

'At approximately 11.30 a.m. this date,—' do you find that in your notes, Mr. Felix?

"A. Yes, sir.

"Q. 'At approximately 11.30 a.m. this date, Dr. Griswold of the Los Angeles County Coroner's Office, contacted us through Deputy Coroner Schwatzberger.' We have to get this into the record anyway, so I will read the whole thing. Follow me on your official copy and if I make a mistake will you correct me?

"A. I certainly will.

"Q. I am reading paragraph one. 'A further check of Abrams effects indicated that he is a student at U. C. L. A. We found a white card bearing the inscription: University of California, Los Angeles, Department of Physical Education, issued to Abrams, Sheldon J. This name is written in ink and below it is a large printed *A* indicating the classification by the university division. No restrictions is also printed on this card. In ink, the date was indicated as 1-30-56. Initials C. A. S. or possibly G. A. L. on the card in ink.'

"A. That is G. A. S. the way I have it here, or possibly G. A. L.

"Q. (Reading further) 'U. C. L. A. was contacted and we found that this is a medical classification after a thorough examination on the date which appears on the card.

" 'We further learned that subject registered in U. C. L. A. on 11-23-54 after completion of courses at the University of Illinois, located at Navy Pier, Chicago, Illinois. He entered in February, 1950, and withdrew June, 1950. He then entered Roosevelt University, Chicago, Illinois, in September, 1950, and withdrew February, 1954, at which time he received his B.A. degree, dated February, 1954.

" 'On 4-21-56, at approximately 10 a.m., a person representing himself as Philip Abrams of 433 Brice, Chicago, Illinois, purporting to be an uncle of the deceased, came to Hq., requesting information regarding the deceased. He was referred to the Los Angeles Coroner's Office in Los Angeles.

" 'At approximately 11.30 a.m., this date, Dr. Griswold of the Los Angeles County Coroner's Office, contacted us through Deputy Coroner Schwatzberger. The doctor advised us that the deceased has expired from carbon monoxide poisoning. He stated that the blood of the deceased had been checked twice and was found to have a high carbon monoxide level—71 percent. He further added, death could result from a 35 to 50 percent carbon monoxide level. *On the possibility of foul play,* Coroner Schwatzberger contacted the Public Administrator, Mr. Parchmont, and a short time later advised us that we were to contact Gates,

Kingsley and Gates Mortuary and have a representative from that company accompany us to 133 Wadsworth, at which time we would be permitted to enter and recheck the premises. The Coroner's Office also requested that Dr. Griswold accompany us and examine the premises.

" 'At approximately 1.30 p.m., in company with Dr. Griswold and a representative from the Gates, Kinsley and Gates Mortuary, we went to 133 Wadsworth. After entering, and with Dr. Griswold's assistance, we located three possible sources that could produce carbon monoxide: one, a small, movable gas heater; two, a gas refrigerator; three, a two-burner gas hotplate.

" 'The building has two ordinary sized windows located on the south wall, one on either side of the only door leading into the building. There is a window approximately 30 inches high and four feet long on the west wall of the building. Located at the northwest corner and on the outside of the room proper (not accessible from the inside of the room) is a lavatory and shower.

" 'The room inside is 10 feet in length and eleven feet in depth, with a slanting roof and ceiling, descending rather sharply from approximately 10 feet in height to approximately six feet in height. This descension is from the south wall to the north wall.'

"I think you said the bed was in the northeast corner of the room?

"A. That is correct.

"Q. (Reading) : 'The furnishings of the room are as follows: a single bed, located in the northeast corner of the building, extending south along the east wall. At the foot of the bed is a crate, 22 x 17 x 11 inches, which appears to be wood and it contains books and papers. Near the southeast corner of the room, and extending along the south wall, is a combination two-burner hotplate, which is enclosed in a wooden cabinet and under the hotplate is space for pots or pans or other small items. Still on the south wall, and directly west of the above-mentioned combination, is a small brown heater. West of the door is a straight-back chair. In the southwest corner of the room is a wash basin. Along the west wall, north of the wash basin, is a round table, 30 x 30 x 22 inches. Next to this table is a Servel gas refrigerator. Next to the refrigerator and near the northwest corner of the room, is a portable clothes closet, 70 x 24 x 22 inches. On the north wall, near the northwest corner of the room, there are four—what appeared to be apple boxes, lying on their sides and stacked one on top of the other. These boxes are completely filled with the aforementioned books. The shelving is inadequate and does not hold all of the books and stacked on top are four piles of books, some of which reach to the ceiling. Next to this is a three-drawer dresser, approximately 28 x 32 x 12 inches. On top of the dresser are numerous papers, an alarm clock, wrist watch, and a small red lamp with a brown shade. Above the dresser is a small mirror, approximately 26 x 17 inches, hanging on the wall.

" 'Located among deceased's papers were envelopes, letters. They were addressed to the deceased and have return addresses—.' ·

"We will omit reading the names into the record, in pursuance of the policy announced this morning.

" 'There were numerous letters that apparently were made to one person, and then distributed to other members of this league found in the room. The majority of these letter were addressed to Max. All of these refer to YSL, ISL, SP, SWP, YPSL and Pacifists.'

"Mr. Felix, I don't know whether your pages correspond to mine or not.

"A. No, they don't. Mine are a little bit different.

"Q. Then I had better let you do this. Will you go back and check and see what is meant by 'this league'?

"A. I had better get over there and check with you.

"Mr. Combs: Off the record while we compare this, Mr. Reporter. * * * On the record, Mr. Reporter. Mr. Felix, does that refer back to the Young Socialist League mentioned in the previous paragraph?

"A. Yes, it does.

"Q. (Continuing): 'Many of them gratefully mentioned the activities of Shelley (nickname of deceased), for his fine activities in the Los Angeles area. One-mentioned that * * * had heard that Shelley regretted that he did not run for an NEC membership at the convention. This letter further boasted of the activities of * * *, and later inquired for the Rochester address of "C." '

"The C is in quotation marks; is that right?

"A. Yes, it is.

"Q. The rest of this report contains a great many names of individuals which will be omitted at this time in pursuance of the policy already announced by the committee. I notice a statement in the report 'Papers pertaining to this case have been placed in an envelope and turned over to the property custodian.' Do you find that statement?

"A. Yes, I do.

"Q. Who was the property custodian? Is he the property custodian in the police department?

"A. Yes.

"Q. Is there anything in any of your reports that would indicate whether or not the gas heater or the gas plate was on when the body was found by Mr. Kaplan?

"A. No, there isn't anything indicated like that in the report.

"Q. Would you look at the next to the last page of the report—on the last page, or the next to the last page, headed 'Investigation by Dets. Chapman and Felix'?

"A. Yes, here it is.

"Q. Would you read that, please?

"A. 'Our examination of the heater and the two-burner hotplate indicated that *both were turned off at the device and also at the wall connection. The gas refrigerator is still in operation and the pilot light is still burning.* (Committee's italics)

"Q. The window was open on the west side of the premises, according to the report given to you by Mr. Kaplan. The body was reported to have 71 percent incidence of carbon monoxide, and yet both gas appliances were turned off, not only at the appliance but at the baseboard?

"A. That is correct.

"Q. The pilot light on the Servel refrigerator was still burning?

"A. That is right.

"Q. Were any photographs taken by the police department at the scene of the death?

"A. Yes, there were.

"Q. Did those photographs include pictures of the interior as well as the exterior of the premises?

"A. That is right.

"Q. Do you have those with you?

"A. Yes.

"Q. I will come around there to the table and you can identify them and we will introduce them in evidence. The pictures of the exterior of the premises were taken by technicians from the Santa Monica Police Department?

"A. They were.

"Q. Will you make those available to the committee?

"A. Yes, I will.

"Q. You don't have them with you at the present time?

"A. No, I don't.

"Q. Would you describe each of the photographs, please, as you hand them to me so that they may be identified for the record?

"A. Here is the one that was near the wash basin, indicating some of the literature that was strewn about the room.

"Q. Were these photographs taken in your presence, Mr. Felix?

"A. Yes, they were.

"Mr. Combs: Mr. Chairman, I will ask that the first photograph showing some of the documents in the room, be marked Exhibit 1 in connection with the testimony of this witness, because we have already received some other exhibits this morning.

"Chairman Burns: They will be admitted in consecutive order beginning with number one.

"Q. (By Mr. Combs): Will you describe the next one, Mr. Felix?

"A. This next one was taken from the door in toward the room, indicating the bookshelf and the little dresserette next to the bed.

"Q. All of these were taken in your presence?

"A. Yes, they were.

"Mr. Combs: I ask this one be received as Exhibit 2 in connection with the testimony of this witness.

"Chairman Burns: Very well.

"Q. (By Mr. Combs): What is next?

"A. Here is one which is a little table with more literature on it. I don't recall exactly where this table was situated, but I believe it was near the east end or the foot of the bed.

"Mr. Combs: I ask this photograph be marked Exhibit 3.

"Chairman Burns: It may be so marked.

"Q. (By Mr. Combs): Were these documents stacked on the table like that when you went into the place?

"A. Yes, they were.

"Q. Would you describe the next one, please?

"A. The next one is a close-up of the books in the apple boxes giving the exact titles of each one.

"Mr. Combs: We will mark this Exhibit 4.

"Q. What is the next one, Mr. Felix?

"A. The next picture would be a shot of the body as it was found when I went into the room.

"Mr. Combs: We will mark this Exhibit 5.

"Q. What is the next one?

"A. This is the shot of the body from the foot of the bed indicating how the body laid from that position.

"Mr. Combs: We will mark this Exhibit 6.

"The Witness: That is about it. These are small ones here.

"Q. Mr. Felix, would you please examine your supplemental report? It is headed 3.19.1.

"A. I have it.

"Q. I will read it and if I make a mistake, will you correct me?

"A. Which one of the supplemental reports are you reading, they are numbered the same?

"Q. This one is No. 56-4253 in the upper right-hand corner.

"A. They are all numbered the same. O. K., swell, I have it now.

"Q. (Reading): 'Supplemental Report, date occurred 4-18 noon/4-20 7:50 A—133 Wadsworth. Victim: Abrams, Sheldon Joseph, 133 Wadsworth. Off.' Does that stand for 'officers'?

"A. That is right.

"Q. (Reading): 'Ortega/Wilkerson, SMPD.' I assume that stands for Santa Monica Police Department?

"A. That is right.

"Q. 'Statement of officers investigating: *Due to above circumstances and large amount of Communist literature in the room, detectives and J. O'Connell (F. B. I.) were notified.* (Committee's italics.)

" 'L. A. Coroner was called and investigation turned over to Mr. O'Connell and Detective Ralph Felix.' Is that a correct reading of that copy?

"A. That is right.

"Q. Mr. Felix, as I understand it, it is not the province of the Santa Monica Police Department to determine the cause of death in a case of this type. Did you make any determination or finding as to whether or not this death was caused from an accident or from natural causes or homicide or suicide?

"A. No. We didn't determine it, we left it that way. However, due to the coroner's report, we did figure it was accidental.

"Q. Did you ever make any effort to determine how a body could absorb 71 percent carbon monoxide when both of the sources of carbon monoxide were turned off, namely, the heater and the stove?

"A. Well, no, I am not qualified for that.

"Q. That is not your province?

"A. No.

"Q. You turned that part of it over to other authorities, did you not?

"A. That is correct.

"Q. When you made these reports that have been read and took the photographs that you took and called in other authorities, so far as you were concerned in the Santa Monica Police Department, your duties ceased. Is that right?

"A. That is right. From all indications at the premises and around the surroundings, checking with the neighbors and all, there was no indication of foul play as far as the Santa Monica Police Department was concerned.

"Q. Did you later call out some representatives of the Southern California Gas Company to check those appliances?

"A. Yes, sir, they were called out.

"Q. What was the result of their investigation?

"A. I never did get a full report from them, but they stated there was no vent on the Servel refrigerator. There were numerous papers and an oilcloth thrown over the vent part of the refrigerator indicating that fumes from this particular place might have stayed in the room.

"Q. Fumes from what?

"A. From the refrigerator.

"Q. From the refrigerator?

"A. The vent from the refrigerator.

"Q. Did their report indicate whether or not there were any leaks in the gas lines that came into the premises?

"A. All I got from them was an oral report, sir. The company man stated there was no indicated leaks.

"Q. No leaks?

"**A. No leaks.**

"Q. The gas used in the Santa Monica area—what kind of gas do you have in your home? Do you have any gas appliances in your place?

"A. Yes, sir.

"Q. Is there an odor to that gas?

"A. Yes, there is.

"Q. It is quite noticeable, isn't it?

"A. Yes, it is.

"Mr. Combs: I think that is all.

"Senator McCarthy: Mr. Chairman, I have a question.

"Q. (By Senator McCarthy): What did the coroner's report show as to the estimated time of death after the body was discovered?

"A. No more than 12 hours, if I recall right.

"Q. Twelve hours?

"A. Yes, sir.

TESTIMONY OF HANNA CLARA KRAUS

Miss Kraus testified that she resided at 6465 Dunsmuir Avenue, Van Nuys, California, and since July, 1948, had been employed in the Senior Medical Records Library, Student Health Service at U. C. L. A. A subpena had been served upon the witness asking her to bring certain records from her office. She identified the records and in that connection testified as follows:

"Q. (By Mr. Combs): Of what do they [the documents produced pursuant to subpena] consist?

"A. What we call an entering physical examination.

"Q. For a student entering U. C. L. A., is an entering physical examination mandatory?

"A. It is for all that we call regularly registered students. They all must have this.

"Q. In connection with what student do these records pertain?

"A. These records pertain to Sheldon Joseph Abrams.

"Q. What is the date on the document to which you are now referring?

"A. January 30, 1956.

"Q. Was that the date of his physical examination?

"A. Yes.

"Q. What is the other document you have with it?

"A. It is a second sheet to the same kind of thing.

"Q. Another part of the same document?

"A. Yes.

"Q. Would you interpret that in lay language for the benefit of the committee? First of all, will you explain the extent of the examination, how thorough was it?

"A. We consider it thorough enough to determine whether he is able to undertake most all activities that the Physical Education Department might require, that he will not pass on disease to anyone else. It is a screening examination, more or less.

"Q. What kind of physical activities?

"A. The Physical Education Department has all kinds, vigorous and less vigorous. It is to know what the students can take.

"Q. If there were any physical disabilities which would preclude the student from engaging in these more violent and vigorous types of physical exercises, that fact would be noted on one or both of the records which you have with you?

"A. That is right.

"Q. Are any such restrictions noted on that, or either of them?

"A. There are no restrictions.

"Q. Would you tell us in lay language, please, as nearly as the subject will permit, what the examination consisted of?

"A. I could read the headings.

"Q. Would you do that, please?

"A. In other words, his eyes were checked without glasses and were fairly good. His teeth and gums and his eyes again, his ears, nose, throat, neck, chest, heart, lungs, abdomen, genitals, penis, back, extremities, posture, height, weight, skin, pulse, blood pressure, urinalysis, and photofluorogram, which is an X-ray.

"Q. In each of those categories, were there any restrictions? Were there any ailments or defects?

"A. None noted.

"Q. None, whatsoever?

"A. That is right.

"Q. So that far as the examination reveals on the date that the same was made, Mr. Abrams was in good physical condition?

"A. Yes. I might add, on the second sheet, our skin tests, a special test for this particular admission, if you want a complete story, were also negative. There are three skin tests and I think they were negative."

TESTIMONY OF DR. GEORGE W. STEVENSON

The next two witnesses, Dr. George W. Stevenson and Dr. Dermot Taylor, were the two best toxicologists the committee could find. They were called to testify for the purpose of exploring the circumstances surrounding the death of Sheldon Abrams, although the committee emphasized several times that the manner in which he died was, in the committee's view, a subordinate element which established a background to the chain of circumstances that lead to the disclosures in the hundreds of documents in the room where the body was found. Since the opinions of these two experts are extremely significant, and

their training and experience in the field of toxicology is of importance
in establishing them as experts whose opinions are entitled to the most
complete credence, their qualifications are given in full. They testified
as follows:

"Q. (By Mr. Combs): Will you give your full name to the reporter,
please?

"A. George W. Stevenson.

"Q. You are a doctor of medicine?

"A. I am.

"Q. You are connected with the University of California at Los Angeles?

"A. That is correct.

"Q. In what capacity, sir?

"A. I am assistant professor of pharmacology and toxicology.

"Q. How long have you held that position?

"A. Since July, 1955.

"Q. Where did you take your undergraduate work?

"A. At Occidental College, here in Los Angeles.

"Q. Where did you obtain your medical degree?

"A. At the University of California in San Francisco.

"Q. You interned where?

"A. At the U. S. Public Health Service Hospital in San Francisco.

"Q. Were you ever engaged in private practice?

"A. I was not engaged in private practice although I did practice
medicine at the Public Health Service for a little over a year in San
Diego after completion of my internship.

"Q. What type of course do you teach at U. C. L. A.?

"A. We teach primarily the medical students in the medical school.

"Q. Would you define, for the benefit of the laymen, which would
certainly include me, what is toxicology?

"A. Toxicology is the study of poisons, their effect upon animals,
people, tissues, and so on.

"Q. Is carbon monoxide considered a poison within the terminology
of toxicology?

"A. Yes, it is.

"Q. What about carbon dioxide?

"A. Carbon dioxide can also be poisonous under certain circumstances.

"Q. How long have you been interested in the field of toxicology?

"A. As a student of medicine you do learn toxicology. You have to
be interested in toxicology in medical school. I also spent several years
in graduate work in chemistry at the University of California at Berkeley. At that time, I was also interested in toxicology. I have had this
job since July of 1955.

"Q. Where is your office at the university located, doctor?

"A. It is located in the Department of Pharmacology at U. C. L. A.
Medical Center.

"Q. Do you conduct your work in toxicology in conjunction with
anybody else? Do you have an associate or colleague?

"A. No. Of course there is always some collaboration in any research
with other members.

"Q. Have you heard of a case involving the death of a graduate student at U. C. L. A. by the name of Sheldon Joseph Abrams?

"A. Yes, I have.

"Q. Did you conduct any investigation of the circumstances surrounding his death?

"A. No. I was never involved in any official way at all.

"Q. I don't mean official, but unofficial?

"A. No, I have had no direct contact in examination.

"Q. Did you examine any documents or reports in connection with his death?

"A. Yes. I examined the police reports concerning the discovery of this man's body.

"Q. I take it, then, you are aware of the fact that death was attributed to an incidence of 71 percent of carbon monoxide in the blood of the student?

"A. Yes. It was reported that he had 71 percent of his hemoglobin as carboxyhemoglobin.

"Q. What would be a lethal accumulation of carbon monoxide in an individual 25 years of age, 5 feet 8½ inches in height, 160 pounds in weight—you heard the testimony of the witness who preceded you, did you not?

"A. Yes, I did.

"Q. (continuing)—Who was in good physical condition. What would be a lethal dose of carbon monoxide in an instance of that kind, if you can give that approximation?

"A. Even though you have stated his age, sex, and so on, it is not possible to give any definite limit. All that can be said is that when carboxyhemoglobin concentration or proportion is in excess of roughly 40, death would be possible. As the percentage increases, say above 50, death is much more likely.

"Q. Would 71 percent be considered a massive incidence?

"A. Yes. It is a very high proportion of carboxyhemoglobin.

"Q. Now, doctor, did you read the police report?

"A. Yes, I did.

"Q. You were not present yesterday when Mr. Kaplan, who was the first person to discover the body, testified; and from whom the premises at which the body had been found had been rented, nor when Ralph Felix, the detective from the Santa Monica Police Department, testified, you were not here then?

"A. No, I was not here.

"Q. But you have read the police report, haven't you?

"A. Yes.

"Q. When did you first receive a copy of that report, doctor?

"A. That was about a week ago; I am sorry I don't remember the exact time.

"Q. That's all right, that is close enough. In that report did you read about the physical description of the premises?

"A. Yes, I did.

"Q. And the fact that at the time that the body was first discovered by Mr. Kaplan, the two gas appliances were turnd off, not only at the appliances but also at the floor board where the gas entered the building. Do you remember that?

"A. Unfortunately, that did not appear in the police report. The gas appliances present in the room were enumerated but there was no mention as to whether or not they were operating or shut off.

"Q. They were off. It was so testified yesterday both by Mr. Kaplan and by Detective Felix. There was a Servel gas refrigerator in this single room, which was 11 x 12 feet in size. When the body was discovered, the pilot light of the Servel refrigerator was burning normally, because the testimony yesterday established the fact that there were no leaks in any of the gas appliances. The gas company checked that at the request of the Santa Monica Police Department. All of them were in good working condition.

"A. I see.

"Q. Doctor, what are the post mortem evidences of carbon monoxide poisoning?

"A. The only positive evidence is the presence of carboxyhemoglobin in the blood.

"Q. Is it not a fact that in cases where there is an incidence of 71 percent, which you have described as massive, that reddish blotches or reddish patches appear over the skin surface of the body?

"A. Yes. It is due to the colored nature of the carboxyhemoglobin itself.

"Q. Do you find the symptoms of bloodshot and blood engorged appearance in the eyes?

"A. Yes.

"Q. How long after death would it be possible for a post-mortem examination to reveal with accuracy the cause of death due to carbon monoxide poisoning?

"A. For months or year. This is a fairly stable complex which is formed unless it is exposed to a high concentration of oxygen.

"Q. Technically, would death by carbon monoxide poisoning be called asphyxial death?

"A. Yes, it would.

"Q. I presume such a death could also be caused by strangulation.

"A. That is right.

"Q. Or suffocation.

"A. Yes, it could.

"Q. Or by carbon dioxide poisoning.

"A. It could be caused by an number of things which exclude oxygen from the tissues.

"Q. In how many ways can death be caused?

"A. Legally, death is defined as a stopping of the heart.

"Q. Death could result from a natural cause?

"A. Yes.

"Q. Or an accidental cause?

"A. Yes.

"Q. Suicide?

"A. Yes.

"Q. Homicide?

"A. Yes.

"Q. Are there any others?

"A. No, I can't think of any offhand.

"Q. I am basing this on the legal report which was read in its entirety into evidence yesterday, but also on the testimony of Mr. Kaplan, who discovered the body, also on the testimony of Detective Felix, who was there in 10 minutes after the body had been discovered; I am basing this next hypothetical question upon these factual elements already before the committee: Assuming that this boy whose health was in the state that has been testified, who was of an age, weight and size I have described, who occupied a room 12 x 11 feet in size in which there were three windows, one open at least an inch, four feet in height and three feet in width, a window which swung out like you would open a notebook so that there would be a space around the window—one witness thought it was an inch and another several inches, but the minimal description was at least one inch—and that there were in the room three gas appliances all in good working condition, namely, a Servel gas refrigerator, a two-plate gas burner, a portable gas heater, the last two being turned off at the two places I have mentioned; that the body of the occupant whom I have described was found clad in pajamas stretched out on the bed; that the post-mortem examination showed 71 percent carbon monoxide poisoning—what would be your opinion as to how death occurred?

"A. I would say, if all these assumptions are correct——

"Q. They are not assumptions, Doctor.

"A. Yes, I understand.

"Q. They were testified to.

"A. Yes. If all these conditions are specified, then it does not seem possible that death could have resulted accidentally from carbon monoxide from a Servel gas refrigerator with the window up and the other appliances off.

"Q. It is your opinion that with 71 percent accumulation of carbon monoxide, death by accidental means would have been impossible?

"A. Yes. May I make a statement in regard to this?

"Q. Certainly.

"A. First of all, with regard to the gas itself, this is natural gas in this area. This gas will not cause death as a result of leakage unless so much gas is present that oxygen is excluded. This takes a terrific concentration of gas. There is no carbon monoxide in this natural gas, so that carbon monoxide can originate only from a process of incomplete combustion on the part of the flame. We have a situation with one flame in the room, of the Servel gas refrigerator.

"Q. That is right.

"A. Fatal poisoning has resulted from the presence in the room of a Servel gas refrigerator, but in all such cases all windows and doors have been closed. This, of course, requires a defective gas refrigerator, so that if this refrigerator was in proper working order, it would not produce an undue amount of carbon monoxide *even if the windows and doors were shut*—thus, death would not be produced. (Committee's italics.)

"Q. Even if the doors and windows were closed?

"A. Yes. *Even if it wasn't in proper working order and released some carbon monoxide, then if a window was open, poisoning should not result either*. (Committee's italics.)

"Q. Even though it was defective, with the window open, still death would not result from that type of accident?

"A. That is right."

TESTIMONY OF DR. DERMOT TAYLOR

"Q. (By Mr. Combs): Will you state your name in full, Doctor?

"A. Dermot Taylor.

"Q. Where do you live, Doctor?

"A. 346 South Anita Avenue, Brentwood.

"Q. What is your occupation?

"A. I am Chairman of the Department of Pharmacology and Toxicology at the University of California here in Los Angeles.

"Q. How long have you occupied that position?

"A. Since July, 1953.

"Q. Where did you take your undergraduate work?

"A. I took my undergraduate work at the Portola Royal School in Ireland and my graduate work in Trinity College, Dublin, Ireland.

"Q. What academic degrees do you hold, Doctor?

"A. Bachelors degree in medicine, surgery, obstetrics, and gynecology. I hold a doctors degree and a B.A. degree from the University of Dublin.

"Q. How long have you specialized in toxicology?

"A. I have been in the field of toxicology since 1945.

"Q. You heard the testimony of Dr. Stevenson who preceded you?

"A. That is correct.

"Q. Have you also examined the police reports of the case of Sheldon Joseph Abrams?

"A. I have examined the police reports that were sent to me by the campus police.

"Q. You are familiar with their contents?

"A. Yes.

"Q. Did you hear the hypothetical question I put to Dr. Stevenson a moment ago?

"A. Yes, sir, I did.

"Q. If I were to put the same question to you, what would be your answer?

"A. I am in agreement with what Dr. Stevenson said.

"Q. Would you kindly amplify your opinion in any way you deem it fit, Doctor?

"A. Bearing in mind that the subject met his death from carbon monoxide poisoning—that seems to me to be clear—and bearing in mind that the window was open and that the only other appliances, the Servel refrigerator was certified as being in good condition, I cannot understand how the individual met his death in this room under those conditions.

"Q. In your opinion, it would not have been possible for his death to have been accidental due to carbon monoxide poisoning of 71 percent from a Servel gas refrigerator with the window open?

"A. That is my opinion.

"Q. That is all, Doctor.

"Chairman Burns: I have a question. If gas leaked into the room in an unburned, natural state, carbon monoxide would not be present?

"A. That is right. There would be no carbon monoxide present in an individual's body.

"Q. (By Mr. Combs): In other words, in order to produce carbon monoxide the gas would have to be burned and thereby exhaust the oxygen in the room?

"A. No, that is not quite the case. The gas would have to be partially burned and the refrigerator would have to be sufficiently defective to prevent complete combustion.

"Q. That clears it up. One other question, Doctor. If death were due to carbon *dioxide* poisoning, what would be the post mortem evidence? Would that be identical with that caused by carbon *monoxide* poisoning?

"A. There would be no resemblance to a pathologist. There would be no carbon monoxide in the blood.

"Q. If gas merely leaked into the room, which is not shown by any of the facts before the committee—as a matter of fact, the exact opposite is true because the gas company certified there were no leaks— but assuming there were—that in and of itself could not have caused this 71 percent carbon monoxide poisoning, could it?

"A. That is correct."

THE ABRAMS DOCUMENTS

In the process of sorting and correlating the hundreds of documents found in Abrams' room on April 20, 1956, the committee was struck by several significant facts. In the first place, as Detective Felix testified, these documents were scattered about the place in the utmost confusion as though someone had been searching through them; in the second place, the committee divided these documents into two main categories: the first comprising reports from the national headquarters of the Young Socialist League at 114 West 14th Street, New York City, N. Y., together with other relatively innocuous documents; and the second group comprising critical letters and papers, such as the minutes of meetings attended by members of the Communist Party in Southern California and the names and addresses of contacts at colleges and universities throughout the United States, coupled with copies of letters sent to and original letters received from such contacts. It appeared significant to the committee that the first category of documents proceeded in steady chronological sequence with no apparent gaps, whereas, in the critical documents there was no such chronology, the documents themselves indicating that in many instances key payers had been removed.

In quoting from and commenting on the contents of the various Abrams documents, the committee will follow its practice of refraining from giving the true names of those individuals whose status has not yet been ascertained, but in all other instances the names of persons mentioned in the documents will be given as they appear.

Sheldon Abrams graduated from Sullivan High School in Chicago in 1949, and enlisted in the United States Marine Corps on February 1st of that year, having received his honorable discharge at Parris

Island, South Carolina, on January 31, 1950. From February, 1950, until June of that year, he attended the University of Illinois, and thereafter continued his undergraduate work at Roosevelt College, Chicago, from September 1950 to February 1954, when he received a bachelor of arts degree. He came to Los Angeles in November, 1954, and worked as a salesman and at other jobs both in Los Angeles and Santa Monica. At the time of his graduation from Roosevelt College, he had been editor in chief of the *Torch*, official student newspaper of that school. During his senior year he received many letters from an individual who was in the United States Army in Korea and Japan, and who, in pursuance of the policy above-mentioned, we shall refer to as Stanley. Since these letters reveal much about the political thinking and activities of Abrams, we quote liberally from the letters received from Stanley and also from the carbon copies of letters addressed to him from Abrams. All of this correspondence occurred in the year 1954.

The first letter indicates something of the rebellious nature of young Abrams while he was at Roosevelt College, his flair for organizing, his interest in radical activities, and his defiance of the administrators of the institution he was attending. He wrote to Stanley, whom he had known as a student at Roosevelt College, as follows:

"Events have occurred so suddenly and with such force that I haven't even had a meal until today since last Monday night, so you can understand why I haven't written.

"Summarily, this is the story.

"There has been considerable talk around school to the effect that the administration has been trying to get rid of Pontius and Hans Tischler of the Music Department. Both received word that due to financial stringency, their contracts would not be renewed. The student council undertook an investigation of the affair, while the *Torch* reported whatever facts it was able to glean. James Messer, a music student, created a new stir when he charged that Creanza, the Dean of the music school, threatened to have his draft board induct him if he, Messer, did not stop leading the 'underground movement' against him. The S. Coun., under Edna's charges of prejudice, undertook an investigation of this case. Edna called for a poll of the music school student body. The poll was halted by Baldulf, who claimed that the senate passed legislation prohibiting polling without approval of the president's polling committee. They then undertook a poll outside the school by sending letters to the entire student body of the music school questioning them on aspects of the school. The returned polls were to be opened, tabulated and then destroyed by Harold Linson. Linson received an administrative order from Sparling calling a halt to the poll. The *Torch*, in the meantime, had started to conduct its own poll, not to determine anything, but rather to see if the administration would try to stop us. That they did, issuing an administrative order citing a nonexistent law prohibiting polls without prior approval. George and the board of editors were then called in to Sparling's office after George informed Sparling that he would disobey the order. After a four hour session with Sparling and Leys, whom he called as soon as we started to embarrass him with questions about academic freedom, freedom of inquiry, etc., we left receiving the promise of expulsion if we published the poll. What occurred during those four hours was one of the most interesting experiences I've ever had.

"Sparling [President of Roosevelt College] is a complete phony, a liar and a scoundrel—as well as a scared 'liberal.' George was absolutely brilliant in his argument, slicing the feeble phrases of Leys and Sparling about the 'sensible limits of democracy,' ethics, administrative prerogatives, etc. We informed them that we were going through with the poll and if they expelled us or suppressed the Torch we would carry the fight to the general liberal society, having already been advised by the ACLU [American Civil Liberties Union] and AAUP [American Association of University Professors] on our proposed plans and having secured their unofficial support. Edna, in the meantime, had been working on Harold Jennis and Saul, whom she changed from a conservative liberal into a flaming radical. He had written George a letter advising him that he was within his constitutional rights in taking the poll. While we were in negotiations with Sparling, a letter arrived to him from Frank Untermeyer of the Political Science Department informing Sparling that he, Untermeyer, had advised George to continue with the poll. Untermeyer, you may know, comes from a millionaire family and has been a secret contributor of large sums of money to the school. Sparling made the mistake of reading the letter to us, and this gave us increased encouragement. Ed then entered the session and announced that he was resigning from the presidency of the student council and expected the entire council to follow him. We suddenly realized we were in a strong position and we hit them all the harder.

"Thursday evening and all day Friday I spent organizing. I had already started an organization on Wednesday 'potential,' which had fifteen members and was growing. We made plans to publish the Torch underground if necessary, and received promises of considerable financial aid, as well as advice from faculty members whom Edna had been telling the story to in her usual persuasive manner. Friday evening, just before we went to press, we were called into the office of a very frantic, frightened fool, Edward J. Sparling. He pleaded with us to consider the good name of the school, showed us his press clippings as a champion of liberalism and begged us to reconsider. We had by this time taken a slew of polls, dug up proof that testing and counseling service records had been open to the FBI, the Messer-Creanza story was breaking with Lerner and three other instructors signing a statement that Creanza had admitted threatening Messer, a faculty group had been secretly formed to appeal to the alumni to halt all contributions to the school, and Leys called the Torch a bunch of revolutionaries.

"At the printers Friday, we suddenly realized that we had forgotten to write a newspaper, and frantically put one together (I'll send it to you Monday) around midnight. Sparling formed a committee loaded in our favor to consider procedural rights of students in poll matters. Sparling withdrew his threat of expulsion, since he saw we were going through with it anyway. It is perhaps inselictious [sic] to be over-elated at this time; the thing could still rebound against us. Nevertheless, we have the knowledge that we have accomplished something quite remarkable in these days of reaction. We have defied, under threat of expulsion, an administrative order. We have, temporarily at least, got a bureaucratic administration and we are hanging on with tight fists. All this accomplished by a handfull of revolutionaries! Amateur revolutionaries at that. The inert mass of students still remain unaware of what has been going on—but Monday, they should get a good idea. What lies ahead at R. C., I don't know. Henry and I have applied for co-editorship of the *Torch* for next semester. We are the only applicants, but nevertheless anticipate some sort of impediment from the publication's board which has been persecuting the *Torch* for some time now. Hank and I are being tried by them Wednesday. Thursday, Lerner and Draper debate 'Can Capitalism Survive' and Friday another anti-Franco rally will be held. I am going to be busier than hell, but will try hard to write you and keep you somewhat, at least, informed on the latest developments. When are you getting a furlough?

"As ever

"SHELLY."

In March, 1954, Stanley wrote Abrams a letter which, the committee believes, fairly illustrates the radical interests of these two young men. He writes:

"The friction between the American troops and the Japanese has reached a maximum point and it is absolutely necessary to get troops out of Japan. In fact, this is one of the moves it is hoped will bolster the Yoshida Gov't.

"The Japanese are the only ones that have had atomic bombs dropped on them. Needless to say they are violently anti-atomic warfare and they view Eisenhower as the devil incarnate.

"The strength of the Japanese left-wing Socialists is largely unassessed since much of it is secret. In terms of culture and social character the Japanese are 2,000 years ahead of the West. Japan is in a sense the most democratic nation in the world. Their democracy is not one of law, but is imbedded in the warp and woof of their society. Even during the war, the anti-war editorials were openly printed in the newspapers. The same thing is true in relation to civil liberties. Furthermore, the Japanese are perhaps the only people in the world who when they decide on a course of action will carry it out to the letter. All Japanese book stores carry a heavy line of Marxist and Stalinist literature. Until recently, there was cooperation between Stalinists and Socialists. The explosions came recently. The big debate in Socialist circles was whether or not to support South Korea and an imperialist war effort. Stalinist infiltraters into the Socialist movement gave the same master race imperialist crypto-Communist pitch they gave in Germany. They have been exposed and the battle is on.

"All Japanese school teachers from grade school through college are solidly left. This is the reason the Yoshida Government recently put through a bill barring teachers from political activities and connections."

On April 10, 1954, Abrams wrote to Stanley, expressing concern about the radical and subversive material in some of the letters, and warning his correspondent to be careful, as follows:

"* * * I was particularly disturbed by your letter in which you stated you believed that your incoming and outgoing mail was being censored. Your flippant attitude (for example, your P.S. to the censor) is an example of rank pureility. [Sic] Your bravado, no matter what you may mean by it, is not the kind of disposition that your situation requires. I frankly don't think your mail is being censored—this is still a democracy, you know, with all its shortcomings. However, if you've given the Army reason to be suspicious through your inability to repress your desire to sound off, it is conceivable that they may be investigating you. God knows, the Army is muddle headed enough and undemocratic enough to take a dim view of a soldier's writing about political subjects, no matter how naive the soldier may be, and no matter how meaningless and transitory the soldier's remarks may be. The point is that the Army does not know you as well as I do. I have seen you espouse some screwball ideas as well as some damn good ones. Some numbskull or opportunistic intelligence officer, however, might be inclined to make capital out of material which I am able to disregard as the rantings of an insecure and maudlin, yet dynamic and prolific person. I thought that the fact that I didn't answer your political comments would be sufficient to refrain you from continuing. Unfortunately, I have to run the risk of sending the FBI sniffing around me by writing this. Yet I am in a hell of a better position to defend myself in the U. S. than you are overseas, so I'll take the chance. Knowing you, I am sure you will construe all sorts of hidden meanings in this, but I assure you, Stanley, it is nothing more than an honest appeal to you to conduct yourself with more discretion. I am not so much worried about your mail being censored as I am by the fact that since you are foolish enough to write such nonsense, most of which I am sure you don't believe—at least not for more than the span of a couple of days, it follows that you must display corresponding foolhardiness in your every day life in the Army. That is what I fear. * * *"

On April 14, 1954, Stanley replied to Abrams as follows:

"Dear Shell: I have a favor to ask of you. The charge that I am a fool could easily be laid against me.

"Enough of this tempest in a teapot I am creating. The favor is that you forget about my friendship or fortune while I am in the Far East.

"There are important things that people must do in the regulating of their own affairs without deploying their energies or time in worrying about a person out of sight and hearing."

But Abrams did not follow his friend's advice and the correspondence continued throughout the balance of the year. In one of the letters written by Abrams, he said:

"I had an interesting experience at Joan's last night. I browsed through several boxes of archives of the old WP [Workers Party]. What a lesson. I saw names of people I know today as writers of sociology textbooks, State Department officials (McCarthy is quite right about the past of some of our government functionaries), writers of bourgeois novels and plays, respectable trade unionists, etc., who a mere 10-15 years ago were sincere democratic politicals. The best laid plans of all mice and some men go the way the forces of history dictate."

In view of the fact that Abrams was actively collaborating with the highest officials of the Communist Party in Southern California by April of 1956, it is interesting to note that in 1954, he as highly critical of the entire Communist movement, and particularly the Stalinists. In another letter to Stanley, he wrote:

"I am afraid I can't understand the basis for your sympathy for Stalinist fronts. It may be true that Stalinists have fought big battles for civil liberties, union organizations, etc. But it should be clear to any thinking person that *they fought these battles for their own political purposes.* Your critical support of Stalinist activities savors of the philosophy of doing evil because good may come of it. The Stalinists acted like Fascists in the 'Minneapolis nine' case. Read Clarence Darrow's words about their conduct in the 'Scottsboro case.' Investigate how they sabotaged the UAW strikes during 1946 and how vigorously they fought for no-strike pledges during the war against the most conservative trade unionists. There are so many instances of their selling out civil liberties and progressive unionism for the sake of totalitarian strings from which they, even though they are less puppets than the Communists in most countries, dance, that they must not enjoy the support of Socialists."

And later in the same letter, he said:

"The Russian Research Center at Yale is composed, as far as I know, mainly of fugitives from Russia and a few former Stalinists. Dallin, Boris Shub, Jerzy Gliksman and that crowd. I would doubt the authenticity of much of their work, although there is probably instructive material being turned out there. The Russian Institute at Columbia is along the same lines. I think that they are working closer with the State Department than Yale. In general, Trotskyists are the best students of the Russian Empire (which you insist on referring to as the Soviet Union and Soviet satellites, etc.) Shachtman, in my opinion, is the American most informed on Russia. He is currently, I hear, living in Mexico with Natalia Trotsky."

In a handwritten postscript to this letter, Abrams added:

"Just read Eisenhower's final denial to the Rosenbergs. The blood-thirsty bastard calls himself 'the most religious man I know.' The death of the Rosenbergs symbolizes more lucidly than any event of recent months, the truly barbarous state of our civilization."

On July 7, 1954, Abrams again expressed concern about the possibility that he and Stanley would be investigated because of the contents of their correspondence. He said in a postscript to this letter:

"P.S. There is no doubt in my mind, if there is in yours, but that our correspondence is being red—excuse me, 'read,' if you are under any sort of investigation."

In August, 1954, Abrams repeats his fear of investigation because of the radical content of this correspondence. He wrote:

"Think you are quite foolish to save my letters. If I said anything of merit there would be reason to do so. I find letter-writing to be an unsuitable vehicle for political discussions. Don't mean to sound like a kid impressed with counter-espionage movies (re: my utterances regarding censorship) but I am afraid you don't understand. The Government doesn't clue you when they are abridging your democratic rights. You and I will probably never know what the Government knows about us right up until the electric chair. * * *"

On August 23, 1954, the depth of Abrams' political education expressed itself in the following statement, which also displayed considerable analytical ability. He declared to Stanley that:

"You advocate, in the face of the most damaging attack the Stalinist hierarchy has ever received, a united front. Now that the tide may be beginning to change (not in favor of America, but against the Stalinists) you want to preserve Stalinism through unity. Now, more than ever before, there is no reason for a united front for Stalinism. Perhaps in the past there was justification for it, imperialist encirclement, etc. But the most damaging blow that Stalinism has ever received came not from the encircling imperialists. *If you study the situation you will see that never has Stalinism been so seriously threatened as it has been recently— not by A-bombs, Marshall Plans, threats from the 'free world,' U. N. concerted action, etc., but by its own slaves.* The revolts in the satellites caused the most far-reaching effects inside the Kremlin that all the machinations of the imperialist encirclers put together. Yes, there may be a case for unity in the face of western imperialism, *but how can anyone who is anything of a Socialist call for a united front against the working class victims of Stalinism?*"

In a later exchange of correspondence with Stanley, young Abrams expressed his pessimistic and somewhat bitter views toward the future of American capitalism. These gloomy, cynical statements forcibly bring to mind similar statements which appeared in the letters written by another student whose flirtation with Communist activities led to his untimely death while he was attending U. C. L. A., Everitt Hudson. In fact, as we will indicate later, the common factors that were present in each of these two cases of U. C. L. A. students, who became embroiled in radical activities and whose mysterious deaths led to a wealth of documentary material concerning far-flung subversive activities in California universities, is indeed striking. For example, Abrams wrote to Stanley:

> "* * * Capitalism is outmoded, reactionary and thus, it follows —is doomed. The backwardness of the country which would enable capitalism to survive and nourish it, perhaps it even needed capitalism, is no more, thanks to capitalism. Capitalism now impedes progress. The industrial revolution was conducted in the name of production. Now the production methods are sufficient to meet the needs of the consuming people. Capitalism is no longer needed and production for consumption is possible."

And further in the same letter:

> "I don't know what the future holds. As I struggle for a realistic Marxist interpretation of events today, I see few tendencies which would indicate that Socialism is on its way. As enthusiastic as I can get about the possibilities of Socialism for America, while in a political discussion, my sense of objectivity remains stronger. I see little possibility (but plenty of hope) for Socialism in America. Barbarism, the little-heralded alternative of Marx, seems far more imminent. As for the rest of the world— the possibility is there—but, to borrow the only realistic phrase in the political consciousness of the average American, 'America is the strongest country in the world'."

In informing his friend about the situation at Roosevelt College, Abrams wrote, in another letter:

> "Will dispense with my traditional apology for answering you late. Things, as you may well guess have quieted down at R.C. It is pretty evident that we have gained a clear-cut victory, however small or seemingly insignificant. It is a victory, for even if we've failed to shatter much student apathy, we've nevertheless proved to some people in the school (and I'm speaking mainly of the liberals among the faculty who have been afraid to openly oppose the administration for some time now) that the administration can be fought and has vulnerable points in its protective strata."

Another letter from Abrams indicated that he was becoming more deeply interested in Marxian ideology, when he described his reading to Stanley, as follows:

> "I have been thinking quite seriously of going to school in New York after graduation. Either Columbia or the new school, which looks mighty interesting. I have been reading political matters studiously lately. Engels 'Ludwig Feurbach,' Lenin's 'Materialism and Empiro-Criticism' and the most valuable book I've ever read 'The Selected Correspondence of Karl Marx & Friedrick Engels.' It's the most illuminating writing I've yet encountered. They answer in their letters every, I repeat *every* criticism of the materialist conception of history that has arisen to date."

THE YOUNG SOCIALIST LEAGUE

The Young Socialist League was formed in 1953 as the result of a merger of the youth section of the Independent Socialist League, the youth section of the Socialist Party of the United States, and miscellaneous pacifists, anti-war anarchists and democratic radical groups of various kinds. The organization, from its inception, was predicated solidly on Marxism, although it professed to be militantly anti-Communist. As we shall see, this anti-Stalinist attitude was sincere and continued until after the important speech by Khrushchev in February of 1946. Since that time, the Young Socialist League has been doing business with both the Trotskyite and Stalinist movements in the United States—the first instance of that kind of collaboration in this country being found in the meeting described by Abrams which he attended in Pasadena and which will be described in his own words in connection with the testimony of Dr. Robert Neumann.

If one can accurately judge from the documents found in Abrams' room, the Young Socialist League was not only a Marxian organization but leaned strongly toward the Trotskyist movement.

Shortly before his death, young Abrams had prepared a speech which he intended to deliver at a Young Socialist League meeting. His death occurred before the speech could be delivered, but a typewritten copy of it was found among his effects. In it he said:

"Since its birth—a little over two years ago, the growth of the YSL has been amazing. Units have been established on campuses throughout the country. Where political organizations are banned by repressive college administrations, groups have set up in the 'off-campus communities,' in the vicinity of the campus. Factions have been created in the trade-union movement and our people have influenced the thinking of young workers in various areas.

"YSL publications, the YSR, the YSC, which appears in LA weekly, the *Anvil*, which although not an official YSL publication, is written mainly by YSLers—these publications have achieved circulation in the thousands.

"YSL members participate as active members of various liberal organizations and civil rights and civil liberties organizations and take part in picket line activities and the like of that.

"I referred to our growth as being amazing. And I think it has been amazing. The effect and influence we have had on campuses and in the shops is far beyond that which even the most optimistic of us had at our birth—and some Socialists can be awfully optimistic. Units from all parts of the country have reported an opening up in the political climate within the past year."

While still at Roosevelt College, Abrams received a letter dated November 8, 1954. It was signed by Max Martin, national secretary of the Young Socialist League, and read, in part, as follows:

"Now that you two are co-organizers (congratulations incidentally) I will follow this procedure in correspondence: address the letter to Shelly and send Jim a carbon, unless some other procedure is preferred by you. You will both also get NAC [National Action Committee] minutes. In regard to your communicating with the NO [national office] I naturally would like to hear from both of you. However, I think it essential that one person be given the definite assignment and have the responsibility of regular communication with the NO. From the fact that you, Shelly, have written so far, and from the fact that you are Chicago area organizer while Jim is in charge of the University of Chicago, I assume that you will be the correspondent.''

Thus, we see from the foregoing that while still an undergraduate student, completing his senior year at Roosevelt College, young Abrams was made organizer for the Young Socialist League for the entire Chicago area, leaving the matter of running the organization at the University of Chicago to someone else. It is clear that Abrams plunged with great enthusiasm into his new duties. His flair for organization quickly manifested itself and he was successful in building up a strong YSL unit in Chicago.

In December, 1954, a letter from Max Martin to Abrams indicated that the Trotskyists were endeavoring to infiltrate the organization. He said:

''* * * There is evidence that the Chicago affair has been handled on a national level by the Socialist Workers Party. Someone here in New York was approached by the New York Socialist Workers Party organizer who seemed to know all about it and also inquired what the attitude of YSL would be toward letting SWPers into YSL elsewhere— N. Y., Milwaukee, etc. All this was done on a tentative, informal, 'I'm not speaking officially, only for myself' basis—but they are feeling things out.''

On December 24, 1954, Howard Mayhew, organizer for the Socialist Workers Party in Illinois, wrote a letter to Abrams, as follows:

"Young Socialist League
  c/o S. J. Abrams, 1400 East 53d Street
    Chicago, Illinois

''GENTLEMEN:

''Your communication of December 21, 1954, inviting the Socialist Workers Party to debate the Young Socialist League received yesterday.

''It arrived too late for the organization to take action on your invitation prior to the date set by you as acceptable for an answer, i.e., Sunday, December 26th.

''Please advise if you are interested in having a representative of the Socialist Workers Party speak before one of your public meetings at a later date.

''Sincerely,

''HOWARD MAYHEW, Organizer.''

ACTIVITIES IN CALIFORNIA

Immediately after coming to California in October, 1954, young Abrams plunged into the task of giving new life to the Young Socialist League Organization in Southern California. He established contact with his comrades who had been operating the organization, and soon rose to a position of control. Soon after arriving in Los Angeles, he wrote to some friends in the East, as follows:

· "Life has been rather pleasant lately, although the novelty of this area has worn itself and I am beginning to get the wanderlust. Mexico pops into my daydreams frequently, as does Europe, but the expenses involved in going to Europe are too much. I'm enamored of San Francisco despite the fact that I am sick of the big city. San Francisco is the most sophisticated and cultured city I've seen and it looks like it would be an interesting place to live. My prospective for the next few years, if not for longer, is to live part of the year here, part in Mexico and part in San Francisco. This is quite feasible as long as the job market is wide open as it currently is. Hardly any problem making money out here at the present time."

After moving to Santa Monica and getting interested in establishing a unit of the Young Socialist League on the U. C. L. A. campus, Abrams wrote to his friends, as follows:

"I'm living now in a tiny cottage just off the beach in a working-class section of Santa Monica. Nice, bright, and cheerful little place, situated in back of another house. I have a lovely patio practically to myself, an elderly Jewish couple for landlords (who are remarkable in that they are as unlandlordish as anyone could be). My comrades call it a real crazy pad (they, like everyone else out here, are all bopsters).

"I'm going to U. C. L. A. at present. My motivations are primarily political, although when I started I had notions of going on for my masters. One week in the barren field of the social sciences convinced me that I don't have that kind of patience or endurance. The unit has needed someone on campus desperately. We've been unsuccessful in attempting to persuade Bob into transferring there from Loyola. I am convinced the only way we are going to get out of the doldrums is to establish ourselves on campus. It looks as though I can be very effective there, despite the notorious Rule 17 which bars all types of political activity. There are 14,000 people on that campus—there must be some good blood there somewhere. I spend most of my time walking around with displaying a pile of *Anvils* and L. A.'s [Labor Actions].

"It's illegal, of course, to sell them, so I merely let them have my copies for what I paid for them. We have another guy there, a real popular boy, president of his fraternity and all sorts of other things. He can be tremendously useful to us and he shows promise. We are having Shachtman speak at the campus YWCA. I met with their rentals committee yesterday and I was frankly amazed when they agreed to rent us the hall. The gimmick was that this is strictly an educational not a political meeting. We are going to have a problem publicizing the thing since leaflets, posters, etc., are illegal. It is even illegal to verbally publicize a political meeting. *Some of our arm-chair revolutionaries want us to conduct a civil disobedience campaign on campus.*" (Committee's italics.)

Following a report submitted to national headquarters of the Young Socialist League by Abrams, he received approval of a program he had outlined in a communication from Max Martin, dated January 19, 1955. Martin said:

"The program you outline re public meetings on campus, Sunday night suppers, Tuesday night classes, socials, and work in the SRP sounds like an extremely good one, one that should really establish the YSL on an extremely high level of functioning. In view of the 'newness' of so many members, I think the desirability of making that 'basics' class a real success is very important."

By January, 1955, Abrams had apparently returned to Chicago, since a communication dated January 20, 1955, on the letterhead of the publication *Labor Action* was addressed to him at 1400 East 53d Street in Chicago. This letter, being signed by L. G. Smith, business manager of the publication, whose address was 114 West 14th Street, New York 11, New York, was addressed to "Dear Shelly" and inquired whether or not the Chicago Young Socialist League unit wanted to assume an obligation to pay for more copies of the publication than it was accustomed to receive, the general idea being that additional free copies would be provided for "promotional and general propagandistic distribution." The letter concluded by saying: "So, let me know. Are the 65 free copies solely for free distribution, or does the unit think it can take on a weekly obligation for the sale of more than the present five copies? Any additional ones will be charged to you at $0.03 per copy."

If the Young Socialist League experienced some difficulty in resisting the attacks of the Trotskyists to infiltrate their organization, the same situation existed in the Socialist Workers Party with regard to members of the YSL—this constant shifting of membership back and forth providing a source of some annoyance to both organizations. Thus, on May 8, 1955, Abrams received the following letter:

"*Shelly Abrams, Executive Committee, Chicago
Young Socialist League*

"DEAR COMRADE:

"We have your letter of May 6th, containing serious complaint about Jim G. which you say may jeopardize the officially recognized status of the YSL on the campus. At the present time, however, we can give you only a tentative reply, as follows:

"Jim G. was a member of your organization when he made application to join the SWP and was accepted. Subsequently, he left your organization; but his relation to the SWP at the same time became a state of uncertainty, which is still the case at this moment. When we learn definitely what Jim G.'s intentions are regarding his relations with us, we shall be able to look into the matter and take appropriate action.

"Meanwhile, we wish to assure you that if your complaint proves to be correct we consider such activity utterly reprehensible.

Fraternally,
HOWARD MAYHEW, Organizer, Chicago SWP."

Abrams had returned to California by December, 1955, since he enenrolled as a graduate student in the Department of Sociology at U. C. L. A. on November 19th, of that year. On January 27, 1956, he received a letter from Max Martin instructing Abrams to contact five individuals. One in San Diego, one in Santa Monica, one in Los Angeles, one in Inglewood, and one in Beverly Hills. Concerning the first person on the list, Martin said:

"He wrote a letter requesting info on the YSL. Am sending him some lit. plus a letter telling him about us. I realize that San Diego ain't exactly in L. A.'s backyard, but if somebody does wander down there he ought to be looked up. Also, you might place him on the Los Angeles unit's mailing list. Also, you might write him, asking if he ever comes up to Los Angeles, invite him to do so, to attend meetings, etc.

"The following are the names of people (who do live in L. A.'s backyard) who have recently subscribed to *Anvil*. In none of the cases do we know how they heard of it, although a reasonable guess is through the ad *Anvil* had in *Expose*, which is a New York published and nationally circulated muck raking (old fashioned variety) newspaper. Why not put them on your mailing list, look them up, telling them that you heard that they are *Anvil* subscribers and that the YSL supports and distributes *Anvil*, etc. It would be wise, at least in the initial interview, to be evasive about how you got their names, since any hostile ones might be able to use their being looked up as a basis for attacking *Anvil*, i.e., say its *just* a YSL front."

On January 28, 1956, a card was addressed to "N. S. Abrams, 1429 Ocean Front, Santa Monica, California," advising him that the next meeting of the young people's organizing committee of the NAACP would be held on Friday, February 3d, 1956, at 2069 South Oxbridge Street, Santa Monica, at 8 p.m., and as a result of this and similar meetings, we have ascertained from the Abrams documents that he became a member of the organization.

On January 28, 1956, Abrams reported to Max Martin in New York that:

"* * * I've discussed trade union questions with people here (and not just the Berkeley people and not just YSLers) and I'm startled at how willingly they are willing to believe anything told them about what we are doing in the shops in the midwest—or for that matter, how readily they will believe anything about how we operate in any arena. As far as the newer people are concerned, I don't think I can blame them for being gullible. They have only a glimpse of what we are, they're remote from the center, they're, in short, isolated."

On February 28, 1956, Max Martin addressed a report to Abrams in which he said:

"Once again let me congratulate you on the various mimeod organizer's bulletins and exec. reports you put out. Not only are they useful for inactive unit members, but they give the N. O. and other units receiving them a real picture of what's going on. I am trying to get other units to emulate you in this. I agree with your diagnosis that Los Angeles needs to work on the problem of a campus base. This, as a matter of fact, is the problem which plagues the whole YSL, and New York in particular. It's something I think will need thorough discussion at the plenum (and/or convention).

"More specifically on your prospects, I think the idea of a 'Chicago approach' broad Socialist Club in Pasadena with the YPSL and some pacificists is a good idea and that it ought to be tried, especially if the relationship with the YPSL-SP has continued to develop along the lines you two wrote about some months ago. Let me know what has been developing along these lines generally and in regard to the proposed club.

"U. C. L. A. Also agree with the 'Berkeley' approach there, except for the following questions, necessitated by the fact that the copy of the report I got lacks the first half of page 5. *Did the exec. decide for the civil disobedience campaign? I have no objections to it in principle, but it seems to me that the practical objections which the report lists some comrades as making bear some weight. Suggestion: why not see if you can make this a joint campaign with the Westwood NAACP. Since your purpose is to get recognition for the YSL via aggressive public activity, you would want to conduct this campaign in the name of YSL and NAACP, not in the name of 'Committee Against Rule 17' or something like that. If NAACP would agree, and if you would get a previous commitment from ACLU to support any case arising out of it (you should try for this in any event), then the dangers referred to would be mitigated and the aims could be served at the same time.*" (Committee's italics.)

In reply to this communication, Abrams wrote as follows:

"U. C. L. A. We are beginning to move here. In my opinion the Berkeley vs. Chgo. approach dichotomy, the more I think about it, although perhaps a fruitful means in which to discuss the Pasadena situation, is meaningless in reference to U. C. L. A. since how we operate there isn't a question of deciding whether activities should be carried out in the name of the YSL or through a broader, more inclusive, politics club-type organization. U. C. L. A. regulations answer this question for us in advance. The so-called Berkeley approach is the only way we can operate on campus at this time, but it is not the result of our choosing this as the wisest of two alternative approaches. I would be in favor of the politics club approach if it were legally possible there. As you know, all political activity is illegal on this campus. There is a development under way which may open the doors for us to undertake an approach different than that which is our primary prospective at the moment. The NAACP is now officially attempting to get recognition on campus through various formal procedures. In the meantime, they are conducting semilegal (publicized only through word-of-mouth and ostensibly spontaneous affairs) meetings on the lawns. We would be crazy if we passed up the opportunity that this development gives us. The NAACP claims to have 150-200 registered members on campus (about 35 attended a lawn meeting last week).

"Dick's call for us to conduct a civil disobedience campaign on campus is foolish in the light of conditions there. *Such a campaign might be successfully carried out by the NAACP, however.*

(Committee's italics) : They have respectability, a good many influential friends, etc., and if the university resorted to coercion the local ACLU would undoubtedly be willing to take the matter to court.

"Am toying with the idea of our holding lawn meetings on the campus a la NAACP. We were disappointed to hear that Shachtman can only give one talk out here since we've procured the campus YMCA for him on the 19th (to my amazement, frankly). At any rate, Ted has agreed to substitute for Max, and so we are going to have a meeting on campus (technically, the Y is 'off campus').

"Pasadena. Dave and Henry got together with a group of our friends there last week and we've finally got something concrete set up. We are going to have a series of discussions which we hope will lead to the formation of a club there. Prospects look good."

Abrams addressed another letter to Max Martin on April 9, 1956, stating that:

"Developments here have been excellent the last several weeks. We recruited three people last week, have a couple more who we may pick up soon, and our contact work has produced a good many new people who are attending various activities and showing interest in the organization.

"U. C. L. A. We picked up two new people here last week, and old SYLer from Detroit, who has been out of contact with the movement several years due to a variety of personal circumstances. We met him about a month ago when he noticed me giving a bunch of literature to a guy on campus. Although at first we were somewhat suspicious because of his appearance out of nowhere, so to speak, we are quite confident of him. Had him meet Joe while he was in town and Joe spoke highly of him. Hard to say just how much we can expect from him, though we have reason to believe he will be very valuable. He's living at the University Coop where we need someone badly. He is willing to function there more or less openly as a YSLer.

"Phil, a young student who sent in an interest blank from *Anvil* sometime back. He attended SLP classes in the Bay area for a couple of years. A member of the *Bruin* staff and popular with freshmen-sophomore students on campus."

Abrams continued to describe the organization of a new YSL fraction on the U. C. L. A. campus as a preliminary move toward defying the university administration and planting a unit of the YSL more or less openly at U. C. L. A. for propaganda and recruiting purposes. The term "fraction" is used in Marxian circles to signify a small proportion of organized individuals who are secretly insinuated into the mass of a larger group for the purpose of influencing the group activities and furthering the particular political line that is sought to be advanced. Thus, when Abrams referred to the planting of the YSL fraction on the U. C. L. A. campus, he meant that the organization was ready to secretly function in defiance of the university's rule, and to

gradually assume a position of open activity at U. C. L. A.
He continued:

"The first major activity of the new fraction will be in connection with a talk Pete will give on campus next week. This will
be conducted like the NAACP meeting I described to you several
weeks back. No further publicity, just word-of-mouth publicizing
of the talk. If this comes off without a hitch, we will consider holding a regular meeting on campus with leaflets and the like.
Whether we do this or not will depend upon the strength of the
fraction, the amount of support we think we can get for defense
in the event of campus police action, etc.

"Joe's talk at the Y last month, incidentally, won us a couple
of friends and we hope to use the Y again for a meeting soon. * * *
I presume you've seen our spring educational program. Originally,
we intended to set up two series of classes—one advanced and one
elementary socialist education. The program we arrived at is one
which integrates basic educational material (historical materialism,
working class, third camp, etc.) within our regular weekly series
of talks. We had 16 people at our meeting educational last
Thursday (the largest meeting we've had within at least the last
year) and I hope I'm not being too presumptuous, I think the days
of meetings of three, four and five people are over."

Among the Abrams documents was a schedule of the educational
meetings and classes described above. The meetings were held at 8939½
Santa Monica Boulevard, Los Angeles 46, California, which was described as the headquarters of the Young Socialist League. The classes
were to commence on the 3rd of April, 1956, and comprised 10 courses
as follows: (1) Socialists in the American Labor Movement, 1936-1946;
(2) The Russian Revolution and Stalinism, Part I; (3) The Russian
Revolution and Stalinism, Part II; (4) The Relevance of Marxism; (5)
Capitalism, International Stalinism and World War III; (6) Socialism
and Democracy; (7) The Decline and Fall of Rome—a Marxian Analysis, Part I; (8) Decline and Fall of Rome, Part II; (9) National
Struggles under Capitalism (Permanent Revolution); (10) The Permanent War Economy. The names of the instructors in each of the classes
were given, Abrams being listed as the instructor for the class dealing
with the Relevance of Marxism and the one dealing with Socialism and
Democracy. His first class was to have been given on April 26th and
the second on May 17th, 1956.

THE NEW UNITED FRONT

We now approach the period after Krushchev delivered his cele-
brated "secret" speech at the Twentieth Congress of the Communist
Party of the Soviet Union on February 14, 1956. This speech, in which
Stalin was castigated and ridiculed in the harshest language, gave the
signal for a new united front movement all over the world, and we
must realize that in analyzing the documents which follow, they must
be considered in the light of insistence both on the part of the Socialist
and Communist organizations that thenceforth they should collaborate
toward a common goal. Thus, among the Abrams documents were two
handbills, each advertising a speech in Los Angeles under the auspices

of the Young Socialist League. The first was to consist of an address by Max Schachtman, national chairman of the Independent Socialist League and American editor and translator of the works of Leon Trotsky, entitled "The Peace Crisis, What Is the Meaning of the Kremlin's New Turn?" Case Hotel, 8 p.m., 11th and Broadway, Los Angeles, California, Sunday, March 18th, 1956; the other handbill stated that a Socialist analysis of the 1956 elections would be given by Theodore Enright, Los Angeles chairman, Independent Socialist League, at 574 Hilgard Street, Los Angeles, Monday, March 19, 1956, in which the would discuss "The Communist's New Entry into the Democratic Party and Its Challenge to the Liberals."

On April 10, 1956, came another report and directive from Max Martin, in which he discussed the question of endeavoring to lure members of the Communist Party into the Young Socialist League. This, obviously, was an extremely dangerous and sensitive situation, particularly in view of the fact that the Young Socialist League, in general, and Sheldon Abrams, in particular, had heaped abuse and sarcasm on the Stalinist movement at every opportunity. Abrams made no effort to conceal his bitter hatred of the Stalinist movement. As will be seen, the Krushchev speech which effected a revival of the worldwide popular front movement, had for its basic purpose an amalgamation of all liberal, Socialist and even Trotskyist groups with the Communist Party. This profound change, coupled with pointed and specific directives from the national headquarters of the Young Socialist League, ordering all subordinate functionaries, such as Abrams, to implement the program by direct action, operated to compel him to reverse his role and now seek to do business with the Stalinists. We shall see how this activity developed.

On April 10, 1956, the following statement was received by Abrams in a directive from Max Martin:

"All comrades everywhere should make all efforts to do some work on the Stalinists, the youth in particular, for this is a period similar to the days of the Hitler-Stalin pact for them. While we won't do any real recruiting out of it, there is an opportunity to intervene, to try and push some Stalinists in a progressive direction. And single recruits are certainly not excluded. To these ends, I had that 'appeal to the LYL' [Labor Youth League] in *Challenge* week before last and will try to have as much stuff in the paper that would be useful as possible."

Martin emphasized and expanded his directives in a communication dated April 14, 1956, directed to all members of the Young Socialist League, and its officers and functionaries in particular. He said:

"DEAR COMRADES: This communication is a follow-up of what I have been saying in my correspondence with the comrades during the past week or so: namely, that it is a *must* for us to do everything we possibly can to attempt to make contact with Stalinists during this period of confusion and turbulence in their ranks.

"The experience in New York last night more than amply confirmed the view that unparalleled opportunities for work on Stalinists exist at the present time. At last night's ISL-YSL meeting, at which Comrade Schachtman spoke on the latest developments in Moscow, a meeting which, by the way, was extremely well attended and successful from a general point of view, we had about one dozen Stalinist youths in the audience. That they were Stalinists, i.e., LYL members among whom there were some who probably were also dual members of the CP [Communist Party], must be stressed. *Stalinists,* not Stalinoids. In addition, there may have been some adult CP members in the audience; we cannot be certain, but we know that there were quite a few people in the audience who were complete strangers to all of the comrades present.

"While we had expected that a Stalinist or two might show up, since the NY unit has systematically been covering CP meetings, Jefferson School lectures, LYL meetings, etc., with distributions of *Labor Action,* special leaflets discussing the dethronement of Stalin, leaflets announcing the Shachtman meeting, etc., and while we had had comrades attending these meetings, speaking from the floor when possible, trying to talk to Stalinists after the meetings, and so forth, we did not expect such a turnout. Only those comrades who have been in the movement for a long time, *and/or who are acquainted with the past attitudes of Stalinists towards Trotskyists can fully realize the significance of such a turnout* (Committee's italics). There are Stalinists today who are willing to listen to us and to discuss with us.

"But they did more than attend. A number of them took the floor during the meeting (they were encouraged to do so and allowed to speak extensively) and some of them revealed that they have great doubts about their movement. In addition, some took literature, one promised to start attending our meetings, a second made a private appointment with one of our comrades for additional discussions of Russia, a third remarked, 'You guys may be mistaken, but I no longer think that you have horns and are monsters,' etc. It is not that they have ceased being Stalinists, for their discussions reveal that they still are and they reveal also that they are ignorant, have distorted conceptions of Socialism, etc. But they revealed that they have doubts and are troubled. One of them took the floor at the meeting and argued as follows: 1. I know and have known all along that Russia isn't democratic and that many, many people, even revolutionists were murdered, and it's true that I never told anyone that I've had these thoughts, I kept it quiet, etc. But then they are building Socialism there, as proved by the growth of industry, and besides democracy will now be introduced. Another stated in a discussion with the undersigned after the meeting: While I don't agree that there has to be the right to organize parties in Russia, I think that Khrushchev should introduce complete democracy in the Russian CP, the right to organize factions, etc. The problem is, I don't know who to believe about Russia, etc. It is impossible to do more than give the barest bits of the flavor of the discussions which a half-dozen of them held for a number of hours with our comrades after the meeting, discussions in which they showed interest in our point of view.

"Now it is not necessary to exaggerate the situation which now exists in order to realize the significance of the above. Nobody can predict that we will definitely break a number of these contacts away from Stalinism and that we will recruit some of them, but on the other hand, it is certainly not excluded that we will. What is certain is that the opportunity for trying and the possibility of succeeding does most definitely exist. Moreover, if we do not succeed in politically winning and organizationally recruiting any of these Stalinist contacts of ours, for they are now contacts, the efforts will have by no means been fruitless. For next time there is some bizarre development in Russia, a month from today or three years from today, and there is turbulence in CP ranks again, what we have said to them today will have an effect then.

"All of our units, groups and friends must make it one of their primary tasks to reach Stalinists and Stalinist youth in this period. And this effort must be made now, for we may only have a few weeks or months before the CP line hardens, the rationalizations are completely worked out, the discussions ended, and things settle down. All units and unit executive committees should discuss at once the question of systematically undertaking this work. Wherever and whenever the CP, LYL, fronts, hold meetings, we should try to distribute *LA* leaflets drawn up discussing the Twentieth Congress. Comrades should attend these meetings, take the floor, repeat the YSL's challenge for the LYL to debate, etc. In addition, all efforts should be made to achieve personal contacts. All comrades who know or can get to meet Stalinists, whether through school or other sources, should try to do so. All comrades in those areas in which Comrade Shachtman will be speaking during the second half of his tour—see *Labor Action* for April 16th for schedule—should make every effort to get Stalinists to attend, via personal contact, and word-or-mouth, distributing leaflets announcing the Shachtman talk at Stalinist meetings. (Comrade Shachtman did an excellent job in dealing with the LYLers during the discussion, making a very good impression on some of them.)

"The Stalinists should be approached in a politically firm but friendly and sympathetic manner. Their sense of dignity and self respect, their feelings that to some extent they may have been deceived by their leaders, their desire for democracy should be appealed to. The following should be stressed: for years you were told that Stalin was a great genius and that everything was fine in Russia. Now you are being told that those tales were just tales but at the same time are expected to believe that Khrushchev will fix everything up on the basis of more evidence than you had for the previous beliefs about Stalin. Why should you take Khrushchev's words for it? What evidence is there that Khrushchev is introducing democracy in Russia, or that Foster is in the CP? Demand deeds, not words. What about the Moscow trials and the other purges? How do you know they weren't frame-ups too? How do you know that the Hitler-Stalin Pact was a good thing? How could this mad man, Stalin, have ruled Russia if it were Socialist? Why won't your leaders debate with the YSL?

"Naturally, the points to be stressed will vary with each individual situation and the individual Stalinist involved. The above are suggestions which may prove effective.

"A last point. All units should examine their literature stocks to see if they have suitable literature for giving such people, such as the special pamphlet issue of *Labor Action* devoted to Stalinism, the pamphlet of the Browder-Shachtman debate, recent issues of *Labor Action,* etc. Units lacking these should order them from *Labor Action Service* immediately. Fraternally, Max Martin."

ABRAMS MEETS WITH TOP COMMUNISTS

Immediately after the reports of the Khrushchev speech reached the United States, Abrams established his contacts with the Communist Party in Southern California. In a letter dated February 23, 1956, written to functionaries of the Young Socialist League in the East, he said:

" * * * We've been having interesting relations with the Stalinists. Just how far the new turn goes, is an open question. Some say it includes approaching the Trotskyists, SP [Socialist Party], maybe even us. * * * The reason that we are involved with them to an extent is that our periphery is almost exclusively pacifist or pacifist influenced, and the Stalinists are making big overtures to them. The result being we've attended several discussion meetings of Socialists, pacifists and Stalinists *and have been having informal meetings with the top leadership of the CP.*" (Committee's italics.)

Perhaps the most critical statements made in any of the Abrams documents were contained in one dated February 23, 1956, describing a Pasadena meeting with some of the Communist Party leadership. This description was contained in a two-page document signed by Abrams and directed to contacts in the East. He said:

" * * * And there were people from the California YPSL, SP, and 15 or 20 pacifists, mostly unaffiliated, and four avowed Stalinists (including the county chairman of the LYL, who was 40 if he was a day). It was very interesting. Although we did a good political job exposing them, we couldn't compete with the Stalinists on the level of moralizing and sermonizing. Early in the discussion (which lasted almost four hours) one of the Stalinists, who claimed that he was a registered member of the French CP, began to criticize the wishy-washy American CP with its constitutional prohibitions against violence and proudly pointed to the French CP which openly advocates force and violence. At that point, * * *, a scribbler for the PW attacked the 'Frenchman' ruthlessly, denouncing him for his advocacy of violence, and said that if he were in the American CP with those views, he would be expelled. Clever, huh? The pacifists ate it up. That was the tone of the conference. The Stalinist line was that they, unlike the Socialists who stood for violent revolution, were the natural allies of the pacifists. We did an excellent political job tearing the Stalinists apart and exposing their demagoguery. But the pacifists fell for the sermonizing and moralizing in the end."

It should be observed that the correct name of the reporter for the *Daily People's World* was given in the document, and the committee's dossier concerning him indicates that he is much more important than is indicated by his position as a reporter for the Communist paper. The committee consulted an expert concerning the proper conclusions to be drawn from the remarks which Abrams made so frankly concerning this meeting when it questioned Dr. Robert Neumann of the Political Science Department at U. C. L. A.

In order to fully understand the significance of this unprecedented move whereby the Communists, who had always detested both Socialists and Trotskyists, were brought together in a common cause, one must first consider the development of this new international Communist line which gave rise to the situation in which young Abrams found himself in February of 1956.

Immediately following the conference at Geneva, Switzerland, attended by representatives of the Soviet Union, President Eisenhower and the foreign ministers from Britain and France, the Communist Party line quickly shifted from one of hostility and noncooperation to one of sweetness and "peaceful coexistence." As is always the case in such matters, the new line was immediately picked up by the organs of the Communist Party of the United States and other countries throughout the world. Particularly in the issues of *Political Affairs*, the new peaceful coexistence line was hammered home for the benefit of the rank and file members of the party. The careful reader is able to discern here the beginnings of the new united front movement. Tentative feelers were being put out by the Kremlin through its propaganda organs in other countries. The Khrushchev speech of February 14, 1956, with its vicious downgrading of Stalin and its condemnation of his rule by terror and his utter disregard for human rights, was merely the emphasis that pointed up the new line and set it uniformly in motion throughout the world.

Let us now examine some of the excerpts that began appearing in the monthly ideological publication of the Communist Party of the United States as early as November, 1955. Oddly enough, the first of these articles was written by Celeste Strack, also a graduate of U. C. L. A., and who was on the editorial staff of the *Daily Bruin* while she was making little effort to conceal her fanatic dedication to the Communist cause. Since her graduation from the university, she has devoted her full time to the Communist Party. On page seven of the November, 1955, issue of *Political Affairs*, she declared:

> "* * * Preparation for future struggle cannot consist in gathering progressives tightly together into a valiant band that will keep its banner flying with the hope that the mass of workers will rally to it tomorrow. It must be found, rather, in fighting together with a majority of American workers today, for the demands they now support, and through the channels they presently utilize while simultaneously pointing to the next steps needed to achieve these demands."

Miss Strack would never issue this sort of a pronouncement unless she first received orders from above. And American Communist leaders never set a pattern for their comrades on a mass scale unless they first have obtained the approval of the Kremlin. What Miss Strack is actually saying amounts to simply this: Comrades: we have received orders to quit acting as a tiny conspiratorial group, looking with disdain upon other progressive and liberal organizations. Henceforth, we must infiltrate into mass organizations, such as political parties and trade unions; we must place our people in positions of control and we must at the same time collaborate with other progressive groups. This is the new line, let us get on with it.

Elsewhere in the same issue of *Political Affairs,* the Geneva Conference was hailed as the shining symbol of a new era of peaceful coexistence, and the issue for December, 1955, carried the same general line in an article by Albert E. Blumberg and Rob Hall on page 11. They declared:

> "* * * The struggle * * * must go on in all popular organizations—especially the trade unions, seeking the expression of this broad aim in speeches, in resolutions, and in delegations to Washington."

Blumberg also had an article in the January, 1956, issue of *Political Affairs,* page 19, where he said:

> "The main task of '56 requires that much more attention be given to the role of the Left and advanced workers, including the Marxists, and to promoting the unity of action of the various groups and elements of the Left."

And, on the concluding page of his article, Blumberg tells his fellow Communists what they must do, as follows:

> "Thus, to further the cause of peace, economic welfare, equal rights and democracy in the '56 elections, all Left and progressive forces should unite:
>
> "(1) To help build, first and foremost, broad mass movements on the issues able to influence the course of elections and to exert increasing pressure on the Administration in Congress which takes office after '56.
>
> "(2) Within this context, to join in the labor and people's fight to oust the Cadillac Cabinet and put a substantial dent in the GOP-Dixiecrat ruling coalition in Congress, directing the sharpest fire against the GOP and its McCarthyite wing and their democratic McCarthyite and Dixiecrat counterparts and at the same time resolutely combating the anti-Geneva policies of many 'Fair Deal' Democrats.
>
> "The party is small in size. But as it strengthens its ties with the masses of the working people, Negro and white, pursues a correct united front policy, and popularizes its views and aims, it will be able to play a vital role in helping to influence the course of events."

The Labor Youth League, youth organization of the Communist Party, received its assignment, too. Martha Stone contributed an article called "The Youth," which appeared in the January, 1956, issue of *Political Affairs* at page 37. And she declared on page 48:

"Our discussions have revealed that by and large the party appreciates the contributions of the LYL. Within this framework, however, much confusion has existed as to how, by what forms, with what tactics can LYL best accomplish its responsibilities. The biggest of these questions centers around the mass policy of the league.

"What motivates the confusion is the feeling that such a policy of mass work undermines the ability of the Labor Youth League to build itself as a mass popular youth organization. The contention is that the main way for the league to influence the fight for youth unity is through the activities which it itself develops.

"In our opinion, such a view is incorrect. It closes its eyes to the reality of the situation among young people today. There is no other section of the Left where we would put forward the idea that the main way to influence the struggle for unity is from outside the main stream of people's organizations. Quite the contrary, we reject any concept which minimizes or takes our focus away from these organizations which must inevitably be a main source of united youth activity.

"Of major consideration is the formation of a teen-age division of the LYL that will function with a high degree of autonomy and through a variety of more flexible forms and activities. The most rapid growth of the LYL can take place today among teen-agers. This is a true reflection of the general experience of other youth organizations."

In an article called "The Labor Merger," by Hal Simon, commencing on page 51 of the January, 1956, issue of *Political Affairs*, this amazing statement appears.

"The Left forces hold no position of leadership in the merged organization. They exist among the rank and file in many unions with varying degrees of influence. However, in all cases, their influence is very limited. The Left has no organized form, no spokesman, nor any voice in the labor movement beyond that of the Communist Party and the *Daily Worker*, the *Daily World*, etc. However, the number of forces, including organized caucuses and local unions that take a consistently progressive position on all questions and will undoubtedly be the heart of the future new Left in the merged organization are already broader than those who agree with the program of our party. Consequently, the fight for a broad coalition policy in the course of struggle around single issues and the uniting of all those forces that tend to take a consistently progressive position will be a prerequisite for the formation of the new Left in the united labor organization."

ANALYSIS OF THE NEW LINE

The foregoing directives are unmistakable. They were preceded by others. This line was the signal for the launching of the second Communist united front movement—the first one having been launched by Georgi Dimitrov in 1935 and discontinued with the opening of World War II. Why has it been revived at this particular time? Why is it concentrated on the United States?

Since 1945, the Soviet Union pushed its foreign espionage activities with almost reckless enthusiasm. The Gouzenko, Hiss, Rosenberg, Fuchs, Pontecorvo, McLean, Burgess, White, Petrov—and other espionage cases did more to jar Americans and Englishmen into an awareness of the Communist menace than all the other Soviet activities combined. The Oppenheimer case jarred us once again.

Our reaction was a swift series of countermeasures: the McCarran-Walters Act, the Smith Act prosecutions, the stepping up of our counter-intelligence activities, the renewed activity of legislative committees investigating Communism. As leader after leader of the Communist Party was hustled off to jail, the movement suffered from a lack of high command. Ever since the early '20's the same people had been running the show: Browder, Foster, Stachel, Hudson, Green, Hall, Ford, Trachtenberg, Bittleman, Bedacht, Weiss, Jerome. These, and a handful of others, have actually run the Communist Party since its inception. As these bureaucrats were arrested, convicted and taken out of circulation, the mass leadership was forced to function from underground positions.

The FBI had started sifting its undercover agents throughout the Communist Party structure years ago, and a cartoon which appeared in a New York publication some time ago, depicted a Communist leader addressing a secret meeting in a cellar as "Comrades—and members of the FBI." Subsequent events have indicated that this was not so far-fetched after all. Deprived of the leadership to which it had become accustomed since the 1920s, the party was driven deeper and deeper underground. Despite the most elaborate precautions, however, government agents continued to secure the innermost secrets of the party. In Northern California, soon after a group of carefully selected members went deep underground to previously prepared positions, the FBI uncovered the entire headquarters, arrested and convicted the leaders and thus gave further evidence of the constant high state of efficiency of our Federal Bureau of Investigation.

These continued Smith Act convictions, the espionage revelations, and the persistent exposure of its activities by federal and state committees harried the party as never before. It was forced to activate its "sleepers" or members-at-large. This elite corps is comprised of people who are highly respected, exert great influence, and who have no record of Communist affiliation or sympathy but are sufficiently dedicated Marxists to carry out party discipline.

These sleepers let loose with a campaign attacking the FBI, the Subversive Activities Control Board, legislative committees, the McCarran-Walter Act, and at the same time hypocritically plugged away for peaceful coexistence with the Soviet Union. This propaganda campaign was set loose from widely scattered sources simultaneously. The national administration was referred to as the "Cadillac clique," a phrase that first came to the attention of this committee during the Los Angeles hearing on the infiltration of the medical profession in 1954. It has since been widely used as a party propaganda phrase. As the year 1955 drew to a close, the American Communist Party found itself running short of both funds and members. It could no longer function through big front organizations, and the tiny, compact units found it most difficult to communicate with each other and at the same time maintain adequate contact with the party's high command.

Thus, the united front was revived as a desperate measure, linked to the Geneva Conference in a transparent effort to portray itself as an implementation of peaceful coexistence instead of an emergency measure to save the party from stagnation. The faithful comrades wormed their way into labor unions, churches, schools, universities, public utilities, professional associations, cultural groups, and media of propaganda. Nor did they overlook the two political parties and, indeed, amazed all students of political science by beginning to collaborate with Socialist organizations and even the hated Trotskyist groups.

Trusted party members were placed in key positions and operated with relative safety because they had no documentable records. The older Communists soon became useless, since their affiliations and activities had been more open, and were carefully enumerated on file cards in the offices of the various official agencies engaged in investigating this particular type of activity. Now the Communist Party mobilized a new group that had no such records; whose members had never been permitted to join the party in the formal sense, and who were contacted by it with the most elaborate caution. These Communists carried on the open work with great care—thereby being forced into a position of relative impotency as far as the open work of agitation and propaganda were concerned, but subtly impeding anti-Communist work at every opportunity.

The effect of the sudden activation of this brigade of Communist sleepers was most apparent. It was seen in the almost frantic campaign of the fellow-travelers, hitchikers, and anti-anti-Communists. These groups used, and continue to use, every possible weapon of propaganda, persuasion and pressure to stifle the factors that have so effectively forced the party underground, broken it into tiny fragments, and deprived it of its accustomed leaders.

This, then, was the real reason for the revival of the united front movement throughout the world and particularly in Great Britain and the United States.

We cannot too strongly emphasize the fact that far from being rendered weak and ineffective, the dedicated, fanatic, hard-core of Communist Party members are much more of a menace today than ever before. Operating from underground positions, utilizing the services of the sleeper apparatus, insinuating themselves into mass organizations, particularly those liberal and progressive movements with which the readers of these reports have become familiar, the Communist Party poses a grim and serious menace. Obviously, the Soviet slaughter of thousands of Hungarians and the uprising in Poland, together with the sudden attack on Stalin, who had for years been revered as the almost saintly leader of the world Communist movement, drove a good many American Communists out of the movement. These, however, have been considered dispensable. They have been expended by the party as not sufficiently steeled as Bolsheviks, not sufficiently dedicated and fanaticised to be worthy to carry on the movement in this Country. The revelations made by witnesses who appeared before us in 1954, concerning infiltration of the medical profession in Southern California, and the testimony in the present hearing by the Chancellor and Dean of Students of one of our greatest universities—these provide eloquent and certainly the most persuasive evidence of the fact that Communist activity in this Country continues to be an ever-present threat to all that we hold most sacred, and which demands constant vigilance in order that we may know something of its techniques and its activities.

Not only in Political Affairs, issued by the Ameircan Communist Party, was the new united front movement proclaimed; the Cominform Bulletin issued from Bucharest set the same line for the Communist Parties of the world. The April 13, 1956, issue, proclaiming:

> "An extremely important question for the development of the working-class movement and the anti-war fight is that of healing the split in the working class of capitalist countries. This calls for rapprochement and cooperation among all workers' parties and trade unions.
>
> "The Twentieth Congress has shown that there are real prospects of united action by Communists, Socialists, and other workers' parties." (Results of the Twentieth. Congress of the CPFU and the Tasks of the Polish United Workers Party, by Edward Ochab, First Secretary, Central Committee, Polish United Workers Party.)

In June, 1956, Eugene Dennis wrote in *Political Affairs:*

> "Not the least important of the new and serious problems we should concern ourselves with as we probe and re-assess the present status and future of our party—is the question that keeps coming to the forefront in respect to the possibility of organizing a new and broader mass party of Socialism.
>
> "One of the unique aspects of political and social trends in the United States in recent years is the revitalization and growth of a number of Socialist-oriented and pro-Marxist currents and groupings.
>
> "* * * Precisely because of the vicious onslaught against our party, some Socialist-minded people have sought other channels, perhaps safer or less vulnerable for Marxist expression."

The whole question was well summarized by an article entitled "Communist Party Discussion Section—Towards a United Party of Socialism" by Nemmy Sparks, which appeared in *Political Affairs* for July, 1956. He declared:

> "* * * during the periods when our party was reaping our most conspicuous successes, as when it stood at the head of the struggle of the unemployed, when it was playing a key role in the building of the CIO unions, when it was attempting to develop American traditions in the modern period, and exerting tangible influence on the political scene in the heyday of the new deal, many individuals did come over from other Socialist movements and schools of thought. . ."
>
> "* * * The historic conditions. deriving from the first World War, the Russian Revolution, and the split in the Socialist movement, have now given way to the new conditions which the XXth Congress described as the era of the world Socialist system. These

conditions make possible a vast new trend toward unity among Socialist-minded people which has already begun to be felt not only abroad but in our own country. The new features of independence and mutual criticism in the relationships among Communist parties also tend to remove barriers between Communists and other supporters of Socialism.

"Would it not bring this perspective nearer, if in various localities Communists would begin talking to other Socialist-minded elements and groupings and begin to explore the areas of common agreement and difference, develop interchanges and public discussion, such as the splendid forum in New York between Norman Thomas, A. J. Muste, Dr. Dubois, and Comrade Dennis?"

We wish to make it very clear at this point that the new united front, Communist style, originated in the Kremlin and carefully tailored to fit the exigencies of the various Communist Parties throughout the world, did not for one instant plan on its members boring their way into mass liberal organizations and then of becoming anonymous therein. This is, of course, completely at variance with Communist technique. The united front operates on the assumption that every Communist who is sent into a mass non-Communist liberal organization will work his way into a position of control, thereby dominating every organization with which Communists come in contact. If the party is unable to infiltrate and use an organization for its own purposes, then it regards the organization as an impediment to the cause of Communism which must be wrecked or rendered impotent. The other liberal organizations, such as the Socialist Party, had no plan for luring Communists away from their own organization and making mere Socialists out of them. But remember well that the national headquarters of the Young Socialist League enthusiastically instructed its members to burrow into Communist organizations, sow the seeds of dissatisfaction, disrupt its membership, and lure the Communists into the ranks of the Young Socialist League. As we have seen above, the Communist Party in this country was extremely sensitive and fearful of penetration by government agents. Time and time again, as Smith Act defendants were brought into court, they sat flabbergasted and stunned when some of their trusted comrades, with whom they had attended meetings a few days preceding the arrest, proceeded to the witness stand, revealed themselves as undercover agents for the Federal Government, and proceeded to give evidence that resulted in the conviction of the defendants with whom they had been intimate in the party.

THE YSL INVITES DANGER

For years the Communist apparatus had become more and more sensitive and alert against infiltration by government agents. Despite its most elaborate precautions, the penetration of its ranks continued. Of all the progressive groups in the United States, the Young Socialist League was the only one that issued an official directive ordering its members to penetrate the Communist Party ranks, sow the seeds of disaffection among its younger members, persuade them to leave the Communist movement and become members of the Young Socialist League. Under the conditions we have outlined, it was only natural that the

Communists should regard this effort at mass penetration of their ranks with the utmost alarm and suspicion. This would be particularly true in cases where members of the Young Socialist League managed to meet—not with merely the rank and file Communists—but with Communist leaders and functionaries, and particularly with members of the Trotsky movement and representatives from pacifist and other liberal organizations. And in the event it was ascertained that a representative of the Young Socialist League was foolhardy enough to describe such a meeting and give the correct names of the persons who attended the same, the natural suspicion might easily develop to a state of utter consternation.

We have shown that the Young Socialist League was essentially a Trotskyist type of organization. It employed members of the Trotskyist movement, such as Shachtman and James Cannon, to speak in its behalf; it welcomed members of the Socialist Workers Party into its ranks; in many instances, some of its members were also members of the Socialist Workers Party or Trotskyist organization. It is, then, necessary that we understand something about the almost indescribable hatred that existed between the Stalinists and the Trotskyists who were found attending some of the meetings described by young Abrams.

The reason for this bitter hatred between Stalinists and Trotskyists lies deep in the heart of the Russian Revolution. Lenin and Trotsky, on the one hand, were educated, brilliant, dedicated, dominant forces in the machinery of the revolution; Stalin, on the other hand, was used largely as a creator of strikes and riots, an organizer, and as a person who—although virtually illiterate—possessed a natural talent for playing one man against another, undermining here and there, capitalizing on sheer terror as a weapon with which to gain his own ends.

Both Lenin and Trotsky were dynamic and moving orators, able to take a place on the rostrum before a large and somewhat hostile audience and move them to great levels of emotional ecstasy and loyalty through the sheer magnetism of their respective personalities. Lenin has always been worshiped by Communists the world over as the founder of Russian Communism and the one individual who personally led the Russian masses out of the bondage of the Czar. Trotsky was the creator of the Red Army, the commissar for war, the brilliant master of Marxian ideology and the individual selected to negotiate the treaty at Brest-Litovsk when Russia withdrew from World War I.

Throughout the early days of the Russian Revolution, Stalin began to nurture a violent jealousy of both Lenin and Trotsky. When he and Voroshilov were in the southern part of Russia during the civil war that followed the Revolution of 1917, Stalin's hatred and jealousy of Trotsky became so intense that when Voroshilov, who was commanding the Red Army forces, received directives from his superior, Stalin would scrawl on the bottom of the order in his heavy, irregular hand, "ignore this."

News of his rebellious attitude reached Moscow, Trotsky reported the defection to Lenin, and Stalin was recalled for discipline. This only served to intensify his hatred of both the other leaders, and when Lenin died in 1924 Stalin immediately set about to undermine him and climb over his dead political body to a position of supreme command in Red Russia. He did this by breaking promises, sending spies throughout the structure of the Communist Party, planting rumors about Trotsky, launching the purge trials that shook the nation from one end to the other. In a previous report, we have explained how Stalin promised Kamenev and Zinoviev that if they would assist him in the elimination of Trotsky as a political idol, the three of them would rule the Soviet Union together. Kamenev and Zinoviev did assist Stalin, as did many other lesser functionaries of the Communist Party. When Trotsky was undermined by the most scurrilous of rumors and gossip, and after his supporters had been scattered to widely separated localities throughout the vast reaches of the Soviet empire, Kamenev and Zinoviev were arrested along with Trotsky, and both of them were summarily shot. Trotsky was then ousted from the Communist Party, exiled from the Soviet Union, and finally was harrassed and harried from one European residence to another. Finally, in 1939, he was apparently safe in a fortified villa at Coyoacan, a suburb of Mexico City. The forces of Stalin were implacable, however, and his arm was long. In the summer of 1940, one of his secret agents assassinated Trotsky, thus removing this hated rival forever.

In a book, *The Appeals of Communism*, by Gabriel A. Almond, Princeton University Press, Princeton, New Jersey, 1954, we find some material that helps to explain why the hostility against the followers of Trotsky continued from the moment of his expulsion from the Russian Communist Party until even after the death of Stalin. A former British Communist was quoted as saying: "For a capitalist or Fascist there is respect and acceptance because he is the reason for your existence. There is no such basis for the existence of social democracy, which is claiming to do what you are claiming to do in a better way. That is why Trotsky and Tito were pursued with such venom."

A former American Communist said: "Hatred for capitalism was never strong enough, but hatred for ex-members was very strong."

A former high-ranking member of the Italian Communist Party said: "I am certain that the Comintern hated Trotsky more than the foreign powers. * * *"

The author summarized the thinking of the former Communists who were interviewed by saying:

"It would appear from our respondents that there were no very clear directives on the question of extra-party friendships, except for extreme cases. Friendships with renegades were strictly forbidden. To be seen with a Trotskyite would constitute a basis for expulsion."

Trotsky was expelled from the Communist Party and banished to Alma Ata in 1927. The reading of his appeal to the assembled delegates to the Sixth World Congress of the Communist International determined several of the American delegates to follow his leadership. They were expelled from the American Communist Party on October 27th, 1928.

One of the expelled leaders, James C. Cannon, has written a clear and accurate account of the long years of bitter rivalry and hatred between the Stalinists and the Trotskyists in America in a book called *The History of American Trotskyism*, Pioneer Publishers, New York, 1944, 116 University Place, New York 3, New York. He wrote:

"The first weapon of the Stalinists was slander. The second weapon employed against us was ostracism. The third was gangsterism." And he continued:

"The fourth weapon and the arsenal of American Stalinists was burglary. They were so afraid of this little group, armed with the great ideas of Trotsky's program, that they wanted by all means to crush it before it could get a hearing. One Sunday afternoon, returning from a meeting of our first New York branch—12 or 13 people gathered solemnly to form the organization and lay the groundwork for the overthrow of American capitalism—I found the apartment ransacked from top to bottom. In our absence they had jimmied the lock on the door of my home and broken in. Everything was in disorder; all my private papers, documents, records, correspondence—anything they could lay their hands on— were strewn on the floor. Evidently we had surprised them before they could cart the plunder away. While I was on tour a few weeks later, they came back and finished the job. This time they took everything."

We point out here that this example of the Communists burglarizing their rival's possessions in order to gain access to critical information and documents is nothing new. There have been innumerable instances of this sort of action, and it will be noted that the documents in the possession of Abrams, whose thinking was shot through with both Trotskyism and Socialism, were scattered about the premises in the utmost confusion, and there were great gaps in a series of critical documents, whereas the noncritical papers flowed along in almost completely unbroken sequence.

Cannon continues to describe some of the more direct activities between his group of Trotskyists and the Communists in the United States, and his descriptions are sufficiently vivid to warrant inclusion at this point.

"We planned a national tour on the same subject. I tried to speak in New Haven, but there we were completely outnumbered. The Stalinists surrounded us and the meeting was entirely broken up. I spoke in Boston; there we made better preparations. I arrived a few days early, went around to a few old IWW friends of mine to see if they could not get some boys from the waterfront to help us uphold free speech. We had about 10 of these lads around the platform. A group of Stalinist hoodlums was also there, bent on breaking up the meeting, but evidently they became convinced that they would get their own heads broken if they tried it. The Boston meeting was a success."

"In Cleveland we had a fight * * * our squadron was ready, waiting for me to give the signal. I finally said, 'OK, go ahead.' Thereupon, they went after Amter and his gang, took them one by one and threw them down the stairs, and cleared the hall and the atmosphere of Stalinists."

"At my meeting in Minneapolis * * * we were taken off guard. * * * The Stalinist gang arrived first, assaulted Oscar Coover at the door with blackjacks, forced their way in and occupied the front seats in a rather small hall. When I rose to speak, they began howling in the manner of Amter and his gang at Cleveland. After a few minutes we tied into them, and a free-for-all fight ensued. Then the cops came in and broke up the meeting.''

"In New York, as we began holding more regular meetings, the Stalinists intensified their attempts to stop us. One meeting here in the Labor Temple was broken up. Their standing plan was to come in such force as to rush the speaker off the platform, take over the meeting, and turn it into an anti-Trotskyist demonstration. They never succeeded in doing that because we always had our guard on the platform equipped with the necessary implements. The Stalinists never reached the platform, but they did start such a free-for-all fight that the cops came in force and the meeting was broken up in disorder.''

''* * * We held a May Day celebration * * * May 1, 1929—the spring after our expulsion. Looking through *The Militant* I saw the announcement of the May Day meeting at the Hungarian Hall and the appended statement that it would be under the protection of the Workers Defense Guard. It was well guarded; our strategy was not to let the disturbers in. Our own comrades, sympathizers and all those who were obviously coming to celebrate May Day were admitted. When the Stalinists tried to force their way in, they met our guard at the head of the stairs, and got blows over the head until they decided they could not storm that stairway.

"The following Friday, I think it was, the Stalinists decided to take revenge on the Hungarian group for their inability to break up the May Day meeting as instructed. The Hungarian comrades were holding a closed meeting—eight or ten people quietly transacting the ordinary business of a branch. Among those present was the Communist veteran Louis Basky, a man of about 50, and his aged father, a man about 80, who is a militant partisan of his son and of the Trotskyist movement. Several women comrades were there. Suddenly the hall was raided by a group of Stalinist hoodlums. They rushed right in and started beating both the women and men, including old man Basky. Our comrades grabbed chairs or chair legs and defended themselves as best they could. One of those present, a woodworker by profession, who had one of the tools of his trade in his pocket, saw a couple of these hoodlums beating the old man. He went berserk when he saw that and went to work on one of the pair. They carried the Stalinist thug to a hospital. He stayed there three weeks, the doctors uncertain whether he was going to pull out of it or not.

"That put a stop to the attacks on our meetings. The Stalinists had brought things near a terrible tragedy and scandalization of the whole Communist movement. They became convinced that we would not surrender our right to meet and speak, that we would stand up and fight, that they could not break us up. Thereafter, there were only isolated instances of violence against us. We did not win our free speech from the Stalinist gangsters by a change of heart on their part, but by our determined and militant defense of our rights.''

"* * * Sporadically, over the entire 13, nearly 14, years of our existence, the Stalinists have resorted to their hooligan attempts to silence us. Each time we not only fought back, but sought the assistance of other groups for cooperative defense. While we never succeeded in forming any permanent united front defense movement, we had partial success on each occasion. It was sufficient to secure our rights, and so far we have managed to maintain them. This is very important to remember in connection with a new attempt of the Stalinists in one part of the country to silence us. At the present time out in California, *The Militant* reports such an attempt and you see our party right back in the groove, forming united fronts running in all directions for support and scandalizing them all over town, forcing the Stalin gang to break down. Our people are still distributing the paper at the forbidden places in California."

"* * * At that time, the Stalinists were exerting extraordinary pressure on the Socialists in order to lay hold of this progressive left-wing movement and turn it back in the direction of reformism by way of Stalinism. * * * The Stalinists had the edge on us to begin with. In the Socialist left wing there were already strong sentiments of conciliation with Stalinism, and the Stalinists were working the demagogic 'unity' slogan for all it was worth. We recognized the problem and realized that if we did not bestir ourselves, what had happened in Spain would happen here."

"* * * This was the time of the Sacramento 'criminal syndicalism trial' of Communist Party members. One of our comrades —Norman Mini—was among the defendants, and because he had turned Trotskyist, not only did the Stalinists refuse to defend him, but they denounced him in their press as a 'stool pigeon' while he was on trial. We came to his aid. The nonpartisan *Labor Defense*, a non-Stalinist defense committee, did very distinguished work in providing defense for Comrade Mini. We exploited to the full all of the political aspects of this situation."

Thus, in criticizing the Communists in the bitter language found in his documents, Sheldon Abrams was merely echoing the general Socialist and Trotskyist attitude of hatred. But, with the Khrushchev secret speech in February, 1956, came orders from headquarters of the Young Socialist League for all of its officers to take advantage of the situation and recruit Communists to the ranks of the Young Socialist League (see letter from Max Martin dated April 14, 1956—just two months after the Khrushchev speech). Other documents show that Sheldon Abrams, following these instructions from his superior in the Young Socialist League, did attend meetings with members of the Communist Party. Six days after the date of the letter from headquarters ordering him to thus contact members of the Communist Party, he was dead.

TESTIMONY OF DR. ROBERT GERHEART NEUMANN

The testimony of Dr. Neumann was preceded by a preliminary statement by R. E. Combs from the committee counsel, as follows:

"* * * This phase of the hearing will deal with what in my opinion is the most important phase, perhaps not quite as sensational as some of the others, but by all means the most important phase of the hearing, and that is an analysis of the documents—not all of them because there were literally hundreds of them that were found in Mr. Abram's room —for the purpose of assisting us to accurately evaluate the political and sociological meaning of these documents; to accurately study the background of the international Communist Party line, and to that end we have asked the assistance of Dr. Neumann of the Department of Political Science of the University of California at Los Angeles. As you will see in a moment, Dr. Neumann is a recognized authority in this field. If the committee will indulge us, I think after Dr. Neumann has been sworn and his qualifications placed in the record, we should have him comment on these things as the hearing progresses, and instead of proceeding by the usual technique of specific questions and answers, it would be a little more informal so that his interpretation and evaluation may be asked from time to time as this part of the hearing unfolds. Is that satisfactory?

"Chairman Burns: I think it would be better that way.

"Q. (By Mr. Combs): Will you state your full name, Doctor?

"A. Robert Gerheart Neumann.

"Q. You reside in the Los Angeles area?

"A. I reside in Los Angeles, sir. I am Associate Professor of Political Science at U. C. L. A.

"Q. What is your residence address, Doctor?

"A. 3282 Grand View Boulevard, Los Angeles 66.

"Q. What degrees do you hold? Academic degrees?

"A. I have a master's degree, doctor's degree, I have a diploma from the Geneva School of International Studies, from the Counsellor Academy in Vienna, and from the University of Rennes in France. I think that is about all.

"Q. I think that should do it. Where did you take your undergraduate work?

"A. In Europe, sir, University of Vienna.

"Q. You have been a member of the faculty at U. C. L. A. in the Political Science Department for how long?

"A. Since 1947.

"Q. What is your specialty in the field of political science?

"A. Comparative government with special regard to Europe, the Middle East and North Africa.

"Q. Have you devoted particular attention to the international Communist Party line as exemplified by the Communist Party of France?

"A. Yes, sir.

"Q. It would be necessary for you to study the development of the Communist Party line in places other than France, wouldn't it?

"A. Yes, because the Communist movement is international. It is not an isolated movement.

"Q. Are you familiar with the Seventh Congress of the Communist International?

"A. Yes, sir. That was the congress where the united front line was brought out.

"Q. Who was the general secretary of the Communist International or Comintern at that time, if you know?

"A. If I remember, that was Dimitrov.

"Q. Georgi Dimitrov. Do you remember that he instituted the policy called the 'Trojan Horse'?

"A. Yes, sir.

"Q. Would you explain that briefly to the committee, please?

"A. The policy which was actually not new at that time is sometimes called boring from within. This was a policy directed primarily toward left wing, social-democratic and liberal movements. It was sometimes also called the united front, earlier version. That version looked toward uniting at the base rather than at the top. This was the reason why the term united front met with a good deal of suspicion on the part of Socialists and liberals because they felt it was another one of the earlier versions. That is why later the 'popular front' was used.

"Q. In both instances is it not a fact that the ultimate purpose of that strategy was for the Communist Parties of the world to insinuate themselves as members into broad masses of liberal, progressive, non-Communist organizations?

"A. Yes, sir, that was true. It also had that desired result. From that time on you have a massive Communist infiltration into the various unions in many countries, in industries, nationalized industries, and so forth. It also had the desired results for the Communist Parties themselves. If I may explain, I have a few figures here.

"Q. Please do.

"A. The popular front was made official about 1936. Here are the figures for Communist membership in France in that period. I am using France because it is strongest and it is the most Stalinist of the Communist Parties outside of the Iron Curtain. Famous words were—if you will forgive me for a moment of levity—'when Stalin gets a cold, Thorez sneezes.' Thorez was general secretary of the French Communist Party and still is. In 1932, the French Communist Party had 25,000 members; in 1934, 50,000; in 1935, 70,000; in 1936, 329,000, a jump from 70 to 329,000 when the popular front was officially established.

"Q. That is a graphic illustration of the effectiveness of the popular front movement as originated by Dimitrov at the Seventh Congress.

"A. The popular front movement not only combines the already existing forces of Socialist, liberal, and Communist groups, but attracts others in addition.

"Q. I think it is important at this stage to show the cleavage, the mark between the two Communist groups, between the members of the Third International and the members of the so-called Fourth International, the Third International being the so-called strict orthodox Communist and the Fourth International being the Trotskyite group. Correct me if I am wrong, Doctor, but is it not true that at the inception of the revolution in Russia in 1917, the two outstanding leaders were Lenin and Trotsky and at that time it was not Stalin?

"A. That is correct.

"Q. At that time Trotsky played the part of commissar for war. He negotiated a treaty with the Germans at Brest-Litovsk and was practically deified throughout the revolutionary period with almost the same degree of adoration as Lenin himself?

"A. Yes.

"Q. Then after the death of Lenin and the ascension of Stalin, through that period, with the help of Kamenev and Zinoviev, Stalin undermined Trotsky and forced him out of the Soviet Union and finally into Mexico where he was murdered in 1940?

"A. That's correct.

"Q. So there was an implacable and fanatical hostility between the forces of the Stalinists and the forces of the Trotskyites, is that right?

"A. That is entirely correct.

"Q. I lay that foundation beacuse of this, that even during the inception of the popular front under the direction of Dimitrov at the Seventh Congress, nevertheless, there was never at that time a collaboration between the Stanlinists and the Trotskyites? Is that right?

"A. That is entirely correct, sir. As an illustration of that, the tactics of the Communists during the Spanish Civil War was directed toward the liquidation of the Trotskyites wherever possible, as in the instance of Andre Marty, sometimes called the 'Butcher of Albacete' who was particularly in the forefront of that.

"Q. One of the worst things you could call a Stalinist in this period was to accuse him of being a Trotskyite?

"A. That is correct.

"Q. By way of background, Dr. Neumann, when Earl Browder, who for some 17 years had been leader of the Community Party of the United States, was expelled from that position and expelled from the party itself, in fact, the day that announcement was made—the announcement that he was a traitor to the cause and should be expelled—did that originate in the United States?

"A. It was first announced in a French publication of which I have some recent copies, called *Cahiers du Communisme,* which may be translated as 'Communist Notebooks,' the theoretical and political monthly of the Central Committee of the French Communist Party. That is the official name. The article was reprinted verbatim in the *Daily Worker* of New York while Browder's name still appeared on the masthead. That was the beginning of the execution.

"Q. The final decision regarding the political liquidation of Browder did not come from the American Communist Party, but from France?

"A. That is correct, sir. The French Communist Party and its agents have often been known as the 'carrier of the word' from Moscow.

"Q. The person who wrote the article which led to the expulsion of Browder was Jacques Duclos?

"A. Yes. He was assistant general secretary of the French Communist Party.

"Q. So if it should develop that a student at the university was meeting in California with a member of the Communist Party of France, this would be a somewhat significant event in your opinion?

"A. Not only significant, but quite serious, because this is the customary way that an important decision occurs, not just a minor one.

"Q. In view of what you have testified to about the relationships between the Stalinists and the Trotskyites, if it were also developed that the same student was at the same time meeting with members of the Trotskyite group, would this give added significance to the situation?

"A. I would be inclined to say so, sir.

"Q. If at the same time at the same meeting there were five Communist scientist students at a scientific institution in the vicinity, would that add some additional weight to the meeting, in your opinion?

"A. Obviously.

"Q. If at the same meeting at the same place there were members of the Young Socialist League present and all people meeting together with a member of the Communist Party of France, would this also be significant?

"A. Yes, it would. At any rate it might be.

"Q. If in addition to that meeting documents were produced from official sources showing that a change in the international party line had been officially announced calling for that kind of a meeting, and pursuant to that direction the meeting was held, in your opinion would that be moved from the realm of coincidence?

"A. I would say it would fit together very well.

"Q. The first international Communist organization was known as the Communist International? The Comintern?

"A. That was the Third International, that is right.

"Q. What organization succeeded that?

"A. The Cominform.

"Q. Are these the organs put out by the Cominform (exhibiting)?

"A. Yes, sir, they are. That is the official organ of the Cominform published first in Belgrade and after the breach with Tito, in Bucharest.

"Q. Those are the last two numbers, are they not, the one in your hand being the first one and the one which precedes it being the second to the last issue?

"A. I can't say for a fact, but it should be because I don't believe that any others have been issued.

"Q. It is a fact because if you will notice in the last one it announces that it is the last issue.

"A. That is correct, April 17th, the announcement of the dissolution.

"Q. The one preceding it is the next to the last issue, is that right?

"A. Yes, sir, the 13th and the 17th.

"Mr. Combs: For the purpose of more specific identification, Mr. Chairman and members of the committee, the first one is entitled 'Workers of all Lands Unite! For a Lasting Peace, for a People's Democracy! Bucharest. Organ for the Information Bureau of the Communist and Workers Parties, Friday, April 13th, 1956.' The second issue bears the same masthead. It is dated Tuesday, April 17, 1956. The leading article on the front page says 'Announcement on the Dissolution of the Information Bureau of the Communist and Workers Parties.' These are only for identification, Mr. Chairman.

THE KHRUSHCHEV "SECRET" SPEECH

"Q. Dr. Neumann, on the fourteenth of last February, something of great importance occurred in the Soviet Union. What was that?

"A. That was the Twentieth Congress of the Communist Party.

"Q. Of the Soviet Union?

"A. Yes.

"Q. Did Nikita Khrushchev make a speech on that occasion?

"A. He made two speeches, an open one, open in the sense it was before the date immediately reported at the beginning and then a secret speech about a week later also during the congress. The secret speech was held only before the delegates from the Soviet Union. The other one before all delegates.

"Q. The open speech was quite lengthy, was it not?

"A. Very lengthy.

"Q. As a result of those two speeches, the overt and the covert, the one that followed, did a change in international Communist Party line result?

"A. Yes, sir. The first speech made only general reference to the cult of personality. It did not bring out anything new because that policy had already gone on for some time. The second speech was sensational because it brought the condemnation of Stalin and a revelation of all kinds of misdoings. Actually, Khrushchev was not the first one to do that. The speech by Mikoyan preceded it and in the opinion of some, propelled it.

"Q. For the record, Mikoyan was a member of the Politburo?

"A. Yes, sir, now called the Presidium of the Central Committee of the Communist Party.

"Q. As a result of those speeches, various Communist Parties throughout the world drew conclusions from them?

"A. Yes, sir. I have here a book published by the Russian Institute of Columbia University which summarizes and brings together the initial reactions to that speech by the Communist Parties of various countries.

"Q. Does that book reflect a change in the so-called popular front?

"A. This book does not as yet, but subsequent developments did.

"Q. I will identify this for the record only at the present time, but I will not introduce it. Have you seen this before? (Exhibiting document to witness)

"A. Yes, sir.

"Q. It is a copy of *Political Affairs*, identified heretofore as the monthly ideological publication of the National Committee of the Communist Party of the United States. This is the speech of Khrushchev. It is entitled 'N. S. Khrushchev's Report to the Central Committee of the Communist Party of the Soviet Union to the Twentieth Party Congress. Foreign Language Publishing House, February, 1956.'

"Here is one entitled 'The Meaning of the Twentieth Congress of the Communist Party of the Soviet Union Report to the National Committee of the Communist Party of the United States of America," by Max Weiss, also printed in 1956.

"Here is another one, 'The Communists Take a New Look, a Report to the National Committee of the Communist Party of the United States,' by Eugene Dennis, General Secretary of the Communist Party of the United States, which appeared in 1956.

"The last is entitled 'Draft Resolution for the Sixteenth National Convention of the Communist Party of the United States, adopted September 13, 1956.'

"There is a statement in one of these Cominform Bulletins and the date of each was *after* the Khrushchev speech of February 14th, you will note—one is by a member of the Communist Party of Poland, Edward Ochab—if I can find it. It has reference to the Polish United Workers Party and in light of what has happened in Poland, I would like to get from you whether or not this is an accurate interpretation of the general party line that ensued afterwards. This article comprises almost the entire page in the *Bulletin* for Friday, April 13, 1956, and is entitled 'Results of the Twentieth Congress of the Communist Party of the Soviet Union and the Tasks of the Polish United Workers Party.'

"A. May I interrupt for a moment, sir?

"Q. Surely.

"A. This is the official name of the Communist Party of Poland.

"Q. (Continuing to read): 'An extremely important question for the development of the working class movement and the antiwar fight is that of healing the split in the working class of capitalist countries. This calls for rapprochement and cooperation among all of the workers parties and trade unions. *The Twentieth Congress has shown that there are real prospects of united action by Communists, Socialists and other workers parties.*' (Committee's italics.) Is that a correct interpretation of the new line?

"A. Yes, sir, I think it is, although Ochab is no longer secretary general. They change their officials quite rapidly.

"Q. There is one here from the first secretary of the Central Committee of the Communist Party of Czechoslovakia entitled 'Twentieth Congress of the Communist Party of the Soviet Union,' by Antonin Novotny: 'Friendly relations between our party and the Communist Parties of different countries which have Marxism-Leninism as an ideological basis are an important factor in the struggle of the peoples for peace and Socialism and we shall therefore steadily strengthen them.'

"And, finally: '* * * The possibilities exist for working out, in the interest of the struggle for peace and the interest of the working people, the basis for cooperation with Socialist circles to whom we extend the hand of cooperation. We shall exert even greater efforts in order to insure that our international relations are also developed through public and cultural organizations.'

"Is that a correct interpretation of the new line, in your opinion?

"A. Yes, sir.

"Q. This was the organ which did the same thing for the international Communist Party movement that *Political Affairs* does for the American Communist movement?

"A. Yes, sir."

Dr. Neumann then commented on the articles that appeared in *Political Affairs* and other Communist organs in the United States for the period immediately preceding and subsequent to the Khrushchev speeches of February 14, 1956. Earlier in this section of the report, these articles have been quoted in full, and Dr. Neumann, in commenting on them, stated that in his opinion they correctly heralded and exemplified the change in the party line and the revival of the united front movement.

His attention was then called to one of the critical documents that has already been mentioned, as follows:

"Q. (By Mr. Combs): Note the date of this, Doctor, February 23, 1956, I will reread it. 'We have been having interesting relations with the Stalinists. Just how far the new turn goes is an open question. Some say it includes approaching the Trotskyites, maybe even us. Anything happening on your end in connection with this? The reason we are involved with them to an extent is that our periphery is almost exclusively pacifist or pacifist-influenced, *and the Stalinists are making big overtures to them.* The result being we have attended several discussion meetings of Socialists, pacifists and Stalinists, and have been having informal dealings with the top leadership of the C. P. I don't know how familiar you are with all this. The first meeting with them was several months ago in Pasadena. * * * and I attended for the YSL, and there were people from the California YPSL, SP, and 15 or 20 pacifists, mostly unaffiliated, and four avowed Stalinists, (including the county chairman of the LYL, who was 40 if he was a day). It was very interesting. Although we did a good political job exposing them, we couldn't compete with the Stalinists on the level of moralizing and sermonizing. Early in the discussion (which lasted four hours), one of the Stalinists, who claimed that he was a registered member of the French CP, began to criticize the wishy-washy American CP with its constitutional prohibitions against violence, and proudly pointed to the French CP which openly advocates force and violence. At that point * * *, a scribbler for the PW, attacked the Frenchman ruthlessly, denouncing him for his advocacy of violence, and said that if he were in the American CP with those views he would be expelled. Clever, huh? The pacifists ate it up. That was the tone of the conference. The Stalinist line was that they, unlike the Socialists who stood for violent revolution, were natural allies of the pacifists. We did an excellent political job. * * *'"

"In connection with this last excerpt that I have read, Dr. Neumann, do you have any comment?

"A. The only comment that occurs to me—the man who wrote those letters is putting them in the language of the revolutionary movement which the Trotskyites stress particularly, since their accusation against Stalin was that Stalinism was a counter-revolutionary doctrine.

"I am also attracted by the date of the last letter, which was after the first Khrushchev speech but before the second one became known. The presence of a French Communist is significant.

"Whatever this writer learned at U. C. L. A. I don't know, but he has learned some dramatics. Whoever he wrote it to, he is trying to put forth his own activities in the best light. Perhaps something can be determined from that point. The fact that there was a meeting between those people is in itself significant, whatever may have come out of it. The Stalinists felt they would not leave themselves open to condemnation or expulsion. A few weeks earlier it would have been quite dangerous to do so.

"Q. Isn't this also true, and please correct me if I am wrong, that from the Stalinist standpoint they were precisely implementing the line which we have developed in your testimony, and the things which I have read into the record today. Here they were meeting with Socialists, there was a member of the Communist Party of France present, there had been collaboration between the Young Socialist

League and the Trotskyite movement, and there was an effort to use the National Association for the Advancement of Colored People as a spearhead for a proposed civil disobedience program which never took place, of course. Isn't it a significant thing, doctor, the fact in light of the statement in the *Cominform Bulletin,* the Khrushchev speech, the *Political Affairs* articles and the documents you have referred to, that here were these people sitting down with top leadership in the Communist Party?

"A. Yes, sir, and also that they were making the overtures. I don't know if this is the time you wanted me to refer to these.

"Q. Yes, I wish you would.

"A. When I had knowledge of these hearings, I got hold of some of the latest issues of publications of the French Communist Party to which I have already referred. *Cahiers du Communisme,* issue No. 3, March, 1956; No. 5 for May, 1956; and a double issue of August-September, 1956—the latest just arrived here. All three of them put this particular attitude in major focus. In No. 3, the major article is by Etienne Fajon, a member of the Politburo and top man in French Communism, 'The Struggle for a New Popular Front and the Lessons to be Derived from the One of Twenty Years Ago.' This is my translation.

"In the issue for May, 1956, an article by another member of the Politburo, a man who is perhaps one of the most intelligent of the Communist leaders, but also the sneakiest, Waldek Rochet, 'Unity of Action Must Impose Peace in Algeria.'

"There is another article here, 'The Problem of Workers Unity at the Present Stage.'

"Here are two articles, one by DeKerze, editor of a Communist journal for farmers caller *Laterre,* meaning 'The Earth;' 'The Alliance Between the Working Class and Working Peasants.'

"Another by Pierre Devio, another Communist leader and Member of Parliament, 'The United Front.'

"I also brought a recent issue of the leading French newspaper *Le Monde,* which is not a Communist journal by any means, for November 9, 1956, report of a debate in the French Parliament, in the National Assembly where the Communists stood up and shouted such things as 'Unity, unity.' The French National Assembly is somewhat unruly at times. The Communists in organization or in chorus fashion often say, 'Union of the forces of the left.' Then Mr. Villion, who is the man who wrote the article, says, 'The working class and *all democratic forces* must get together tomorrow in a salutary union.' (Committee's italics.)

"These remarks often don't make any real sense in terms of what went on before. These are prepared remarks beforehand, and they require some sort of action to push them forward. It is an organized effort. It is not something that came over them suddenly. It is a very logical development, since Khrushchev's and Bulganin's visit to Tito, descending out of invitations to Socialists, to Catholics, to anyone who would listen, to coalesce, have united front tactics on this, that or the other level, promising all kinds of confessions if they will only get together.

"You are probably familiar with the House Un-American Activities Committee's article called, 'The Great Pretense,' about 39 people who tried to interpret the meaning of the Twentieth Congress of the Communist Party. They didn't get together on it, but they agreed on the one point.

"Q. Were you a contributor to that also?

"A. Yes, I was.

"Mr. Combs: As I have said, Mr. Chairman, there were literally hundreds of documents which came into the possession of the committee. It would be futile and cumulative to endeavor to go into all of them at this time. The names have been placed in alphabetical sequence. They are being studied for whatever action may be needed. I think the important thing to develop at this hearing has been developed, to wit, that here is a boy who had been engaged in a rebellious attitude toward the administration of Roosevelt College where he was a student and editor of the student paper, and that he quarreled with the administration of that university over an administrative matter, namely, whether or not two members of the faculty should be retained or discharged. The folder in my hand, which is his academic record, bears out exactly what he said in his letter, that his major interest at U. C. L. A. was not academic, but political. This record shows he never attended any classes at all. He merely registered. He did no academic work. His full time was devoted to the activities of the Young Socialist League. The letters include many written to contacts in universities all over the United States. The replies he received from those contacts indicated that the same sort of activity was being carried on there that has been exemplified by the last excerpt which I read of his meetings here with the top leadership of the Communist Party of Los Angeles County. The recruiting of five Stalinists from Cal Tech, his letters which were received and letters he sent to the Trotskyite movement, the fact that a member of the Communist Party of France was present, and so on—as Dr. Neumann has so ably and graphically indicated, these are indicative of what Stalinists are doing pursuant to this new party line, reaching out and making common cause with Socialist groups, Trotskyite groups, and so on.

"Q. Dr. Neumann, do you know of any other period in the history of international Communism where the Stalinists and the Trotskyites have thus collaborated?

"A. No, sir, I don't.

"Q. This is the first time?

"A. I am surprised to find it. This is a very recent development, obviously, because even in Khruchshev's speech in Bucharest the Trotskyites were singled out for an admittedly milder form of condemnation, but still condemnation. This is a late development.

"Q. And quite significant, doctor?

"A. Yes, sir.

"Q. One more question. Dr. Neumann, what, in your opinion, would be the probable effect of this revival on an extended scale of the united front? With what success do you predict this development will meet? Do you have any comment to make as to how successful it will be?

"A. This must be speculative.

"Q. Of course.

NEW COMMUNIST THREAT

"A. But it could meet with very considerable success. There are a number of people in all countries who are attracted to radical leftism but who have been repelled by this bickering between different groups. There are sometimes almost ecclesiastic instances of minor points of difference. They would find it easier now to come together. Others are looking for a way of taking some action. There are large left-wing groups. Then there are those who may be classified as permanent malcontents in this country where these groups are relatively small, and I am not a specialist on American political economic movements at all. It is perhaps a little more difficult to answer. We do have this evidence in France. In the last French elections on January 2 of this year in France, the Socialist Party refused common cause with the Communist Party in the election. But in a number of federal organizations, for a department is something like a county, they disobeyed and did run on common lists with the Communists. That occurred in the East and in the Moselle Department and in several others, such as Lorraine. Here not only did the Communists obtain the combined vote, but they gained many more votes. This type of union is very attractive, therefore, it is a matter to be taken quite seriously.

"Q. It also affords pretty good cover on occasion?

"A. That is correct. And as the tragedy of the popular front in France and Spain shows, it gives the whole movement respectability. It makes it French, German, and Spanish rather than a Russian movement. The Communists, of course, are very experienced in using covers of any kind * * * this is no small matter."

When Abrams became interested in radical activities at Roosevelt College, he joined the Young Socialist League there, and successfully led a group of his colleagues in defying the authority of the college administration. He was then elected organizer for the Young Socialist League in the Chicago area and through that organization was put in contact with leaders of the Trotskyist movement. Indeed, the YSL itself was heavily flavored with Trotskyism. Most of its members, (including Abrams) were avid readers of Marxism and admirers of the late Leon Trotsky and his disciples. The voluminous correspondence carried on by Abrams and the dominant Trotskyist nature of his books and papers established this fact beyond dispute.

For several months following his assumption of duties in Illinois as YSL organizer, Abrams followed the usual YSL-Trotskyist line of expressing his hatred toward Stalin and his Communist followers in the most violent terms and at every opportunity. There is no evidence of his meeting even casually with any Communist before he came to California.

His enrollment as a graduate student in sociology at U. C. L. A. was no more than a gesture, for, as he expressed it, his interest was political rather than academic. As YSL organizer for the Los Angeles area, Abrams plunged at once into his new work. The university would not allow the YSL to function on the campus since its rule, heretofore mentioned, prevented that or any other extra-university organization from being officially recognized by the administration. Abrams readily discovered, however, that there was a facility made to order for his purposes. As he reported to one of his superiors in a letter from which we have already quoted, dated February 10, 1956: " * * * Schacht-man can only give one talk out here since we've procured the campus YWCA for him for the 19th (to my amazement, frankly). At any rate, Ted has agreed to substitute for Max, and so we're going to have a meeting on campus (technically, the Y is 'off campus')."

The University Young Women's Christian Association is located at 574 Hilgard Avenue, Los Angeles 24. Its building is "dedicated to the youth of the campus," and is situated directly across from one of the main entrances to the university. Abrams had, among his other papers, a folder marked "YWCA Meeting Forms," and in the folder was one of the mimeographed circulars distributed by the University YWCA which read, in part, as follows:

"The University YWCA recognizes the fact that avowed Marxist, Stalinist, or other Communist groups on the campus or elsewhere, are opposed to the freedom of the individual and to the Christian religion, upon which the YWCA is founded. There is impressive evidence that some of these groups follow the directives of a foreign nation which advocates the overthrow of our form of government by force. There-fore, the YWCA must consider itself in a different relationship with these groups than with other campus organizations.

"It is neither possible nor appropriate, however, for the YWCA to determine which groups are Marxist, Stalinist, or Communist in this day of shifting alignments. For this reason, all rental, lecture and/or discussion groups that wish to use the YWCA for open meetings at the established rental rate will be required to devote the first five minutes after their meeting is called to order by their chairman, to a statement of policy and principles by a YWCA representative designated by the cabinet. This statement will include the fundamental beliefs of the YWCA in the United States in regard to individual freedom, and to the individual and public responsibility which should be concurrent with this freedom."

It appears to the committee that if the representatives of the Uni-versity Young Women's Christian Association does no more than read a statement about civil rights, freedom of speech, patriotism, and con-demnation of Communism, and then turns its facilities over to members of the Communist and Trotskyite movement, its procedures in this regard are in bad need of an overhauling. Any casual student of Marxism, indeed, any real apostle of freedom, knows that the followers of Leon Trotsky are devoted to the principle of permanent revolution, and are, in this respect, advocates of a more violent and immediate unlawful overthrow of the Government of the United States than are their Stalinist brethren. So far as we can ascertain, once the creed of the YWCA and the United States is read from the rostrum, the meeting is then thrown open to all who are willing to pay the rental for the hall, a fact which caused Abrams considerable amazement. It causes us some amazement, too.

We have seen how the YSL was toying with the idea of launching a campaign of civil disobedience on the U. C. L. A. campus, somewhat like the defiant campaign that Abrams had undertaken at Roosevelt College; that the idea was, however, relinquished in favor of using the NAACP as an unwitting tool for campus agitation, and that the YSL leadership that would manipulate this campaign from concealed positions were confident that the American Civil Liberties Union would protect the NAACP from any recriminations on the part of the university administration.

We have already quoted, to some extent, from an excellent treatise called *The Appeals of Communism* by Gabriel A. Almond, Princeton University Press, Princeton, New Jersey, 1954. The author and his associates conducted interviews of many former members of the Communist Party, making a scientific and statistical analysis of the results. Since some of the conclusions affect factors which were found to be common in most students who became interested in the Communist movement, we deem it worthwhile to cite the following excerpts:

"* * * The young intellectually interested student, seeking a meaningful interpretation of the world and his mission in it, busily sloughing off the layers of parental or clerical admonition and rapidly absorbing magnificent and sweeping ideas, was readily attracted to the 'Socialist Club' or the 'Student Union' where he found spirits who shared his confusion and his interest in finding a gratifying intellectual and moral order. Most of these students who came into the party via anti-Fascist student societies of one kind or another, left it when they left the university or soon thereafter, when the enchantments and transports of student life fell afoul of the requirements of career and family and of more mature views of what prospects the world held open. It is technically correct to describe these students as alienated from their families and their communities and unsure of their values, but it would be incorrect to view them as permanently alienated, as being capable only of 'mass behavior.' For, in actual fact, like the immigrants and children of immigrants who found in the party a momentary stopping place in the difficult and painful process of cultural adjustment, so many of the university students who joined the party were engaged in a process of self-discovery and reality testing in which this experience was but an incident.

"This should not be construed to mean that these individuals were innocent dupes of the party. On the contrary, in a great many cases * * * they were persons with strong and compulsive needs to attack authority and established order."

"* * * For most of the respondents, therefore, joining the party cannot be described as a single act in time, but rather as a process involving a series of decisions stretching over a period of time. Even for those joining the party or the Young Communist League directly, the act of formal affiliation was infrequently accompanied by an awareness of the esoteric characteristics of the movement. Furthermore, these 'front organizations,' or the party unit themselves with which our respondents affiliated * * * were often locally influential groups. The student respondents, for example, were often confronted with influential, 'Socialist societies. * * *'

"It would appear, on the basis of our interviews with British and American professional and middle-class respondents, that the kind of intellectualization which seemed to enhance susceptibility to Communism in these countries was one of two types. It was the intellectual self-intoxication, for example, of the young college student, or self-taught person, whose mind was filled with an excited confusion and who saw in the party and its doctrine a system which provided answers.

Or it was a kind of cognitive and evaluative distortion which served to rationalize powerful needs for the expression of resentment, needs for relativeness and acceptance, or needs to overcome feelings of weakness and inadequacy. In the first case, joining might be described as a consequence of error; in the second, the most powerful pressures for joining were compulsive and in large part below the level of the individual's awareness.''

How many of these common factors fit Abrams? He was ''a young intellectually interested student, seeking a meaningful interpretation of the world and his mission in it,'' as is amply evident from the letters he wrote to his pro-Communist friend in the Army. He was ''rapidly absorbing magnificent and sweeping ideas,'' and ''was readily attracted to 'the Socialist club','' or ''locally influential groups,'' to wit, the Young Socialist League, ''where he found spirits who shared his confusion and his interest in finding a gratifying intellectual and moral order.'' All of these elements are abundantly established in Abrams, as shown by his correspondence, as well as by the books he pored over, Socialist, Communist, Trotskyist, Marxian works—he read them all. His ''strong, compulsive need to attack authority and established order'' is clearly illustrated by his letter to his Army friend in which he exultantly described how he led a handful of revolutionists in a campaign of rebellion and definance against the Roosevelt College administration.

RECAPITULATION

Those who have read the committee's previous reports will realize that the Communist Party has always employed the tactic of infiltrating mass organizations and seeking to manipulate them for its own purposes; and one of the more important purposes is to recruit new members. This is especially true of liberal groups which are relatively easy for the Communists to infiltrate. But the Communists are always the ones who do the infiltrating, and manipulating, and the recruiting. One of the most cardinal precepts of Communism is its elaborate mechanism of precaution against having its own ranks penetrated by wreckers, counter-revolutionists, or government agents.

The whole period of the Soviet purge trials from 1935 to 1939 came into being largely because of an almost morbid dread of counter-revolution on the part of the Kremlin; and the real reason for the maintenance of a gigantic secret police system is based upon the same obsessive dread.

Yet here, immediately after Khrushchev's secret speech in February, 1956, the Young Socialist League boldly instructed its officers to penetrate the Communist ranks, raid its membership, and take every possible advantage of the period of confusion that permeated the Communist ranks immediately after the Khrushchev speech was delivered. And, consequently, we find Sheldon Abrams, who had written so bitterly of his animosity toward Communism, not only attending meetings with top Communist functionaries in Southern California, but writing detailed accounts of these meetings, with the correct names of the Communist officials who attended! In the Abrams case, we find overwhelming evidence of collaboration between the members of the Communist Party and Socialists, pacifists and Trotskyists. The profound significance in this change in attitude on the part of the Communist Party and its success in attracting to itself these other liberal and radical groups, has been amply shown in the testimony of Dr. Neumann and by the documents that have been quoted heretofore. It means the launching of a new united front movement, and a repetition of the old Trojan Horse policy of the late Georgi Dimitrov, and a resumption of the subtle process of the infiltration of mass organizations for the purpose of manipulating them for the hypocritical purposes of world Communism. Those who have read the committee's report concerning the death of Everitt Hudson will find many elements that are also found in the Abrams case. In both instances, these young men did not directly enter the Community Party. Hudson eventually became a Communist, but Abrams, although meeting with high-ranking officers of the Communist Party in Southern California, never took the step of formaly affiliating with the party, so far as we know. In each case, the students were first attracted to progressive campus organizations; in each instance, the student lived away from his family; in each instance, there were abundant and intimate contacts with Communist Party officials; in each instance, there was a death surrounded by a series of baffling circumstances.

The committee wishes to emphatically point out, at this juncture, that no student organization of a Marxian nature at any university can possibly function very long or very successfully without adult direction. As a matter of fact, in the Marxian way of things, no Communist organization of students is *permitted* to function without adult leadership and absolute discipline on the part of the student members. To contend that there are no adult Communist members of the faculty at the University of California—or any other university—where a unit of young Communist students is also operating, would be simply ridiculous. The committee is quite aware, and the university administration has stated quite frankly, that there is, and probably always will be, a problem of Communist infiltration at the University of California. It certainly is not unique in this regard. The committee does know, however, that the incidence of Communist infiltration has been decreasing, and that the university administration has been cooperating for several years with this committee for the purpose of taking every possible preventive measure to eliminate it altogether. The problem still exists, and will be far more difficult to meet now that the signal has been given for Communists all over the world to engage in the new united front tactic of sliding their members unobtrusively into other mass organizations, adopting their protective coloration, and functioning with renewed fervor from these concealed positions.

The committee wishes to indicate its conviction that young Abrams did not die from natural nor accidental causes, nor did he commit suicide. It should be quite obvious, we take it, that if all three of the gas appliances were turned on and the windows to the tiny room that he occupied were closed, that death could have occurred to Abrams in a relatively short time and leave an evidence of 71 percent accumulation of carbon monoxide in the hemoglobin. The operation of these three appliances together would, of course, account for the sudden rise of carbon monoxide in the room, which was attested to by the

Los Angeles County Health Department. We wish to emphasize, however, that all three appliances were *not* turned on at the time of Abrams' death; that one of the windows *was* open, thus providing ventilation; that there were no noxious fumes being emitted from the Servel gas refrigerator, because that fact was attested to by a representative of the Southern California Gas Company to the Santa Monica Police Department; that the burning of the tiny flame in the Servel refrigerator would be comparable to someone sitting up all night in Abrams' room holding a burning cigarette lighter, as compared to the fumes emitted by a blast furnace if all three of the appliances were going together. The expert opinions given by Drs. Taylor and Stevenson are quite clear, quite positive, and speak for themselves. The committee is in complete accord with the testimony and opinions given by these two outstanding experts.

In the U. C. L. A. *Daily Bruin* on April 25, 1956, the following item appeared in the column entitled "Grins and Growls." It was signed by Mark Golden and Ed Schaupp, and was entitled "No Mystery Here." One of the statements in the article, which we have italicized, strikes the committee as most peculiar. We quote the article in full:

"The death of Shelly Abrams was surrounded by such an air of mystery that his friends feel the need to clarify the matter. Contrary to the lurid, sensational reports which appeared in some newspapers, his death was accidental, and was certified as such by a coroner's jury. His death was caused by carbon monoxide poisoning *from one of three gas appliances* (Committees' italics.) in his tiny, badly ventilated room. Contrary to the inuendoes in at least two newspapers, his senseless, tragic death had nothing to do with his political activities.

"Shelly was a member of the Young Socialist League, a Socialist organization dedicated to the formation of democratic, socialist society. Although he and the organization he belonged to were staunchly anti-Stalinist, there is no basis in the implication that he was the victim of a political assassination. He would not have wanted, nor do his friends want his death to be used to persecute either his political friends or opponents.

"Contrary to the impression given in several newspapers, Shelly was not the center of a dark underground force at U. C. L. A. He spoke and acted openy [sic]. Little mystery surrounded his life; none should surround his death. Mark Golden, Ed Schaupp."

The fact that only one of the three gas appliances in Abrams' room was burning at the time of his death was revealed solely in the police report. That report was not made available to inquisitive U. C. L. A. students, and the first time there was any public disclosure of the fact that only the flame in the Servel gas refrigerator was burning at the time Abrams' body was found, was during the committee's hearing. The confident and positive statement that death was caused by carbon monoxide poisoning from one of three gas appliances would indicate that Messrs. Golden and Schaupp know a great deal more about the source of gas which caused 71 percent carbon monoxide in the decedent's hemoglobin than they do about his "staunchly anti-

Stalinist'' attitude. Either these two were aware of the fact that Abrams was meeting with the top Communist leadership in Southern California and prefer not to disclose their knowledge, or they are unaware of the fact, and consequently are in considerable ignorance about the real nature of Abrams' contacts and activities immediately preceding his death.

NATIONAL ASSOCIATION FOR THE ADVANCEMENT
OF COLORED PEOPLE

Among the documents found in the room of Sheldon Abrams was a letter dated February 10, 1956, and consisted of a carbon copy of a letter addressed to one of his contacts from the East, which was in the nature of a report. This letter mentioned the efforts of the National Association for the Advancement of Colored People to get recognition by the university authorities and establish a chapter of the organization on the U. C. L. A. campus. It will be recalled that this effort was referred to by Dean Hahn, who explained in some detail why the university was prohibited by its regulations from giving official recognition to the NAACP or any other organization not officially connected with the university. Abrams expressed the opinion that the NAACP, being a respectable and liberal organization, might be used as an unwitting tool by the Young Socialist League in connection with a program for a demonstration of civil disobedience on the campus. Pertinent excerpts from the copy of this letter are as follows:

''* * * there isn't a question of deciding whether activities should be carried out in the name of the YSL, or through a broader, more inclusive, politics club-type organization. U. C. L. A. regulations answer this question for us in advance. *The so-called Berkeley approach is the only way we can operate on the campus at this time* (committee's italics), but it is not the result of our choosing this as the wisest of two alternative approaches. * * *

''There is a development under way which may open the door for us to undertake an approach different than that which is our primary perspective at the moment. The NAACP now is officially attempting to gain recognition on the campus through various formal procedures. In the meantime, they are conducting semilegal (publicised only through word of mouth and ostensibly spontaneous affairs) meetings on the lawn. We would be crazy if we passed up the opportunity that this development gives us. The NAACP claims to have 150-200 registered members on campus. * * *

''Dick's call for *us* (committee's italics) to conduct a civil disobedience campaign on campus is foolish in the light of conditions there. *Such a campaign might be successfully carried out by the NAACP however.* (Committee's italics.) They have respectability, a good many influential friends, etc., and if the university resorted to coercion the local ACLU [American Civil Liberties Union] would undoubtedly be willing to take the matter to court. Am toying with the idea of our holding lawn meetings on the campus a la NAACP.''

The committee has never conducted an investigation of the National Association for the Advancement of Colored People, although it has been familiar with the activities of the organization in California for many years and has been fully aware of the fact that this, like other liberal organizations dealing with civil rights, has long been another target for Communist infiltration. The committee wishes to make it plain that its sole purpose in investigating the National Association for the Advancement of Colored People in connection with this hearing was because of the fact that it was mentioned in the carbon copy of the letter quoted above, and also because the committee wished to ascertain the extent of Communist infiltration into the organization in Southern California and elsewhere throughout the State. The National Association for the Advancement of Colored People developed from a conference called on February 12, 1909, and almost 10 years before the Communist Party of the United States was organized.

Immediately after the American Communist Party commenced to function, however, it launched a campaign to stir up discontent and rebellion among our Negro minority. That campaign has never ceased. The committee has, in previous reports, shown in detail how the Communist Party has been especially eager to work among minority racial groups in this country. Through a powerful front known as the International Workers Order, recently defunct, a medium was provided whereby Slavs, Russians, Jews, Germans, Scandinavians, Negroes, and others, were urged to meet and generally absorb the Communist line of hatred toward the United States and admiration for the Soviet Union. This front organization, operating behind the respectable facade of an insurance-fraternal organization, amassed millions of dollars in capital and was enormously successful in spreading Communist propaganda and drawing racial minority groups into the orbit of Communist activities.

The effort to infiltrate and control the NAACP was high in priority on the Communist agendum, all the more because the attempt to infiltrate and control the National Negro Congress had met with considerable success.

In 1935 the Communist Parties of the world sent carefully selected delegates to attend the Seventh Congress of the Comintern at Moscow. The representatives sat listening with rapt attention while Georgi Dimitrov explained to them the strategy of the united front. He explained the idea by addressing the delegates as follows:

> "Comrades, you remember the ancient tale of the capture of Troy. Troy was inaccessible to the parties attacking her, thanks to her impregnable walls. And the attacking army, after suffering many sacrifices, was unable to achieve victory until with the aid of the famous Trojan Horse it managed to penetrate to the very heart of the enemy's camp.
>
> "We revolutionary workers, it appears to me, should not be shy about using the same tactics with regard to our Fascist foe, who is defending himself against the people with the help of a living wall of his cutthroats.
>
> "He who fails to understand the necessity of using such tactics in the case of Fascism, he who regards such an approach as 'humiliating,' may be a most excellent comrade, but if you will allow me to say so, he is a windbag and not a revolutionary, he will be unable to lead the masses to the overthrow of the Fascist dictator-

ship.'' (*The United Front: The Struggle Against War and Fascism* by Georgi Dimitrov, General Secretary, Communist International. Report to the Seventh World Congress of the Communist International, August, 1935. International Publishers, Inc., New York, 1938, pages 52-53.)

This concept of the united or popular front originated with Dimitrov, and this crafty Bulgarian Communist, who headed the Comintern longer than any other of its officials, saw to it that the attending delegates received the necessary guidance to enable them to put his strategy into immediate action.

When the American delegates returned, they supervised the launching of the new united front in this country. Carefully trained Communists were sent into innumerable mass organizations, the more liberal the better. New front groups sprang into operation designed to attract well-meaning but politically myopic celebrities, college professors, writers, actors, and professional people. At the same time, the drive to foment trouble among the Negroes and to capture their organizations was redoubled. In some places the effort was highly successful—and there is no doubt that some NAACP chapters were Communist-dominated and some of the officers were caught up in the network of front organization and fellow-travelled for a considerable period of time from one to another. As the Communists intensified their efforts to infiltrate the NAACP, that organization intensified its consistent anti-Communist position. It has never been cited as subversive by any official agency, so far as we know; certainly not by any congressional committee nor by this committee, nor by the Attorney General of the United States in his list of subversive organizations. And, as we have seen, it has been a prime target for Communist infiltration for 37 years.

During the period prior to 1935, the American Communists had expressed contempt toward the NAACP as being a reactionary organization and of the following an ''imperialist policy, softened with meaningless mumbles of protest'' (*Negro Liberation*, a Communist pamphlet by James S. Allen, 1932.) Whenever a Negro was arrested for a serious offense, the Communists immediately seized the opportunity to depict him as a martyr to capitalist brutality, whipping up dissension and providing ammunition for propaganda. Walter White, when acting as executive secretary for the NA•ACP, commented on the Communist Party's strenuous campaign to capitalize on the famous Scottsboro case by declaring publicly ''that at least some of the Communists did not want the nine boys saved, but fought instead to make martyrs of them for the purpose of spreading Communist propaganda among Negroes'' (*Harpers,* December, 1931) ; and in his autobiography White castigated the attitude of the Communist Party toward the American Negro minority by denouncing the ''cynical use of human misery * * * in propagandizing for Communism.'' (*A Man Called White,* 1948.)

In 1949, the NAACP sponsored a civil rights mobilization on a national scale, and many liberal organizations participated in this movement. The executive director of the Civil Rights Congress demanded that his group be included. In a reply, the NAACP's executive secretary, accurately diagnosing the Civil Rights Congress as a Communist front, addressed the following letter to its secretary on the letterhead of the NAACP:

"November 22, 1949. Mr. William L. Patterson, Executive Secretary, Civil Rights Congress, New York City. Dear Mr. Patterson: I have your seven-page letter of November 14th, which obviously is not merely a request for information on the Civil Rights Mobilization of the NAACP, and an offer of cooperation. It is plainly a declamation on the current philosophy of the Civil Rights Congress on what it chooses to classify as civil rights.

"Although your letter was not labeled as an open letter, we have since learned that it was mimeographed and strategically, if not widely, distributed. This tactic is not either surprising or alarming, and merely tends to confirm our estimate of the real purpose of the communication.

"Without using up seven pages we can say at once that the NAACP Planning Committee, which carried out the mandate of our annual convention, agreed not to include the Civil Rights Congress on the list of organizations to be invited to participate.

"We remember the Scottsboro case and our experience there with the International Labor Defense, one of the predecessors of the Civil Rights Congress. We remember that the present Civil Rights Congress is composed of the remnants of the ILD and other groups. We remember that in the Scottsboro case the NAACP was subjected to the most unprincipled vilification. We remember the campaign of slander in the *Daily Worker*. We remember the leaflets and the speakers and the whole unspeakable machinery that was turned loose upon all those who did not embrace the 'Unity' policy as announced by the Communists.

"We want none of that unity today.

"We of the NAACP remember that during the war when Negro-Americans were fighting for jobs on the home front and fighting for decent treatment in the armed services, we could get no help from the organizations on the extreme left. They abandoned the fight for Negro rights an the ground that such a campaign would 'interfere with the war effort.' As soon as Russia was attacked by Germany they dropped the Negro question and concentrated all effort in support of the war in order to help the Soviet Union. During the war years the disciples of the extreme left sounded very much like the worst of the Negro-hating southerners.

"American Negroes, and especially the NAACP, cannot forget this. It seems to us to prove conclusively (even if there were not mountains of additional proof) that the organizations of the extreme left, when they campaign for civil rights, or in behalf of a minority, do so as a secondary consideration, activity upon which is certain to be weighted, shaped, angled, or abandoned in accordance with the Communist Party 'line.'

"We can have no truck with such unity.

"We are wary, too, of your asserted devotion to civil rights. We recall clearly that when the Minneapolis truck drivers were indicted, tried and convicted under the Smith Act, neither the

Civil Rights Congress nor its predecessor, nor the Communist Party or its associates made any move to assist them.

"The Civil Rights Congress did not provide tens of thousands of dollars in bail. The Stalinist organizations across the country were not circulating petitions, invading meetings and demanding the passage of resolutions, nor were they conducting picket lines. This line of action—or, better, inaction—indicated to any thinking person that the Stalinist groups are for civil rights for some people, but not for all. The Minneapolis men were not Stalinists, therefore not a hand was lifted to aid them. If the Smith Act is a monstrous piece of legislation when used against the 11 Communist leaders, as you so loudly proclaim, it was no less monstrous, no less an instrument for the suppression of civil liberties when used against the Minneapolis men.

"We reject such a 'part-time' concept of civil liberties.

"We of the NAACP recall, also, the most recent attacks on our association by the Civil Rights Congress and by you as its executive secretary in connection with the Trenton case. Last spring the NAACP, the Civil Rights Congress and one or two other organizations held a joint meeeting in Newark, New Jersey, on the Trenton case. After one of our attorneys had spoken, addressing herself to the case and to the supposed unity of action in the interest of the defendants, you took the platform and devoted the major portion of your talk to a vitriolic attack upon the NAACP, its policies, procedures and philosophy. In the course of that talk you are reported to us as having stated that the NAACP should be put out of business. This was but one more demonstration of the kind of 'unity' that can be expected from the Civil Rights Congress.

"In the present Civil Rights Mobilization we have no desire for that kind of cooperation, or that kind of 'unity.' We do not believe it will contribute to the success of the campaign. On the contrary, we believe it will be a distinct handicap. The organizations sponsoring the Civil Rights Mobilization are seeking the enactment of civil rights legislation to the end that minority groups may be more fully protected in their rights under the American Constitution and the American concept of a democracy. We do not believe, in the light of the consistent performance of the Civil Rights Congress and its associates, that this is their end objective. This was the basic consideration in the decision not to list the Civil Rights Congress as an organization to be invited to cooperate.

"Very truly yours,

"Roy Wilkins

"Acting Secretary
National Association for the Advancement of Colored People
20 West 40th Street,
New York 18, New York."

In 1954, the West Coast Regional Office of the NAACP, located at 690 Market Street, Suite 322, San Francisco, California, became concerned over the activities of three Communist front organizations and three publications. Two of the latter were organs of the Communist Party and the third was the propaganda organ for the Trotskyites. In order to warn NAACP members against the overtures of these subversive groups and publications, Mr. Franklin Williams, West Coast Regional Officer of the NAACP, issued the following circular:

"Keep your eyes wide open.
"Don't get sucked in!
"These groups, organizations and publications are attempting to mislead the Negro community: California Labor School, Civil Rights Congress (CRC), (National) Negro Labor Council, *The Militant* (newspaper), *People's World* (newspaper), *Political Affairs* (magazine).
"They say they are 'working for your civil rights,' but they work among us in the interest of the Communist Party or other subversive and un-American movements.
"Check and double-check before you sign petitions, attend meetings, serve on 'defense' committees, or join or contribute to questionable organizations.
"Keep your eyes wide open.
"Distributed as a public service by:
"West Coast Regional Office.
"NAACP.
"National Association for the Advancement of Colored People.
"690 Market St., Suite 322, San Francisco 4, YU kon 6-6992."

This single sheet circular was widely read by members of the NAACP throughout the entire West Coast and provoked an angry retort from *The Militant,* 116 University Place, New York 3, N. Y. We quote this letter in full, not only because it is extremely pertinent at this point for the purpose of showing the attitude of the NAACP toward subversive organizations, both Communist and Trotskyite, *but also for the purpose of showing from a source of the greatest reliability, that through 1954, the Communists and the Trotskyites detested each other,* as they had since Trotsky was driven from the Soviet Union shortly after the death of Lenin. It is indispensible that the reader thoroughly understand that the fanatic hatred between these two Marxist groups originated with the expulsion of Leon Trotsky from the Soviet Union and did not terminate until the downgrading of Stalin by Khruschev on February 14, 1956. Prior to this significant date, there was no active collaboration between the two groups, although each of them were diligently cooperating with other liberal and progressive organizations of all descriptions. The letter from *The Militant,* written on its letterhead, is as follows:

"WEST COAST REGIONAL OFFCE NAACP
"SAN FRANCISCO, CALIFORNIA, April 6, 1954

"DEAR SIRS: We demand a public retraction and apology for the infamous and slanderous attack you have made against *The Militant.* We also believe that you owe an apology to the members of the NAACP and the American people at large for using the most contemptible McCarthyite methods in the attack on this paper.

"On March 28th, at a Fight for Freedom Rally sponsored by the NAACP in Oakland, California, your officers distributed a leaflet listing six organizations and publications which are accused of 'attempting to mislead the Negro community.' Five of these were Stalinist or Stalinist-dominated; the other was *The Militant.*

"This list has now become known in the Bay area as the 'NAACP's subversive list' or 'William's Subversive List' (after Franklin H. Williams, secretary-counsel of your office, who inspired it).

"With this name goes the odium that is attached by every serious opponent of McCarthyism to the whole concept of 'subversive' listings.

"Your office may not know it, but several national conferences of the NAACP have denounced and called for the withdrawal of the Attorney General's 'subversive' list as a violation of democratic rights and traditions.

"By imitating the McCarthyites, who pinned the 'subversive' label on their opponents without evidence, your office has weakened the fight against 'subversive' lists in general, and has disgraced the creditable record of the NAACP on this vital question.

"Your leaflet claims: 'They say they are working for your civil rights, but they work among us in the interests of the Communist Party or other subversive and un-American movements.'

"*The Militant* strongly objects to being linked in this manner to the Stalinists. Although we defend the democratic rights of all persecuted groups, including the Stalinists, *we are and always have been politically opposed to the Stalinists because of their false and treacherous policies* (Committee's italics.) During World War II, for example, the Stalinists called on the Negro people to bury their fight for equality and advocated the suppression of *The Militant,* because we urged the Negro people to continue the fight against Jim Crow without compromise.

"Our record in this fight is without a blemish, and began long before there was a NAACP West Coast Regional Office. No one can point to a single struggle of the Negro people that we did not support without reservation. Despite our differences with the NAACP leaders, freely expressed in our columns, we have defended them and the NAACP against all their white supremacist enemies.

"Our distributors and readers support every progressive struggle of the NAACP, and many of them are among the most loyal and devoted members of that organization. On some occasions the NAACP first learned about certain Jim Crow injustices and atrocities from *The Militant,* and thanked us for our services in bringing them to their attention. All this is a matter of record, which we can prove from our files. Consequently, it is deceitful for your leaflet to imply that *The Militant* is trying to 'mislead the Negro community' when we take pride in the civil rights fight and present our Socialist program to promote that fight.

"And it is slanderous for your leaflet to label us 'subversive and un-American.'

"By what authority did you dare to make such an accusation? You were not assigned such a function by the members or branches or conferences of the NAACP when you were appointed or elected to your post. Nobody authorized you to pass on the loyalty or other characteristics of *The Militant*.

"The national NAACP has correctly condemned the Attorney General's 'subversive' list because it is arbitrary, because no evidence was ever given for the designations, because no listed organization ever has been given a hearing at which it could defend itself.

"Your own 'subversive' list is no better. It is just as arbitrary, just as high-handed, just as much a violation of decency, to say nothing of democratic procedures.

"In 1952, the Attorney General of Michigan, operating under the notorious Trucks Act, which has been denounced by the NAACP, stuck the 'subversive' label on the Socialist Workers Party, a political organization *The Militant* defends.

"The Socialist Workers Party, aided by a citizens committee which included prominent officials of the N. A. A. C. P. in that state, took the fight to court. After almost two years of litigation, the Michigan attorney general was forced to publicly admit in court on September 19, 1954, that he lacked 'sufficient proof to establish the fact, if it exists,' that the S. W. P. is 'subversive.' As a result, he agreed to discontinue efforts to bar the S. W. P. from the ballot.

"Do you have any more 'evidence' to support your monstrous charge against *The Militant* than the Michigan attorney general had against the S. W. P.? Do you have any evidence at all against either *The Militant* or the others on your list? If not, then you are duty bound to withdraw the charge. We promise you that we will not rest until you have done so.

"Your leaflet adds: 'Check and double-check before you sign petitions, attend meetings, serve on "defense" committees or join or contribute to questionable organizations.' You call the publication of this leaflet a 'public service?'

"No, actually, it is a grave public disfavor. What such statements do is to contribute to the spirit of hysteria and conformism that the would-be Fascist dictators of this country are trying to spread. By creating fear and caution in this manner, you weaken not only democratic tradition, but the struggle for Negro equality.

"Only last June, the National Conference of the N. A. A. C. P., in its resolution condemning McCarthyism, warned, 'already there is discernible a pattern which tends to link the advocacy of full equality for Negroes and other minorities to subversion or "un-Americanism."'

"It condemned the 'atmosphere of inquisition' in which people become fearful that that they may be labeled 'Red' or 'subversive' if they sign petitions, attend meetings or join organizations fighting for Negro equality.

"Your leaflet, encouraging timidity and suspicion, re-enforces this 'atmosphere of inquisition.' Instead of helping the N. A. A. C. P. to grow in numbers and effectiveness, your leaflet tends to frighten people away from the N. A. A. C. P.—which, as you know is considered 'subversive' by the white supremacists.

"The 1953 national N. A. A. C. P. conference resolution against McCarthyism specifically singled out book burning as an instrument of thought control and racist reaction. Franklin H. Williams, it is reported, violated both the spirit and letter of that resolution at your Oakland rally when he warned the audience against *The Militant* and urged those who had purchased the paper before coming into the hall to throw their copies in the ash can on the way out.

"Who authorized Williams to tell the Negro community what papers to read or not read? Where did he get the effrontery to try to interfere with the right of N. A. A. C. P. members to buy and read whatever papers they want? It's true that Williams didn't tell the audience to burn *The Militant,* only to throw it away unread; but McCarthy didn't care what happened to the State Department's books either, as long as they would be kept unread.

"We don't ask Williams to endorse *The Militant.* We don't ask him to agree with what it says. We don't even ask him to read it. But we emphatically demand that he stop misusing the authority of his N. A. A. C. P. post to foist his reading habits and prejudices on others.

"Incidentally, Williams did not invent 'the ash can for *The Militant.' This was invented by the Communist Party, and has been a fixture at their public meetings for more than two decades.* It is a scandal to see it transferred to an N. A. A. C. P. meeting too. (Committee's italics.)

"Williams merely borrowed this 'device' from the Stalinists, just as he borrowed 'subversive' tag from the McCarthyite witch-hunters. Like the McCarthyites and like the Stalinists, he tried to discourage the people from even reading news different from his own. It is his personal right to do this, but he does not have the right to use the authority of the N. A. A. C. P's. name to aid him in this shameful game.

"We know why Williams issued his 'subversive' list. He is frightened by the malignant growth of McCarthyism, which emboldens the worst anti-Negro, anti-Jewish and anti-labor sentiments and movements. Instead of working harder to defeat McCarthyism, he hopes to make himself and the N. A. A. C. P. 'respectable' and escape the blows of McCarthyism by imitating it and joining it in attacking political opponents on the left.

"But McCarthyism will never be stopped that way. No matter how moderately the N. A. A. C. P. behaves, Byrnes of South Carolina (who is guilty of 'McCarthyism at its worst,' as Walter White said) continued to attack the N. A. A. C. P. and to 'hope' that it will be dissolved or destroyed. Appeasement of Facism never helps anyone but the Fascists. The American Civil Liberties Union's repeated attacks on Communism don't stop McCarthy from repeating the lies that the A. C. L. U. is a 'Communist Front.'

Williams' 'subversive' list won't satisfy the Fascists, who have the N. A. A. C. P. on their own list, and it can do nothing but damage to the cause of the N. A. A. C. P.

"For the above reasons, we demand that the West Coast Regional Office publicly detract its slanderous attack on *The Militant* and put an immediate stop to the publication and distribution of the leaflet in which it appeared.

"We hope that the members of the N. A. A. C. P. branches on the West Coast will discuss this question at their meetings, oppose Williams' 'subversive' list, let their opposition be known, and take steps to insure that there will never be a repetition of the scandal that has been committed in the name of their organization.

"If the West Coast Regional Office does not act to correct the injustice and the damage inflicted on this paper, *The Militant* will be compelled to take other measures to achieve this end.

"Yours truly,

"GEORGE BREITMAN for
The Editorial Staff
"The Militant

"Copy to National Office, N. A. A. C. P."

This letter is a typical piece of Trotskyite propaganda. Regardless of its claim about the action of the Attorney General of Michigan in 1952, the facts remain that the Socialist Workers Party, which is simply another name for the Trotskyites, is listed as a subversive organization on practically every official list in the United States—including that issued by the Attorney General of the United States. We cannot refrain from adding, parenthetically, that this list of subversive organizations issued by the United States Department of Justice is not indiscriminately thrown together, as the writer of the letter alleges, but is compiled only upon a meticulous check of evidence gathered by the Federal Bureau of Investigation, which has operated in the field of countersubversive activity with amazing efficiency and consistent care to protect the civil liberties of all organizations, publications and individuals it is called upon to investigate.

This committee has repeatedly referred to the *Socialist Workers Party*, or Trotskyites, as a subversive organization.

On June 26, 1956, the Forty-seventh Annual Convention of the NAACP was held in San Francisco. Among the other resolutions passed at that convention was an anti-Communist resolution, as follows:

"In common with the rest of the free world, the National Association for the Advancement of Colored People rejects the program and aims of Soviet Russia and of the international Communist movement. The cause of the National Association for the Advancement of Colored People is a sacred one, vital not only to the future of 16 million Negro citizens, but also to the well-being of all Americans and to the achievement of a democratic American society. The members and the leaders of the National Association for the Advancement of Colored People must zealously protect the association and all of its units from Communists, and their sympathizers, who attempt to exploit the just grievances and legitimate aspirations of the American Negro in the interest of Russian imperialism.

"As in the past, the association will employ every reasonable measure in keeping the democratic organizational principles to prevent the endorsers, defenders of the Communist conspiracy from joining or participating in any way in the work of the NAACP.

"The new 'line' of the Communist Parties throughout the world, and especially in the United States, is by infiltration to insinuate their programs on non-Communists and even anti-Communist organizations. We know that the Communist leadership in America has directed its representatives to seek to involve NAACP units in a 'united front' program. This we absolutely reject.

"The leaders and the members of the association must be even more vigilant now than ever before in preventing Communist infiltration, because Communists today operate under many disguises and false fronts.

"In accordance with the Boston convention resolution of 1950, the official policy of the National Association for the Advancement of Colored People continues to be that no branch or state conference, youth *or college chapter* (committee's italics), will endorse, support or participate in, or cooperate in any way with Communist organizations, Communist-controlled organizations, and/or persons who are prominently identified with the Ku Klux Klan, White Citizens Councils, Fascists, Communist-front or Communist-line organizations, or groups known to be dominated by Communist leadership and policy, and that Communists are ineligible for membership in the NAACP."

TESTIMONY OF ASSEMBLYMAN WILLIAM BYRON RUMFORD

For the purpose of assisting the committee in determining the efforts made by student organizations to infiltrate and control the NAACP at the University of California in Los Angeles, and to determine the degree to which Communists had succeeded in infiltrating the organization state-wide, the committee asked Assemblyman William Byron Rumford of Alameda County to appear before it and testify. Assemblyman Rumford, a highly respected member of the State Assembly for eight years, and widely known for his anti-Communist attitude, appeared pursuant to subpena and told the committee that he resided in Berkeley, was a pharmacist by occupation, affiliated with the NAACP about 22 years ago and had been continuously affiliated with it ever since. Assemblyman Rumford stated that he had been vice president of the Alameda County branch of the organization and educational chairman of that branch and at the present time is regional treasurer of the NAACP. In response to a question about efforts of the Communist Party to penetrate the organization, Mr. Rumford testified that such efforts had been made and continued:

"However, it is difficult to point out who is and who is not a Communist other than the fact their line is the same and their methods of operation are the same. We have tried in every way, and I think we have been successful in removing any individual from any position of power within a chapter. If we know he is, we will try to get him out.

In some instances, we have even lifted the membership of a certain person whom we felt, after a trial, was known to be of Communist background.

"Q. (By Mr. Combs) : So you have implemented your policy of anti-Communism by direct action?

"A. Yes, we have, definitely.

"Q. Has the chapter with which you are affiliated issued written material from time to time warning the membership against attempts by Communists to infiltrate and use the organization for their own purposes?

"A. Yes, we have. Directives from both the national office and from the regional office have been sent to the chapters in our area warning them against the possible infiltration of these persons who are desirous of destroying the effectiveness of the National Association for the Advancement of Colored People. I think that is important. I think we should have in the records that the objective of these people is not to strengthen the organization, but in essence it is to destroy it, because in its purpose of destruction they will render the association noneffective and reduce the possibility of securing rights for all Americans.

"Q. In connection with your own experiences as a member of the State Legislature, have you personally encountered obstructionist tactics by Communists and Communist organizations in connection with their efforts to exploit the colored people?

"A. Yes, I have. I have handled many a piece of legislation in Sacramento which deals with strengthening the democratic processes so that all persons, regardless of color, will receive adequate treatment and do away with second-class citizenship. I handled the bill to outlaw discrimination in the National Guard, which was one of the pieces of propaganda used by Communists in their effort to obstruct this legislation, but in their efforts they weren't particularly anxious that this legislation be voted.

"Q. Was it voted?

"A. Yes, it was voted.

"Q. It is now in effect?

"A. It is now in effect."

At the conclusion of his testimony, Mr. Rumford stated:

"I have nothing further to add, Mr. Chairman, other than the fact I think the people themselves are becoming wise to the new philosophy of the Communist Party, where they no longer are fighting the leadership of the NAACP, but they are now giving us more or less the kiss of death if they can get that close to us, and infiltrate and take over whoever they can. We have been very successful in stamping out their attempts to take over. We still, however, must keep constant vigilance for this effort. It is a pleasure for me to have the opportunity to come before this committee.

- "In closing, Mr. Chairman, with reference to the efforts we are putting forth for the full extension of American citizenship for democracy to all citizens, I would like to say we hope the people understand—those who are not affiliated with our organization, that it is a difficult thing to work for the full and complete citizenship through the courts and all, and to attempt at the same time to keep these people out of our organization. There are times when they have tried, as they did in the Assembly, to make it appear they are behind our organization, but they are not. There is an attempt to retain the status quo and to keep the tools of agitation in operation.

"Q. (By Mr. Combs) : In your view, is that one test between a sincere liberal and a Communist? You said the actual Communist effort with relation to the NAACP, in your opinion, was not to help it, but to damn it with faint praise, infiltrate it and take it over and rack it and keep the racial agitation going?

"A. To destroy the NAACP if they can.

"Q. Whereas, the sincere liberal does not seek to create agitation but to dispel it?

"A. To dispel it and resolve it.

"Q. Has that been your experience?

"A. That has been my experience wherever we have achieved and were able to pass legislation, such as in Sacramento, to remedy the situation. As to the weaknesses of our democratic processes, we have moved ahead and we have thus taken from the Communist group these tools of agitation by which they foster and develop discontent.

"Q. Were you here yesterday, Mr. Rumford?

"A. I was.

"Q. When Dean Hahn and Chancellor Allen testified concerning conditions at U. C. L. A.?

"A. I was.

"Q. You recall they made no claim that their situation was antiseptic. They said it had improved, but there was a problem?

"A. There always will be.

"Q. Is that also applicable to the NAACP? You still have a problem of Communist infiltration?

"A. They will never give up."

TESTIMONY OF FRANKLIN H. WILLIAMS

Mr. Franklin H. Williams testified that he resided at 4160 Caulombe Drive in Palo Alto and that his office address was 690 Market Street, San Francisco; that he was an attorney, admitted to practice in the States of New York and California, and that he has resided in this state since October, 1950. Mr. Williams further testified that he was the superior policy and administrative officer of the West Coast Region for the NAACP, having under his jurisdiction the area comprising the territories of Alaska and Hawaii, and the States of Oregon, Washington, Arizona, Utah, Idaho, Nevada and California.

The witness traced the origin and development of the NAACP, setting forth its benefits, privileges, and objectives, stressing that these objectives were to be obtained in a lawful manner and in conformity with the Constitution and laws of the United States. In discussing the Communist program to infiltrate the NAACP, Mr. Williams documented his testimony with a series of exhibits which were placed in evidence, and several of which were mentioned heretofore. In this connection, Mr. Williams stated:

"It was at the Sixth World Congress of the Communist International in Moscow that the party affected an interest in the Negro, which was to manifest itself in a pro-segregation resolution in the year 1930. That resolution reads in part:

" 'The main Communist slogan must be: the right of self determination of the Negroes in the black belt. Complete right of self determination includes also the right to governmental separation * * * the right of the Negroes to governmental separation will be unconditionally realized by the Communist Party * * * the Communist Party must stand up with all strength and courage for the struggle to win independence and for the establishment of a Negro republic in the black belt.'

"Thereafter, the entire party apparatus began to grind out tons of propaganda on 'Negro self determination.' Responsible Negro leadership within the NAACP and those heading up respected church, labor and fraternal organizations saw easily through this not even thinly-veiled alien replica of our home grown racial segregation. They rejected this proposition with the same vigor as they were fighting indigenous Jim Crow.

"Undaunted by the Negroes' rejection of Communism and his faith in American democracy, the party stepped up its efforts to recruit our largest minority, capitalizing fully upon the tragic depression years and the generally deplorable condition of civil rights.

"Seeking to alienate Negroes from their leaders, particularly those who would not be seduced by the 'united front,' NAACP officials, churchmen and labor leaders were denounced as 'bourgeois reformists,' 'tools of the capitalists,' and 'allies of the lynching forces'."

Mr. Williams then proceeded to discuss the problems his organization had experienced in California, referring to cases where, with callous hypocrisy, the Communist apparatus milked every major case where a Negro had become embroiled with the law in some serious offense, draining the incident of every vestige of its propaganda value and then completely ignoring the individual involved. In this connection, Mr. Williams declared:

"Communist-front organizations, such as the International Labor Defense, and the late Civil Rights Congress, exploited civil rights cases involving Negroes with callous and unabashed dispatch. We have had some recent examples of this in California. Negro victims and defendants were left to languish in jails or were sacrificed to execution while their Communist-front 'defenders' raised large sums over their names and dead bodies and attempted to recruit new followers for the party out of the verbal gore and half-truths their propaganda mills ground out."

Mr. Williams further testified that at national conventions of the NAACP in 1950, 1951, 1952, 1953, 1954, 1955, and 1956, the organization had issued positive and emphatic statements regarding its anti-Communist policy, submitting written exhibits to document his statements, as follows:

"Meanwhile, NAACP leaders and *Crisis* (official organ of the NAACP) editorials repeatedly pointed out the danger of Communist attempts to infiltrate this organization and urged the membership to be on the alert to keep them out of our ranks.

"I would like to present to the committee and for your perusal and inclusion in the record a mimeographed letter of November 7, 1955, beginning: 'Dear Branch President,' and concluding 'Fraternally yours, Roy Wilkins, Executive Secretary.' At the bottom of page 2, after stating that 'the Communists are now in a period of what might be called good feeling and cooperation, they are trying by every method to get on with and into organizations that are not Communist * * * it thus becomes the duty of every branch of the NAACP to be on the alert to see that no persons of questionable reputation as to past activity and organizational connections are permitted to edge their way into positions in our branches where they will have authority or any control over policy. We cannot hold any witch hunts. We cannot go around accusing people of being Communists or fellow-travelers unless we have iron clad proof. Usually, that is not possible to secure. But we do have the duty of retaining control of our NAACP branches and seeing to it that execution of policy is in the hands of those who will faithfully carry out the NAACP program and not twist it to serve another program. In other words, while some fellow-travelers may become members here and there, since our association is loosely organized and all those who say they support our program and pay dues may join, our responsible branch officers and alert membership must use special care to see, first, that these people do not become members and in the event they should manage to do so, that they not come into positions of influence and authority in branch matters. If, after all these precautions, these persons engage in conduct judged to be inimical to the best interest of the association, steps should be initiated in accordance with the Boston resolution to oust them from membership.'

"Changes in the Communist Party's line and strategy were discussed in articles, directives and NAACP workshop. This resulted in our local leadership developing into a solid phalanx, highly impregnable to seizure and control.

"Here in California and wherever the issue confronted us in the Far West, we effectively enforced NAACP policy and evoked administrative remedies. We fought successfully against attempts to gain control of our units and we stand ready to cut down any attempts in the future of the Communist Party or any of the subheads of this ideological Hydra or its agents to infiltrate or seize our branches."

In discussing the Socialist Labor Party, or Trotskyite organization, and its publication *The Militant,* it was necessary to obtain from Mr. Williams the same sort of clarification that had bothered Dean Hahn— to-wit, the distinction between the *Socialist Workers Party,* and the *Socialist Labor Party,* which is a non-Marxian organization. In this connection, Mr. Williams testified as follows:

"Q. (By Mr. Combs) : Excuse me for interrupting at this time, but for the clarity of the record, what organization publishes *The Militant?*

"A. I believe *The Militant* is a publication of the Socialist Workers Party.

"Q. There is a Socialist Labor Party, too. Is that right?

"A. I believe there is.

"Q. What is the Socialist Workers Party?

"A. Well, I don't consider myself a political scientist, but I will give you my impression on the basis of observation.

"Q. That is all we want.

"A. My impression is, it is Trotskyite, which in my opinion is as subversive as the Stalinists and apparently, from everything we have been able to observe, is presently working hand in glove with the Stalinist movement.

"Q. Do you know when this new line originated?

"A. As far as the civil rights fight is concerned, it seems to have been reflected in the last couple of years in articles in *Public Affairs* calling for a new united front.

"Q. Do you mean *Political Affairs?*

"A. *Political Affairs.* It was a couple of years ago that the attack on our leadership sort of levelled off. At one time we were called Black Fascists, Negro Imperialists, and now all of a sudden, we are pretty good fellows. We may be misleading our people, but we are not Fascists.

"Q. You are not being fooled, of course?

"A. Of course not. May I continue?

"Q. Certainly.

"A. The general intelligence of our leadership regarding the Communist Party provided such an effective bulwark against left-wing inroads that the party was forced to set up competing organizations under its direct control. These short-lived organizations were known to our leadership for what they were before the Government took steps to place them on its subversive list. Among these were the American Negro Labor Congress, League of Struggle for Negro Rights, National Negro Congress, and the recent Civil Rights Congress.

"Persons identified in a continuing and/or official capacity with these now defunct groups were denied membership and positions of trust within NAACP branches throughout the nation. This proved such an insurmountable problem to the party that it was forced to reassign known left-wingers to cities and communities where they hoped they would not be thus stigmatized. Being a national organization with branches in more than 1,000 cities and counties, the NAACP often thwarted this strategy. The Communist publication *Political Affairs* lamented the effectiveness of our strategy in a back-handed manner in its March, 1955, issue, in the following language:

"'The NAACP is viewed by the Negro people as their own organized mass weapon which has won important battles for them in recent years. If the Negro people have transformed the NAACP into a mass organization of struggle very much different from what it was in the thirties, how can we reconcile this fact with the character of the NAACP leadership? For the majority of these leaders remain what they always have been, reformist supporters of the white ruling class. But there has also been one change. In order to remain leaders of the Negro people, these leaders have been compelled to take a more militant stand. Had they not done so, the initiative and leadership exercised by the Communists would have resulted in the whole Negro liberation movement being organized and led by the working-class ideology and leadership of our party.

"'The mass organizations of the Negro people do exist. The central task is to influence these in a correct direction and not that of building new ones which further separate the left-minded workers from the mass.

" 'However, when they disagree in estimating the various causes for the present reformists domination of the mass movement and our relative isolation from it, no one can deny the main point we are making—that the present situation is quite different from that of the past and requires a quite different approach.'

"After the Communist Party was driven underground, it became increasingly difficult for an organization like the NAACP to keep its finger on the left-wing's pulse. The association is not equipped nor is it constitutionally authorized to conduct investigations per se of groups or individuals. When the party no longer operated in the open, we had to plan our counter-strategy out of anticipation rather than from direct information based on case incidents.

"No longer could we call a spade a spade, to wit: one who walked, talked, and looked like a duck could no longer be called a duck. One became liable to damage suits and recovery of such damages by a person who openly associated with Communist activities a few years before and who still maintains an active identification with known front groups. The Communist Party cards were gone down that mysterious drain with the party membership lists to the underground.

"Whoever or whatever drove the Communist Party underground also merits the dubious credit for making it next to impossible to ferret the left-wing out into the daylight for an open and democratic fight.

"This is the current predicament of non-Fascist groups and organizations throughout the Nation.

"We must now speak in generalities where we could have called names and cited details. We must now gear our terminology to the libel laws and plan our strategy to expose a phantom camouflaged in the martyrdom of the many persons innocently labeled with a legal weapon called libel. The Communists and their sympathizers move about their business of old under a cloak of immunity to challenge and contest our democratically constituted organizations.

"Further, it distresses NAACP leadership no end to find the association being made to defend itself against the ridiculous charges and innuendoes that it is possibly subversive or that it is a tool of the Communists.

"Much of this is being heard from official quarters and the White Citizens Councils in the South, as well as from the Fascist groups here in the far West.

"I would like to submit to the committee several pieces of the type of literature being distributed in and about the West Coast making direct or indirect references to the NAACP and its program."

(The witness submitted to the committee for its consideration and possible investigation the names and addresses of several organizations situated in Southern California and which are currently engaged in circulating literature and other propaganda material accusing the NAACP of being a subversive organization. The documents were introduced in evidence in connection with Mr. Williams' testimony.)

"Neither the United States Attorney General or the House Un-American Activities Committee includes the NAACP on a list of subversive organizations. Both the House and Senate Committees empowered to investigate subversive activities have at times been headed by avowed white supremacists and declared enemies of the NAACP. * * * The NAACP has never been called before either of these committees, because there has never been any evidence of Communist domination.

"Many famous Americans have held a membership in the NAACP, some of them serving as officers or members of the National Board or of special committees. Others have been presidents of local branches. Some have expressed their appreciation of the work of the NAACP in addresses before association conventions. * * * J. Edgar Hoover, whose business as head of the Federal Bureau of Investigation is to know who is and who is not a Communist, has said: 'Equality, freedom and tolerance are essential in a democratic government. The NAACP has done much to preserve these principles and to perpetuate the desires of our founding fathers.'

"The press of the country, including the pro-segregation newspapers of the South, has generally recognized that the attempt to pin the Red label on the NAACP is a fraud. Writing in the *New York World Telegram and Sun* of May 19, 1956, Frederick Woltman, who won a Pulitzer Prize in journalism for exposing Red infiltration, said that of the various organizations the Communists tried to penerate, 'the NAACP was one of the least receptive.' Further, he wrote: '* * * NAACP's top leaders have sternly resisted Communists inroads. Not only are they opposed to the philosophy and strategy of Communism, but they realize the Communist's first allegiance goes to Russia and world revolution. And that the Red tag would mean the kiss of death to their entire movement. Consequently, the Communists have waged intermittent war on Roy Wilkins, the late Walter White, and other NAACP officers.'

"Other newspapers have editorially dismissed the charge of Communist domination.

Mr. Williams was then shown certain documents which he identified, and which contained statements by official Communist sources concerning the current party line toward the NAACP. These publications were obtained at the Progressive Book Store, 1806 West Seventh Street, Los Angeles, California, which is an outlet for Communist propaganda in the southern part of the State. The documents included: *Resolutions for the Sixteenth National Convention of the Communist Party of the United States*, adopted September 13, 1956; *Political Affairs* for February, September and April, 1956; *The Meaning of the Twentieth Congress of the Communist Party of the Soviet Union*, by Max Weiss, issued in 1956.

Elsewhere in this section there is reproduced an angry letter addressed to the regional office of the NAACP in San Francisco by the Trotskyite organ, *The Militant*, occasioned because Mr. Williams, in his capacity as the top official of the West Coast Regional Area of the NAACP, had characterized the Trotskyite organization, the *Socialist Workers Party*, as subversive. The committee desiring to show that a similar experience occurred with the Communist newspaper in San Francisco, questioned Mr. Williams, as follows:

"Q. (By Mr. Combs): Next is a copy of a letter apparently signed by you on the letterhead of the National Association for the Advancement of Colored People, 690 Market Street, 3332, San Francisco 4, California, dated March 5, 1956, and addressed to the Editor of *People's World,* 590 Folsom Street, San Francisco, California. I show you a carbon copy of that letter and ask you whether or not the original thereof was dictated and signed by you and mailed to the address shown therein under your direction?

"A. Yes, sir, it certainly was. It reflects my then and present attitude concerning the *People's World.*

"Q. Do you have any objection if I read it into the record?

"A. Absolutely none, whatsoever.

"Q. It is a short letter. It reads as follows:

" 'In your edition of February 5, 1954, without authorization, permission or knowledge of this office or of any official of the West Coast Region of our association, you published a picture of our regional officers with an accompanying article in which our program was prominently discussed by your writer. I am writing for myself, my staff, and for each of our regional officers to protest this unsolicited and undesired publicity.

" 'Inasmuch as our policy regarding the *People's World* precludes our sending any more news releases or photographs to your publication, it should be obvious to you that any coverage of affairs, events, conferences or meetings sponsored by our organization is considered undesirable by us.

" 'In addition to our fundamental rejection of and disagreement with your editorial philosophy, we have noted your consistent and apparently purposeful misrepresentation of the news—especially when it involves an issue of civil rights. We have no desire to be a party to either.

" 'Therefore, it is hereby requested that in the future the *People's World* cease using the name of the NAACP and its officers, in their official capacities, in your publication's columns. Failure to comply with this request will necessitate our calling upon all units of the West Coast NAACP to bring this matter to the attention of the general public.'

"Q. You were writing this letter in your official capacity?

"A. Yes, I was. This created quite an exchange and debate concerning whether or not we were violating any concept of freedom of the press. We didn't consider that the *People's World* is a newspaper at all. We consider it a house organ, the official organ of a political party. It does not and could not, in our opinion, conceive that it had the same privileges as the average newspaper as we understand it.

"Q. Is it your opinion that the Communist Party is a political party?

"A. It is my opinion that the Communist Party, as such, is an international conspiracy. The Communist Party, U. S. A., is part of an international conspiracy, acting under the direction and control of the U. S. S. R. to carry out whatever their designs may be in a particular situation.

"Q. Of which the *People's World* is the California organ?

"A. It is the official organ. We never considered it to be a newspaper. We don't send our press releases to them. I have had arguments with good friends of ours as to whether they should sit at our press tables at meetings.

"Q. We have had the same points raised.

"A. I would not consider a magazine which carries the line, and we have an official line and policy that we carry out, that if somebody whose purposes we were opposed to agreed for us not to sit at their tables, I wouldn't consider it to be an invasion of the freedom of the press."

In discussing the activities of the NAACP at U. C. L. A., Mr. Williams was questioned and responded as follows:

"Q. (By Mr. Combs): By the way, Mr. Williams, is there a unit of the NAACP at Westwood, to your knowledge, where U. C. L. A. is located?

"A. We have student groups. Here is the structure: we have chapters in some 1,500 communities, then we have youth groups in these communities. Where there is a college, we attempt to have a college chapter. It is under the jurisdiction of the local adult branch. We presently have a group at Westwood. We consider it a U. C. L. A. chapter of the NAACP.

"Q. When did that originate?

"A. Their charter was issued—I will ask the president of our Los Angeles branch.

"A Voice: About 1955, September or October.

"Q. Did anything come to your attention concerning the problem of subversive infiltration at that time or even thereafter, with reference to that particular chapter?

"A. No, sir.

"Q. There never did?

"A. No, sir.

"Q. About how many members does that chapter comprise at the present time?

"A. Two hundred sixty-seven members.

"Q. It is not an on-the-campus recognized organization?

"A. No, sir.

"Q. Because, if you will recall, yesterday it was explained by the Dean of Students at the university, no political or religious organizations of any kind are officially recognized by the university administration.

"A. Yes, sir.

"Q. So while it exists in connection with students, it does not exist on the campus in a physical sense?

"A. No. Not in terms of campus recognition. There is a problem which exists at many state universities, not only in California, but they have a rule which prohibits on-campus recognition of groups affiliated with national organizations which have a national policy, for example, the Newman Club.

"Q. There is a law which prohibits any organization from using the name of the University of California in any way at all, as was explained yesterday?

"A. That is right.

"Q. (By Chairman Burns) : In your experience, Mr. Williams, have you found Communist penetration in any of your local branches to any degree?

"A. Yes, sir. The Communists substantially infiltrated and took over Tempe, Arizona, branch back in the early '50's. We lifted its charter. We ascertained the infiltration by the nature of the resolutions and some of their actions. On the basis of that, we lifted the charter and reorganized it and it presently exists as one of our good chapters. There was a time when to determine rather easily the extent of the degree of Communist infiltration I would go in and speak to the group, and if I didn't get a rise out of them, that would be one thing. But today they sit and applaud you. *I would say the Communist Party is still making a threat to infiltrate the NAACP as well as the Young Democrats and the Young Republicans.* (Committee's italics.)

"Q. At the universities?

"A. And the universities. If they can hide behind the skirts of legitimate organizations, this is the place they want to be. You may be assured the Negro community, especially the NAACP, learned of the real motive of the Communists. During the war when we were struggling for FEPC, in the period of the united front, Vito Marcantonio was in Congress and Ben Davis was in leadership in New York State Government. They were all vigorous leaders for legislation for fair employment practices, something which we badly needed because we were not permitted to work on defense lines in many cities. * * * Then Russia entered the war on the side of the Allies. Their great desire was to open up the second front to relieve pressure by the Germans on the eastern front. Our fight for the FEPC went down the drain and we became Black Fascists, un-American-like Fascists and imperialists because we were still struggling for fair employment practices.

"Chairman Burns: They said you were impeding the war effort?

"The Witness: That was the party line after Russia entered the war. We have had this sort of thing happening down through the years. They have used the Negro civil rights causes, deliberately misused them.

"For example, during the FEPC campaign in the State Legislature, we put out a publication program. We wanted to influence the representatives to show them what the merits of the FEPC were. We printed up our publications; we had a California Committee for Equal Employment Opportunities, with an address down at the bottom, of a group in San Diego called the Southland Jewish Organization, or something like that, which printed a publication exactly for the same type, the same capitalization, the same layout, and at the bottom it said, 'Return to Southland Jewish Organization.' When we took our problem to the Legislature, we also took our publication and we found on the same desks of the legislators were copies of the publication containing the name of the Southland Jewish Organization. Immediately to the unsuspecting legislators this became a Communist operation rather than a legitimate operation of a democratic organization.

"When we have had NAACP mass meetings in the neghborhood of universities or colleges or in metropolitan areas, *The Militant* people are out in front passing out sheets or organizations are passing out

the *People's World* all over the place. There is more Communist literature on the floor than NAACP literature. So an innocent passerby
would think you had a Communist meeting. The best thing they can
do for us is to leave us alone and fight their own Communist cause.

"Q. (By Mr. Combs): Which is precisely what they will not do.

"A. Right. The less the *People's World* mentions us, the better for
us, and the more they fight me, the better for me.

"Chairman Burns: In more than 20 years in this work while the
Negro people have been a particular objective of the Communist Party,
they have made less progress in that direction; is that correct?

"The Witness: We have had to fight the enemy to the right and left.
We have had to fight to be Americans. We had to fight to be recognized in World War II. You know the stuff of which our people are
made. * * * May I make one more remark? The president of our
local branch called to my attention that perhaps some people got the
wrong impression from what was said yesterday about white members
in the NAACP. The NAACP is not a Negro organization. Our president is presently a non-Negro. Our board is inter-racial. Our staff is
inter-racial. We have found in our struggles non-Negroes who have
identified themselves with us, some who have been more vigorous than
Negroes. It was unfortunate that anyone was left with the impression
that a white person interested in civil rights would not be welcome.

"Mr. Combs: I think it was quite clear what Dean Hahn meant
was that disruptive elements went into it for the deliberate purpose of
disrupting the NAACP.

"The Witness: We have some white Communists come in to disrupt
the NAACP the same as another organization. Thank you, very much,
for giving me the chance to appear."

PROPAGANDA AT SAN FRANCISCO
PUBLIC LIBRARY

On August 17, 1956, Senator Hugh M. Burns, chairman of the committee, received a letter from the city librarian of San Francisco, a Mr. L. J. Clarke. Mr. Clarke advised Senator Burns that the San Francisco Public Library had received an unsolicited assortment of books from the National Library of Peking, Peking, China, and that "before passing on the final acceptance of this gift, the Library Commission is wondering whether in any way these books might, through legislative investigation by your honorable body, be considered subversive."

On August 27, 1956, Senator Burns replied to this letter and advised Mr. Clarke that, "It appears to be propaganda material; however, we will make an extensive study of the books and advise you as soon as possible. The next time that Mr. Combs, our counsel, is in San Francisco, we will ask him to call on you to discuss the matter."

Accordingly, an analysis was made of all of the material received by the library, and the following report was submitted to Mr. Clarke on October 2, 1956:

Pursuant to your letter of August 17, addressed to Senator Burns as chairman of the California Senate Committee on Un-American Activities, and his reply thereto, I have examined all of the books mentioned in your letter and have prepared a report concerning those which, in my opinion, contain subversive material. The committee does not undertake to act in the role of a censor in this matter, but is merely expressing an opinion, as you requested.

There are certain factors that should be considered in connection with these books. The first is that Red China has been thoroughly Russianized. Soviet technicians have supervised the building and operation of China's industrial plants, as well as the building of her highways, railroads, flood control projects, and her agricultural program. The educational system has been reoriented under Russian direction, and her police system, her channels of communication, her press, her cultural development—all have been carried forward under the supervision of Russian experts. Thus, China is dependant on the Soviet Union for not only technical advice, but replacement of parts that are only obtainable from Russia, and that are essential for the continued operation of her basic economy. This fact, long known to experts, was re-emphasized in the *Saturday Evening Post* articles by Robert Gurllain, which appeared commencing in the issue for May 19, 1956, under the title, "What I Saw Inside Red China."

Thus, it is not peculiar that the propaganda and subversive content of the books in question is geared to suit the exigencies of the world Communist line as determined by Moscow, and that it will immediately be recognized as bearing the unmistakable Soviet flavor. It should also be pointed out that many of the books examined, especially those by Mao Tse-tung, Chou En-lai, and other Chinese Communist functionaries, have long been available at the Communist Book Store, 1408 Market Street in San Francisco. The Geneva Conference and the speeches delivered by Nikita Khrushchev at the Twentieth Congress of the Communist Party of the Soviet Union caused profound changes in the international Communist line. The first was a new attitude of sweetness and peaceful co-existence on the part of the Soviet Union. The second was the repudiation of the ruthless regime of Stalin, and the launching of the so-called united front.

This tactic had been tried during the late '30s with astounding success, and consists of the Communists insinuating themselves into liberal and progressive organizations and attempting to swing them as closely as possible to Communist objectives.

These changes are largely responsible for the sudden increase in propaganda materials that have been directed into the universities and public libraries throughout the United States since the Geneva Conference and the Khrushchev speech of last February. The foregoing comment will also explain why this subversive material is not confined to Chinese problems, but includes world matters that are of more concern to the Kremlin and world Communism than any single country. I trust that these introductory comments may make the following report more intelligible.

I. **The China Pictorial.**   This is a magazine about the size of *Life*, and presents the same slick, expensive format. It is profusely illustrated and is issued monthly in the following languages: Chinese, Mongolian, Tibetan, Uighur, Korean, English, Russian, French, Japanese, Indonesian, and Spanish. It is frankly a propaganda publication. The following excerpts are typical of its material that I consider subversive:

"* * * To safeguard Asian and world peace, the Chinese peoples shall strengthen their efforts for the liberation of Taiwan (Formosa). Taiwan is Chinese territory. The extermination of the people's enemy Chiang Kai-shek, is the internal affair of the Chinese people. But the American aggressive bloc persists in their unjustifiable intervention, concluding with Chiang Kai-shek's the 'Mutual Security Treaty' and extending a line for the supposed defense of America into our territory. Could there be any banditry any more outrageous than this?" (January, 1955, p. 4.)

"It is common knowledge that the U. S. policy of embargo has served only to cut off the West from its traditional Eastern markets, has destroyed normal relations of international trade, reduced the size of the capitalist world market and caused economic hardships both for Western capitalist nations and for Asian nations that are producers of raw materials." (*Ibid.*, p. 27.)

The caption quoted below appears above a photograph of a mass meeting of several hundred Chinese Communists. They are shown responding to a speaker, their arms upright, and their fists clenched. The caption reads:

"The signing of the 'Mutual Security Treaty' between the U. S. Imperialists and the traitor, Chiang Kai-shek, on December 2, 1954, has aroused the wrath of the Chinese people. Meetings of protest were held in all parts of the country pledging their determination to liberate Taiwan." (*Ibid.*, p. 36.)

On the following page are pictures showing maneuvers of the Red Chinese naval vessels, and a picture of three sailors shoving a shell into the breech of a cannon. The caption states:

"Naval exercises for Taiwan's liberation. Commanders and fighters of the Chinese people's liberation army are intensifying their military training for the liberation of Taiwan and to smash the 'Mutual Security Treaty' concluded between the U. S. aggressors and the traitorous Chiang Kai-shek clique." (*Ibid.*, p. 37.)

"We will never allow the Wall Street atom-fiend's intrigues to succeed. Dreaming that they can always sit beside their treasure houses with dollars in one hand and bombs in the other, they squeeze the fruits of labor out of others and ruthlessly destroy lives, driven by their greed for 'easy' money. Meeting with frustration, they want to set the whole earth ablaze." (*Ibid.*, March, 1955, p. 2.)

In discussing the Bandung conference on Asian-African affairs, held on April 18-24, 1955, the following comment is made:

"The American ruling circles, in their efforts to enslave the Asian and African peoples and to intensify preparations for war, harbor extreme enmity toward the efforts of the Asian and African countries to maintain independence and peace, and to promote friendly cooperation. Before and during the conference the United States Government used all means to obstruct and disrupt the conference, in order to induce differences, create splits and cause the conference to end up in ill will." (*Ibid.*, May, 1955, p. 4.)

Commenting on the removal of the Tachen Islanders to a place of safety and refuge on Formosa, and in connection with a series of photographs, this caption appears:

"In February, 1955, instigated by the U. S., and helped by her armed forces, the Chiang Kai-shek troops who are occupying the Tachens and other islands, forcibly uprooted some 20,000 peaceful inhabitants and took them to Taiwan." (*Ibid.*, p. 26.)

"The United States Government directly participated in this criminal act. * * *"

"The disaster inflicted on the Tachens and other islands is further evidence that the U. S. imperialists and the Chiang Kai-shek brigands are our most brutal enemies bent on destroying the peaceful life of our people." (*Ibid.*, pp. 26-27.)

During July and August, 1955, the Fifth World Festival of Youth and Students for Peace and Friendship was held at Warsaw, Poland. This affair, as were its predecessors, was dominated by Communists. In describing it, this comment appears:

"Despite the fact that the U. S. Government is remilitarizing Japan in an attempt to make her the springboard for an invasion of China and the Soviet Union, the youth of Japan, China, and the Soviet Union sang in chorus the song, 'Never Let the Atom Bomb Explode Again!' " (September, 1955, p. 39.)

An article entitled "A Student Comes Home From America," by Hsieh Chia-lin, is prominently featured on a two-page spread with five photographs which show: (1) The author with 21 other Chinese students recently returned from the United States; (2) The author showing his parents some pictures he took during a tour of New China; (3) The author being escorted about Peking University by the head of the Department of Physics at that institution; (4) The author with his wife and son after his sojourn of eight years, during which he was obtaining a technical education in the United States; (5) The author with three colleagues experimenting with microwave measurements at the Institute of Physics of the Academic Sinica. The author wrote:

"I went to America in 1947, to study physics, and in June, 1951, I received my doctors degree from Stanford University. At that time China's new government had been established for more than a year and I was elated by its achievement. In August, 1951, I applied to the U. S. Government for an exit visa to return to China; but all I got in the way of an answer were obstructions from the American Immigration authorities and the Federal Bureau of Investigation. It was not until July this year that I and a few others were finally allowed to leave the United States. Even so, during the voyage, U. S. officials and Chiang Kai-shek agents again attempted to intimidate and impede me by concocting a story that my family had been 'liquidated'." (*Ibid.*, November, 1955, pp. 22-23.)

An article entitled "Long Live the Spirit of Bandung!" comprises four pages, replete with illustrations, commemorating the first anniversary of the Bandung-Indonesia Conference. After declaring that the solidarity between the Asian and African countries is unbreakable, the article states:

"* * * The American war-mongers are raising a hue and cry about bringing the world to the 'brink of war' in a vain attempt to cover up the failure of their policy of 'positions of strength' in the Asian and African regions. They frantically try to smear both the 'Bandung spirit' and the 'Geneva spirit' in the hope of obliterating them from the people's memories and checking their influence. The American war maniacs openly backed up the colonial powers in their cruel suppression of the enslaved nations, but, in actual fact, they themselves are stepping into the shoes of the old colonial powers and doing everything they can to deter many nations and countries in Asia and Africa and various parts of the world from their efforts to regain their national sovereignty. The military maneuvers on the Asian seas and the S. E. A. T. O. conference at Karachi, both directed by the U. S., clearly indicates that under the cover of 'alliance' and 'defense' these forces are actually preparing for war and trying to hold fast to the colonial system. * * *" (*Ibid.*, April, 1956, p. 5)

II. **People's China.** This is also a well-printed, profusely illustrated magazine, with a world-wide circulation. It carries on the theme that the United States is an imperialist, war-monger, exploiter-nation; while the Soviet Union is a peace-loving, anti-colonial nation. It attacks the F. B. I., the Immigration Service, and American institutions in general. The effect of these publications, printed in many languages and widely circulated in those countries where hatred of the United States can best be fanned into flames, is too obvious to require comment. Here are some examples:

"A Chinese Student Comes Home," by Tsien Hsue-shen carries on the theme of persecution of Chinese students who happened to be in this country when the Korean War occurred. The fact of their detention is well established. The reasons for their detention were precisely the same as those in China that impelled the detention of American citizens in that country at the same time. Since the author of this particular article taught at the California Institute of Technology at Pasadena, and his predicament received considerable attention in the press, it is appropriate to quote from this article at some length. The author is described as having come to the United States for the purpose of studying aerodynamics. He arrived in 1935, taught at the Massachusetts Institute of Technology, and in California headed the educational and research program of the Guggenheim Jet Propulsion Centre at Cal-Tech. Since his return to Communist China, he has headed the Applied Mechanics Department of the Chinese Academy of Sciences. He describes being "forcibly detained" in the United States, restricted to Los Angeles County by Immigration authorities, and expressed immense relief at being able to return to Red China, where there were, as he put it, no "lurking F. B. I. men."

This article fails to point out, for obvious reasons, the fact that American authorities stated that the author was a member of a Communist unit in Southern California, and that of his trunk contained much secret, highly sensitive material. Dr. Tsien's account follows:

"I decided to return to China in 1950. In August that year, I booked a ticket on a Hong Kong bound airliner and sent my books and research notes ahead for delivery by ship. I was about to leave when the U. S. Immigration Service ordered me to remain. My books and research notes were held, ransacked by the F. B. I. agents and later screened by the customs. In September, the same year, I was arrested and sent to a detention center on a false charge that I was a Communist and had attempted to smuggle secret scientific documents to China.

"For 15 days I was kept under detention. I was forbidden to speak to anybody. At night the prison guards would switch on the prison lights every 10 minutes to prevent me from getting any rest. This ordeal caused me to lose 30 pounds during that short period.

"As a result of protests by faculty members and students at the institute where I held a professorship, I was finally released on bail of $15,000 put up by friends. I may add that the false charge against me was finally exposed when three years later they finally admitted that my books and notes contained nothing secret.

"My troubles, however, were by no means over. The U. S. Immigration authorities prohibited me from traveling beyond the boundaries of Los Angeles County and ordered me to report to them every month.

"I was also trailed by F. B. I. agents who time and again broke into my office and home. These men also censored my letters and tapped my phone calls.

"Despite my unavailing protests, this kind of life continued for five years, until last August when the U. S. Immigration Service finally had to allow me to leave.

"I have nothing against the American people, whom I got to know intimately and got to know and love deeply during my long stay in the United States. As for the U. S. Government, the way it treated me and many other Chinese civilians in the United States speaks for itself." (February, 1956, pp. 20-26.)

Editorial comment on the same topic appeared in the magazine under the heading "They Still Can't Come Home—Persecution of Chinese Students in the U. S. A." It stated:

"When the Korean War began, the U. S. Immigration Service started interrogating Chinese students to discover what they thought about the Chinese People's Government. These grillings sometimes lasted five or six hours.

"In August, 1951, an order was issued forbidding Chinese students to leave the United States. Some who were already on their way home were intercepted and brought back. At the same time the students were refused extension of their visas and required to report regularly on their personal activities to the Immigration Office.

"From that time on F. B. I. agents created an atmosphere of terror among them. They frequently questioned Chinese students about the views of their fellow students and spread false reports to prejudice them against the new government in their homeland. Students who asked to be deported were imprisoned.

"Even after the Geneva talks began, because of the persecution, students feared to apply for permission to leave and land themselves in further trouble. * * *

"Dr. Chen Neng-kuan, who worked in the Westinghouse Electric Corporation in Pittsburgh and has just managed to return, stated in his interview: 'It will take more than a notice in a post-office to undo the sheer terror created by the F. B. I. in the mind of any Chinese suspected of sympathy with his homeland. * * *'" (February, 1956, p. 41.)

A 16-page supplement entitled "Political Report" by Chou En-lai at the Second Session of the Second National Convention of the Chinese People's Political Consultative Conference, January 30, 1956, was included with the February, 1956, issue of this magazine. Chou En-lai is the Moscow-trained Premier of Communist China, and his report is loaded with vicious attacks against the United States. He describes the "Camp of Peace, Democracy and Socialism Headed by the Soviet Union," as opposed to the "U. S. Aggressive Circles," which are exploiting and enslaving the undeveloped countries and fomenting an imperialistic war.

"I Accuse!" is the title of an article by Mrs. Liu Yung-ming, the wife of another Chinese student who came to the United States to study civil engineering at the University of Missouri where he received his master's degree. He was in this Country when the war broke out in Korea, and after a mental breakdown he was sent to an institution for proper treatment. This situation was seized upon for propaganda purposes, and when Liu returned to China his wife wrote this article for foreign distribution. It should be noted that although the article is accompanied by an excellent photograph showing Mr. Liu Yung-ming happily chatting with his family, the article was written for him by his wife. (April, 1956, p. 35.)

An article entitled "Taiwan Under U. S. Armed Occupation," is plainly calculated to undermine confidence in the American soldier. The following is a typical excerpt:

> "U. S. Gangsterism. The Americans, lording it over the island, oppress and humiliate the Chinese people who live there. Wei Ta-wei, an airman who recently flew over to the mainland, has told the press of many incidents which he himself witnessed. At the beginning of November last year, two American soldiers ignited fireworks in a small shop in Chunghua Road, Taipeh, and caused a fire which burned it down and injured the proprietor.

> "Last spring, on a road near Kaohsuing, an American soldier threw a woman he had raped from the car he was driving. She suffered head injuries and was found covered with blood. These were only two of many such occurrences. Even the Taiwan papers published news of atrocities committeed by American soldiers.

> "* * * G.I.'s are always trying to fool around with decent women, bullying the children or beating up Chinese, and such incidents always draw angry crowds. But because the American troops, both officers and men, are armed, and because the Chiang Kai-shek police have orders to protect them for the sake of the 'friendship between the two countries,' these ruffians escaped scott-free." (May, 1956, pp. 29-30.)

One may wonder why, if accounts of these alleged daily incidents of brutality and misbheavior are in fact published in the Formosa press, such accounts were not used instead of the story by a deserter from Chiang Kai-shek who had recently joined the Chinese Communists.

III. **China Reconstructs.** This is another expensively printed monthly magazine, with an abundance of illustrations and an abundance of vitriolic material directed against the United States, of which the following are examples:

"The First Five Years," by Soong Ching-ling, in which she declares, among other things:

> "There are some elements in international life, however, that seek gains from hardships rather than from friendship. The United States Government in particular has tried to poison the mind of the American and other peoples against us, to overthrow us by economic and military means and to prevent the new China from taking her rightful place in international organizations. The attempt to invade us through Korea met with miserable failure.

So will the efforts to steal our territory, Taiwan." (January, 1955, p. 4.)

Soong Ching-ling is another name for Madame Sun Yat-sen. Chiang Kai-shek is her brother-in-law. A university in the Soviet Union is named in her honor, and she is one of the most influential and widely read Communist functionaries in China. She is noted for her bitter hatred of Chiang Kai-shek, regarding him as a traitor to China, and her antagonism toward the United States and the western nations is equally venomous.

Holland Roberts formerly taught at Stanford University, and during the past several years has headed the California Labor School in San Francisco. The latter institution has been characterized as a Communist school by the California Senate Committee on Un-American Activities, and later by both the House Committee on Un-American Activities and the United States Department of Justice. Roberts is also head of the American-Russian Institute at San Francisco. The April, 1955, issue of this magazine contains a letter from Roberts, expressing a desire to visit Communist China and congratulating the magazine on its contents. His letter appears on page 38. Mr. Roberts has already visited in the Iron Curtain region, and led a delegation into the Soviet Union several years ago.

The May, 1956, issue of this magazine, page 12, contains a story by one Lei Wei. He was a member of the Chiang Kai-shek naval force, and was sent to San Diego Naval Training Station for instruction. According to him, the things he read in American newspapers, and the things he saw while in the United States persuaded him that he would undoubtely fare better in Red China, so he deserted and fled to the mainland.

IV. **Women of China.** Three copies of this magazine, August, 1954, June, 1955, and spring, 1956, contain typical but relatively innocuous material attacking the United States and praising the Soviet Union and the nations under its sphere of influence.

V. **Chinese Workers March Toward Socialism.** This book was published by the Foreign Languages Press at Peking in 1955. It contains a chapter headed: "We are Determined to Liberate Taiwan." The following is an excerpt which is typical of the tenor of the entire chapter:

"Taiwan is an inalienable part of China, and this is a world-recognized fact. The Cairo Declaration and the Potsdam Declaration, both of them solemn international agreements, affirmed this fact. China's territorial integrity will never be complete as long as Taiwan remains to be liberated. Therefore, to liberate Taiwan, to protect the sovereignty and territorial integrity of our country is the firm policy of the Chinese Government and the entire Chinese people. This is our sacred task, and it is not only necessary for our security and territorial integrity, but also necessary for the peace of Asia and the world." (*Ibid.* p. 84.)

"Taiwan is the inviolable territory of China. The people in Taiwan are an integral part of the Chinese population. The liberation of Taiwan through whatever means is China's domestic affair, and the Chinese people will never allow any interference by foreign powers. No foreign power has a right, in any case, to interfere in the affairs of the Chinese People's Republic. The Chinese people are determined to liberate Taiwan which will surely be restored to China." (*Ibid.* p. 88.)

VI. **Folk Arts of New China.** Foreign Languages Press, Peking, 1954. In the Soviet Union the cultural arts are regarded as propaganda weapons. Music, literature, the theater, and painting are carefully supervised for the purpose of taking advantage of every opportunity to infuse a class struggle concept wherever possible. In the introductory portion of this report it was seen how China has been Russianized, and in this book we find added evidence of the truth of this statement. The preface states:

"In these talks [at Yenan in 1942] Chairman Mao epitomized the attitude of the New Democracy towards art. It is an attitude of the deepest respect for the arts and crafts of the people. * * * This is an attitude that calls, in the first place, for the mastery of the old arts, for a thorough understanding of their content and form, their techniques, and at the same time a profound understanding of the viewpoint of modern China, the viewpoint of Marxism-Leninism, an understanding of the role of art in the China of today advancing through the transitional stage of the People's Democracy toward a Socialist society.

"But this can be no armchair understanding. Chairman Mao Tse-tung called on the artists to plunge wholeheartedly into the revolutionary struggle, whether this be the armed struggle or on the front of peaceful construction. He called on them to master Marxism-Leninism in practice, and so to serve the workers, the peasants and people's fighters, the mass of the people in their advance to freedom." (P. 6.)

The chapters of this book constitute excellent examples of how Marxian propaganda can be injected into every phase of life. The class in woodworking, for instance, would hardly be considered a suitable vehicle for propaganda by the layman, but a skillful teacher delivers little lectures on the localities that produced various woods. This affords him an opportunity to describe the underpaid workers who felled the trees, the enormous profits made by the mill owners, the exorbitant price of lumber that deprives the common man of adequate housing, etc. So it is with this book, which is another example of the familiar Communist propaganda technique used throughout the world.

The waist drum is a crude Chinese instrument used in ancient folksongs for centuries. The first chapter in this book is called, "The Rhythm of the Waist Drum." The first two paragraphs carry the party line, as follows:

"The sound of the tocsin was the herald of the French Revolution. The rythmic beat of the waist drum is the symbol of victory of the Chinese people.

"As the people's armies advanced from the countryside to liberate the cities, they took with them the militant, courageous, exciting beats of the waist drums. * * *" (P. 8.)

The subsequent chapters are handled in the same manner. In obedience to the directive issued by Mao Tse-tung, the whole ancient culture of China is reoriented to carry the Marxian line, which has thereby been infused throughout the entire cultural life of the country.

VII. *Chinese Literature, Number One, 1956.* This book was published by the Foreign Languages Press at Peking, and does for folk stories precisely what *Folk Arts of New China* does for the waist drum. Each of these ancient tales is given the Marxian twist, also in strict obedience to the mandate of Mao mentioned above.

VIII. *Dragon Beard Ditch, a Play,* by Lao Sheh, Foreign Languages Press, Peking, 1956. This long dramatic work is purely propaganda, characteristically praising the East and damming the West.

IX. *Spring Silkworms and Other Stories,* by Mao Tun, Foreign Languages Press, Peking, 1956. This work contains 13 short stories by Mao Tun, whose real name is Shen Yen-ping, and who has, since 1949, been Communist China's Minister of Culture. It is, then, not strange that one finds that even the spring silkworms have been made to function in a manner compatible with the Marxian way of life. The same is true of all the other 12 tales, except one.

X. *The Sun Shines Over the Sangkau River,* a novel of Chinese land reform, by Ting Ling. Foreign Languages Press, Peking. This is a long, dreary saga of Communist agricultural measures intended to advance China's food production, settle the housing problem, and redistribute land in accordance with the exigencies of the new regime. It is strictly a propaganda work, and in places highly hostile toward the western powers.

XI. *The Hurricane,* a novel of Chinese land reform, by Chou Li-po. Winner of the Stalin Prize, 1951, published by the Foreign Languages Press, Peking, 1955. This novel, like the preceding one, contains precisely the same propaganda and subversive material.

XII. *Chinese Students,* published by the All-China Students Federtion, July, 1955.

> "We want peace. But we will never beg for it at the expense of our territory, for by doing so we should not have peace but encourage aggression. That is why all Chinese students, together with the whole population of China, oppose the occupation of our territory, Taiwan, by the armed forces of the U. S. A. In order to safeguard the sovereignty and territorial integrity, in order to defend the peace of Asia and of the whole world, we are determined to liberate Taiwan." (P. 34.)

XIII. *Changes in Li Village,* by Chao Shu-li. Foreign Language Press, Peking, 1953. This, also, is a novel about Chinese land reform, and, like the others, contains the same type of propaganda.

XIV. *Building a New Life: Stories About China's Construction.* This book, published by the Foreign Languages Press, Peking, 1955, contains articles by a variety of authors. It depicts the Soviet Union as a benevolent power that gently assisted China toward a new way of life, Russian-style, and depicts the United States as a world's rogue-nation, engaged in thwarting all progress, encouraging imperialism, and fomenting World War III with sadistic pleasure.

XV. **The White-haired Girl, An Opera in Five Acts,** by Ho Ching-chih and Ting Yi. Stalin Prize winner, 1951. Foreign Languages Press, Peking. This is a propaganda piece, containing the usual line of praises for the U. S. S. R. and venom for the U. S. A.

XVI. **The Plains Are Ablaze.** A novel of the Communist libera-tion of China, by Hsu Kuang-yao. Foreign Languages Press, Peking, 1955. This book contains the saga of the Chinese Communist Eighth Route Army, also praised in books by the late Agnes Smedley. It is characteristically sprinkled with the same sort of subversive and propa-ganda materials that have been found in the other books discussed above.

XVII. **Registration, and Other Stories.** This book contains pieces by a variety of authors, and was also published by the Foreign Lan-guages Press, Peking, in 1955. It may be described in the same terms as the books listed above.

XVIII. **China, Land of Many Nationalities.** This text, by Wang Shu-tang, describes China's national minority groups, taking advan-tage of the opportunity to direct the familiar type of critical comment against the United States for persecuting the Kao-shan minority on Formosa [Taiwan] and virtually holding them as prisoners. This book, also, was published by the Foreign Languages Press, Peking, 1955.

XIX. **Steeled in Battles.** A play by Hu Ko, a former member of the Communist army. Foreign Languages Press, Peking, 1955. This book contains the same sort of propaganda about the invincibility of the Red Army, and expresses the same sort of contempt for the non-Communist powers as the other volumes described above.

XX. **The Struggle for Red China.** The Foreign Languages Press, Peking, published the second edition of this work in 1953. It is actually a collection of the speeches, statements, and articles of Madame Sun Yat-sen, written under the pseudonym, Soong Ching-ling. The author spent many years studying the world Communist movement in Moscow, is the sister-in-law of Chiang Kai-shek, as has already been stated, and is an extremely influential person throughout the entire Communist world, and especially in Asia. She dedicated the book "To the Korean People's Army and the Chinese People's Volunteers—Valiant Pro-tectors of the People's Cause."

The following statements are typical of those that appear through-out this book:

"In June, 1950, American imperialism launched a war of ag-gression against the democratic People's Republic of Korea. This war presented a serious menace to China's borders and to world peace. The Chinese people started a campaign to resist American aggression, aid Korea, protect their homes and safeguard their country, organizing volunteers to aid Korea on the battlefields. This just action of the Chinese people has struck a heavy blow at the American aggressors and helped powerfully to guarantee the peace of the world.'' (Introduction, p. XIII.)

A particular vicious attack is made against the United States in a chapter headed ''The Difference Between Soviet and American Foreign Policies,'' which originally appeared in *People's China*, Vol. 2, January 16, 1950. The first two paragraphs of this chapter set its entire tone:

> ''Chairman Mao Tse-tung, in his now historic speech of July 1, 1949, pronounced that the New China, the People's Republic of China, would lean to one side in all matters, foreign and domestic. That is the side led by the great Soviet Union under the leadership of the mighty Stalin. That is the side of peace and construction. That is the path joyously followed and ardently studied by the overwhelming masses of the Chinese people.
>
> ''Events in the world have proven, and are every day verifying, that this is the only side to which progressive countries can lean. For there are merely two choices at hand. One is the Soviet Union. The other is represented mainly by the United States, Great Britain and France. As we have contact with these two sides through their foreign policies, we quickly see that they are as different as day is from night. One has all the brightness of day and the warmth of the sun. That is the Soviet Union. The other is as forbidding as a wintry night with all its coldness. That is the imperialist band led by the United States.
>
> ''By comparing these two choices, it is easy to see why in actuality, survival and revival of oppressed nations necessitates leaning to the side of the Soviet Union.'' (Pp. 228-229.)

Madame Sun speaks about the impending economic crash faced by the United States, about the unemployment ''reaching into figures like 6,000,000, with 10,000,000 workers only partially employed,'' (p. 232), and then continues with an angry diatribe, as follows:

> ''The bigger the profits get, the more the people in the United States are suppressed. Civil rights are beaten down and discarded. The police actively show they are mere tools of the vested interests. They protect only the hand that feeds them sop, rather than the people, as was demonstrated in the Peekskill incident. Educational standards are constantly attacked through the intimidation and firing of teachers and professors who object to the fascisization that is taking place. Science is closeted and put under lock and key, the latter in the hands of the financial wizards who control everything else. They do not even allow their imperialist partners to take a peek, as we have seen from the recent breakdown of atomic energy conferences held in Canada between the United States and Great Britain.'' (P. 233.)
>
> ''Thus, our comparison is complete. The imperialist band led by the United States financial groups is a hindering clod in the way of man's progress, both at home and abroad. The Soviet Union, however, lends a helping hand to struggling young nations both within her borders and without, until they can navigate their own way.'' (P. 238.)

Another composition of Madame Sun's first appeared in the *Kwang-ming Daily,* organ of the Democratic League of China, on October 11, 1950. Here are excerpts:

"The United States provides the typical example [of an imperialist regime]. The Wall Street rulers of this country are now engaged in a planned, concerted attack against the popular movement to secure signatures for peace. They mark this vital campaign as a Soviet instrument. What they do not tell their people is that the Soviet Union certainly does not use peace to mobilize the people. Factories, mines and mills over that vast Socialist country are working 'peace shifts' in honor of peace, to forward the concept of peace. On the opposite side, the United States is using war to mobilize its people, to re-arm, to destroy innocent millions, to reduce to rubble whole cities and industries. Since this is such an unpopular road to travel, the American people are being led down it blindfolded, their rulers using every possible camouflage and deceit.

"The plan of the American imperialists is quite obvious. Their Defense and State Departments instigated the aggression in Korea. They provided Wall Street's political arm with the incident that it needed to 'demand preparation for any eventuality. * * *' "
(P. 264.)

The following appears in one of Madame Sun's pieces which is called "Thirty-three Years of Progress":

"When you consider these and the many other victories won by the Soviet Union, how great looms the contributions to mankind by the great October Socialist Revolution and the 33 years of progress! They expose the fact that bourgeois thought is founded in fable, whereas people's states operate only in terms of the welfare of the masses. They finally resolve to the conclusion that capitalism leads to war, whereas Socialism works only for peace.

"Just to make a comparison. Witness the invasion of Korea by the military forces of the United States. Mark its economic penetration of Western Europe and Southwest Asia. Witness the sending of technicians and industrial help from the Soviet Union to the Eastern European democracies and people's Asia. Mark the constant flow of cultural groups and professors from the great Soviet Land to its friends. Compare the decadent economy of the United States and its frantic preparations for war with the blooming life in the Soviet Union and its breath-taking construction of dams, huge irrigation canals, plantings of whole forests, controlling nature at every turn for the benefit of man." (P. 272.)

Under the heading "For Peace in Asia, the Pacific Regions of the World," Madame Sun wrote this:

"Japan, against the expressed will of its people, is being re-militarized by the United States and prepared once again as a base for aggression; crude, ruthless, economic and political pressure is being exerted by the American Government on certain Latin America and Asian countries in an effort to force them into the war camp; American generals continue to pour salt into a nasty wound of their own making, further frustrating the Korean truce talks, stepping up their criminal bombing of the aged, the women and children in Korean cities already reduced to rubble, applying their so-called military pressure by bombing peacetime installations. This is in addition to their already mountain-high list of iniquities, topped off by the most vicious—germ warfare." (P. 391.)

XXI. *Political Report Delivered at the Second Session of the Second National Committee of the Chinese People's Political Consultative Conference, on January 30, 1956.* In this report, Premier Chou En-lai declares that during the period immediately following World War II, "* * * the international forces of peace and the international forces of war have been engaged in acute struggles which progress in a see-saw fashion, and the international forces of peace have increasingly gained the initiative." (P. 4.) Elsewhere in his report, Chou makes it crystal clear that the leader of the forces of peace is the Soviet Union, and that the leader of the forces for war is none other than the United States. Throughout the 48 pages of this report, the Premier continues to excoriate the U. S. and to wax ecstatic about the glorious U. S. S. R.

XXII. *Report on the Work of the Government, Made by Premier Chou En-lai at the First Session of the First National People's Congress of the People's Republic of China, September 23, 1954.* Foreign Languages Press, Peking, 1954. This report, while much the same as the one considered above, contains some choice language that may be well to quote, in view of the high position of the author.

"In June, 1950, the United States Government launched a war of aggression against Korea and at the same time occupied China's province, Taiwan, leaving the Chinese people no alternative but to launch the great movement to resist American aggression and to aid Korea. The victorious struggle waged by the Chinese People's Volunteers and the Korean People's Army compelled the United States in June, 1953, to accept an armistice. Now more than a year has elapsed and the United States Government still refuses to settle the Korean question peacefully.

"Because of the truculent policy of sabotage pursued by the United States Government and the Syngman Rhee clique, the Geneva Conference failed to reach agreement on the peaceful settlement of the Korean question." (*Ibid.*, p. 47.)

Chou En-lai pursues this line throughout the remainder of the report, blandly ignoring the United Nations' verdict about which nation was the aggressor in Korea, and the fact that U. N. troops were the ones that took the field. Chou closes by again reverting to the "liberation of Taiwan" and accusing the United States of trying to start a third world war.

XXIII. *China and the Asian-African Conference.* Foreign Languages Press, Peking, 1955. This book comprises the speeches delivered by Premier Chou En-lai, in the last of which he fires a characteristic propaganda blast at the United States.

XXIV. **Fourteen Booklets** by Mao Tse-tung, 1953-1956. Foreign Languages Press, Peking, 1956. Mao Tse-tung is the chairman of the Communist Party of China. The power he holds is comparable to that exercised by Stalin or any other head of a Communist Party in a government where there is only one political party, and that party operates the government on a totalitarian basis, obtaining obedience through force. These booklets are considered together, because they are all subversive and can also be procured at the Communist Book Store in San Francisco. Mao's writings have been translated into many languages and circulated throughout Asia. His treatise on how the Chinese Communists successfully used guerrilla warfare in their conquest of China is especially popular in India.

XXV. **Daily News Release,** edited and published by the Hsinhua News Agency, March to October, 1955; January to April, 1956. Each issue of these compendia contains a section headed: "U. S. Aggression," under which is listed every news dispatch of a propaganda character from Iron Curtain countries, from India and other countries throughout Asia where the United States is unpopular. These are lumped together each month, and the collected whole is then bound and distributed where it will do the most propaganda harm to us and the most good to the Communist world. Here is an example of propaganda by reiteration: the same themes are hammered home over and over again. Everything that could be possible construed or contorted into an anti-American statement is handled to that end; everything beneficial to the United States is simply omitted. These compilations are voluminous, and nothing could be gained in quoting from them. Each of them is, in my view, subversive to the best interests of the United States.

> Very truly yours,
>
>   R. E. COMBS, Counsel
>   Senate Fact-Finding Committee on
>   Un-American Activities

Since the Geneva Conference there has been a veritable flood of this type of propaganda coming from behind the Iron Curtain, and especially from Red China, and finding its way through our customs service and into the libraries in cities and universities throughout the country. Only constant vigilance on the part of the recipients of this unsolicited material will prevent it from finding its way eventually, unclassified and unnamed as propaganda material, to the libraries and thence accessible directly to the public. The committee believes that this type of material should be designated as propaganda, and it congratulates the board of the San Francisco Public Library, and Mr. Clarke, the librarian, for having been so alert in this instance.

INFILTRATION OF PUBLIC UTILITIES IN CALIFORNIA

Ten years ago, the committee commenced an investigation of subversive infiltration into various public utilities. These concerns, usually characterized by inseparable connection with the public interest, dealing in the sensitive areas of communications, the generation and distribution of electric energy, the production and distribution of natural gas— all provided natural targets that are highly attractive to subversive elements.

A preliminary survey revealed to the committee that all of the utilities had chief special agents who could see that the company rules were carried out, and who could find out who had been stealing company property, but did not have any specially trained personnel for the purpose of preventing subversive infiltration. Consequently, after a more intensive investigation had been completed, the committee found colonies of Communists buried deep in the heart of some of our largest and most sensitive public utilities. After a series of public hearings, resulting in the elimination of many individuals who invoked the Fifth Amendment when asked about their Communist affiliations and activities, the companies employed experts who had F. B. I., military or naval intelligence experience, and handed over to them the task of protecting the utilities against infiltration. In many instances, when employees with long documentable records showing subversive activities were revealed, the individuals were subpenaed before the committee and subjected to detailed interrogation. As we have explained in previous reports, many of these individuals were discharged by their employers after the hearings, and after the witnesses had invoked the Fifth Amendment on questions dealing with their past subversive connections.

This investigation is still continuing. We are glad to report that in every major public utility in California adequate precautions have been taken through the employment of experts for the purpose of thus providing the companies with the means of protecting themselves against subversive agents who are constantly endeavoring to insinuate themselves into positions of strategic importance.

An illustration of how enormously important this matter is now becoming, and the tremendously vital public interest involved, can be seen in the fact that every defense industry in the State of California—and elsewhere, for that matter—which has a defense contract with the United States Government, is required by law to maintain the most scrupulous vigilance to guard itself against this very type of infiltration. Further, these defense industries are required to protect themselves by the installation of adequae physical facilities, such as high wire fences, uniformed guards at all entrances, protection of its presses and electrical facilities and other critical components, so that a continuity of operation can be guaranteed. All of these concerns are enabled to operate because of the electric energy supplied to them by the great public utilities in this State. And yet, until a few years ago, these utilities were almost completely open to infiltration. Disruption of the flow of electric energy into the southern part of this State would immediately put every defense plant out of commission. Despite all of the elaborate precautions required on the part of each individual defense plant, the technicians inside would have to light candles or turn on flashlights in order to grope their way to an electric switch, and when they managed to find it, it would, of course, be dead. Without any lights in the plant, without any electricity to operate the machinery, the flow of critical materials would be as effectively stopped as though the entire facility had been blown up in an explosion. The presence of a subversive agent in a position that would enable him to monitor the long-distance telephone calls between the critical agencies of this Country dealing with our defense effort and discussing other classified information, could be of enormous detriment. In addition, the technicians whose skill enabled them to keep in proper working condition the facilities that would permit such communication and the undisturbed distribution of electric energy, natural gas, and continuous supplies of domestic water, must be men whose loyalty is unquestioned; at least men who have no documentable records of subversive affiliation or activity. In line with the committee's continuing investigation of these highly important matters, it examined two employees of the Southern California Gas Company in Los Angeles, Vincent C. Gribben and Leland R. Waterman.

Mr. Gribben, who appeared before the committee on August 6, 1956, represented by his attorney, Mr. Leo Branton, made a very brief appearance. He testified that he resided at 1817 East 134th Place in Compton, California, had lived there five years, was a crewman and had been employed in that capacity by the gas company for approximately 10 years. He refused to answer any questions concerning his alleged affiliation with the Communist Party and the Communist Political Association and we are reliably informated that he was thereafter discharged by the company.

TESTIMONY OF LELAND R. WATERMAN

Leland R. Waterman testified that he lived at 1336 Sutherland Street, Los Angeles 26, having resided there for approximately 14 months. Prior to that time, he lived at 1600 Lucretia Avenue, Los Angeles 26, was employed by the Southern California Gas Company as an instrument repairman and had been an employee of that concern for approximately 17 years. Mr. Waterman was represented during all stages of the interrogation by his attorney, Mr. A. L. Wirin. The witness readily admitted his own membership in the Communist Party, but steadfastly refused to give any information whatever concerning any one else he might have known in the movement—even by inference. We are informed that Mr. Waterman was also discharged by the Southern California Gas Company immediately following the hearing. His testimony may be summarized below, and will provide the reader with valuable information concerning the extent of infiltration in at least one of the major public utilities in this State. We wish to point out, in all fairness, that this hearing had been preceded by a hearing involving the Pacific Gas and Electric Company in San Francisco several years earlier, and that several individuals with documentable Communist records were also found to be employees of that institution. They also invoked the Fifth Amendment and were discharged by the company. The same situation has been found to exist with the Pacific Telephone and Telegraph Company, and, to some extent, with the Southern California Edison Company.

The fact that the committee devoted a 1956 hearing to employees of the Southern California Gas Company should not be taken to indicate that this is the only public utility with a problem of subversive infiltration, or that this committee is by any means finished with this investigation of the subject.

Waterman testified that he joined the Communist Party in about 1943. At that time, he was working in the compressor station of the gas company—attending to equipment that supplemented the delivery of gas at times when the load was unusually heavy. He did not go to the party headquarters on his own volition, but had been actively solicited for membership; (recruited), to use the party parlance. He attended a couple of meetings while living in Alhambra and went to beginners classes at the Workers School in downtown Los Angeles. These classes were held once a week for about 10 weeks and involved not only lecturers but the study of an official textbook known as *An Official History of the Communist Party of the Soviet Union.* Waterman said there were about 10 other beginners in his Workers School class.

Having completed this course of study, Waterman was regularly received as a Communist. He paid regular dues, attended party meetings once a month in the homes of other party members who belonged to his unit. He took little active part in these Alhambra meetings, however, regarding himself as a novice who was more interested in observing than participating actively in these early meetings.

When Waterman moved from Alhambra, "* * * We set up a new club, an industrial club or a trade union club, or something like that." This, as is made clear in previous reports, was a customary Communist practice. If several party members belonged to the same trade union or worked for the same concern, they were organized into a separate club or unit because of their mutuality of interests. Thus, the inevitable responsibilities of recruiting new members, strengthening the influence of the Communist unit in the non-Communist union or management organization, and of expounding the current party line, could best be handled.

This witness was adamant in his refusal to name others whom he knew as Communists and even declined to knowingly give any information concerning the size of this new industrial portrayed union unit. In this connection, his testimony was as follows:

"* * * I think when I moved into Alhambra, or moved from Alhambra, rather, that we set up a new club, an industrial club or a trade union club, or something like that.

"Q. In Los Angeles?

"A. Yes.

"Q. It was with them that you were affiliated?

"A. (Witness nodding head.)

"Q. Did you ever hold any office in it?

"A. This was a very, very small organization or club.

"Q. How many people?

"A. I think this narrows down the area again.

"Q. You have volunteered the fact that it was a small club and I am merely following your own response, Mr. Waterman. How small?

"A. I think the exact number is a question that is one I would decline to answer. It was just small.

"Q. You decline for the reasons heretofore given?·

"A. Yes, sir. We weren't able to function on the basis of regularly elected officers and to keep those officers for a period of time.

"Q. How many officers would you normally have had if the club had comprised 50? How many officers would you have had?

"A. I don't recall at the moment.

"Q. A chairman, or something similar to a chairman?

"A. Probably a chairman.

"Q. A secretary to take minutes?

"A. Probably.

"Q. A person to collect dues, a financial secretary?

"A. Probably.

"Q. An educational secretary?

"A. Yes, something like that with that function.

"Q. That would be one, two, three, four. You would have about five officers normally, would you not?

"A. I believe in a club of the size of 50, there would be five or six officers.

"Q. Yes, five or six. So you did not have more than five or six in this club, did you? If you did not have enough to elect any officers and the normal number was five or six officers, then you did not have more than five or six, obviously. Now, did the membership of that club comprise persons who were employed by the Southern California Gas Company as you were?

"A. This is a form of identification, Mr. Combs, therefore, I decline to answer."

It should be made clear here, that among the other grounds invoked by this witness for his refusal to answer questions about persons other than himself and the Communist Party was the Fifth Amendment which provides that a witness cannot be compelled, in a criminal proceeding, to give testimony that might tend to incriminate him. Chairman Burns uniformly ruled that the ground was not sufficient, and instructed the witness to answer these questions in every instance.

It would appear to the layman that five or six Communists in a union or management of an organization of several thousand would be insignificant. Yet statistics show that very frequently several of such cells or units are operating simultaneously, and that there are at least 10 fellow travelers or sympathizers who are more or less amenable to party discipline for every actual Communist member. Furthermore, it is not the numerical strength of a subversive unit in a large non-Communist organization which is important, but rather the quality of the membership of that unit, the degree of discipline under which they work, and the strategic positions which they occupy. At the time of the revolution that overthrew the Czarist regime in Russia in 1917, the entire upheaval was accomplished at a time when there were only 11,000 Communist Party members in all of Russia. A Communist-controlled group of 60 would be a formidable force, indeed, with their specialized training in propaganda, strike strategies, and parliamentary procedure; with their complete obedience to discipline and their conviction that any methods must be used to further their objectives—such a relatively small force can exert an enormous influence. We have described in other reports the exact processes by which tiny, compact Communist cells have managed to dominate entire unions, and through them exert constant pressure on the employer organizations.

The new unit, explained Waterman, met on an average of once a month, mostly in his home. Bearing out the not unnatural assumption that the members comprised his fellow workers, he was asked:

"Q. * * * How would you communicate the information that there was going to be a meeting to the other members of the club?

"A. By telephone or contact.

"Q. By personal contact?

"A. Personal.

"Q. Was it difficult for you to make personal contact and advise them of the fact that there was going to be a meeting?

"A. Not too.

"Q. Who presided at the meetings in your home? Well, I will withdraw that. Let me reframe it this way: did you preside at the meetings in your home?

"A. Sometimes.

"Q. Did you do that pursuant to the consent of the people who were the other members of the club there? Were you elected in any way, or did you simply do it by a sort of tacit consent?

"A. As I said before, our club was so small as to make regular officers difficult, so that there was no steady, recurrent repeating. Someone would be chairman for an evening and someone would be by tacit agreement, as you say, assigned to make a certain report or something like that, so there was no steady functioning officership.

"Q. Did you procure party literature to be disseminated at these meetings?

"A. I believe that party literature was available at these meetings. I don't recall procuring it myself.

"Q. Did you get any of it yourself?

"A. How do you mean did I get any of it myself?

"Q. Did you ever get the literature and take it to your home so that it would be available at the time you had the meetings?

"A. I don't recall that I did.

"Q. Do you know whether or not there was a Communist book store in Los Angeles at that time?

"A. A Communist book store?

"Q. * * * Did you ever hear of a book store in Los Angeles known as The Progressive Book Store?

"A. Yes, I have heard of that.

"Q. Where was that located? Was it on West Seventh Street?

"A. I believe so.

"Q. Did you ever go to that store?

"A. As an individual, yes, sir.

"Q. That is what I mean.

"A. Oh, yes. Yes, sir.

"Q. For the purpose of getting party literature, I presume?

"A. And also children's records.

"Q. Yes, but you also got party literature, did you not?

"A. My answer to that question earlier was a truthful one. I don't recall that I ever went to this place and got party literature for any club or organization.

"Q. No. I mean for any purpose, Mr. Waterman.

"A. I bought various pieces of literature and Red material some of which I am sure—let's say it was this way, some of which could by no remote stretch of the imagination be considered Communistic. I bought a book there, *The Rennaissance of American Poetry*, as well as other literature which certainly has been identified as Communist Party literature, yes.

"Q. You did get Communist Party literature at that store, did you, from time to time?

"A. This literature was available to anyone.

"Q. That was not the question. The question was whether or not *you* got party literature at that store.

"A. I am having trouble identifying literature.

"Q. I will be glad to identify it for you.

"A. Fine.

"Q. Did you ever get a copy of the *Daily Worker* there? Let me go on: *Political Affairs*, the *Monthly Communist*, the *New Times*, the *Daily People's World*—did you ever get any of that material, or a copy of the *Communist Manifesto* or any of the works of Engels, Lenin, or Marx?

"A. I believe I have purchased some of the literature you describe there."

Waterman made it amply clear that he was not disillusioned with the Communist Party or the Communist movement at the time he ceased being an active member. As he put it: "Disillusioned with the Communist Party? I can't honestly say that I was disillusioned because of anything that had happened to me, or that I didn't believe at that time in the same things that I had believed in earlier."

The party tried to reactivate him for a period of six months—but he testified that he nevertheless ceased all active participation with the movement and has not been a member of the Communist Party since about December, 1951, or during the early part of 1952.

When questioned about whether he attended Communist meetings elsewhere than in Alhambra and Los Angeles, Waterman again, perhaps unconsciously, linked such meetings with his union activity.

"Q. * * * Mr. Waterman, did you ever attend any Communist meetings during the period of your membership at any locals other than Alhambra and Los Angeles?

"A. I don't believe so.

"Q. Are you quite certain?

"A. Well, I was very active in the union and it occurs to me that in moving about I occasionally made trips to San Francisco, Fresno and such places, but I don't believe I ever attended a Communist meeting per se in this movement."

Waterman's testimony concerning the union to which he belonged and his activities in it, is illuminating. He said:

"Q. What is the union that you belonged to and were active in?

"A. The Utility Workers of America, CIO.

"Q. What is the local?

"A. 132.

"Q. Was that local comprised of employees of the gas company?

"A. Central Division, Los Angeles, sir.

"Q. Did you ever hold office in the local?

"A. Yes, sir.

"Q. About what date and what were they?

"A. Within three months of my joining the union or approximately three months of my joining the union, I was elected president.

"Q. Three months after you joined?

"A. Yes, sir.

"Q. How long did you continue in that office?

"A. To the best of my recollection, I was elected president by referendum ballot for two terms.

"Q. Would that be two years?

"A. Yes, I believe so. Now it is possible I was in my third term or in the second term, I don't recall, when delegates to a council which was formed to coordinate the efforts of local unions throughout the gas company—the council was formed and I was elected. I wasn't the first secretary-treasurer of it, I believe I was elected either the second or third secretary-treasurer of that council for a period of somewhere in the neighborhood of two years and served as a member of the negotiating team. But that was not an automatic function of my office, I don't believe.

"Q. The negotiating team that dealt with the employer?

"A. They met with management representing the union, yes, sir.

"Q. I see.

"A. I also held the office of vice-president in the local union when I was secretary of the council, I believe.

"Q. Now, please tell us, if you will, which offices of those you have mentioned you held in the union at the time when you were also a member of the Communist Party?

"A. All of them.

"Q. Did you ever hear the term 'Communist fraction' used?

"A. Yes, I have heard the term used.

"Q. What did it signify to you during the period of your membership as a Communist?

"A. A small group of, let us say, a Communist fraction, as I recall it, a small group of Communists within an organization.

"Q. Within a non-Communist organization?

"A. Yes, otherwise.

"Q. It would not be a fraction otherwise?

"A. Otherwise it would not be called a fraction—a small group of Communists in an organization who met as Communists and put forward or urged the adoption of policies that they had formulated in fraction meetings.

"Q. In other words, a fraction would be a small group of Communists who would meet privately for the purpose of formulating activities to be put into operation within the framework of a large non-Communist organization in which they worked?

"A. Well, without knowing the detail as to the type of activities, yes, I think that is it."

During Mr. Waterman's testimony it became quite evident to the committee that he was never disillusioned with Communism, quite aside from the statement he made to that effect. He continued to subscribe to the Communist newspaper and was receiving it at his residence even at the time he was appearing before the committee. His rapid rise in the trade union to which he was affiliated and his position of authority —not only in the union but also in the Communist Party—amply illustrated his capacity for leadership. When he moved from Alhambra to Los Angeles he became affiliated with a Communist industrial unit, and the committee feels quite justified in drawing the inevitable conclusion from his testimony that the Communist meetings were held in his residence in Los Angeles, that he presided at most of them, that he procured Communist literature at the Progressive Book Store on W. Seventh Street, that he informed the other members of the time and place of the Communist meetings, and that his activity in union matters was contemporaneous with a similar or greater degree of devoted activity in the Communist Party.

Waterman's steadfast refusal to mention the names of persons he had known to be Communist Party members is an indication of the fact that he could be hardly disillusioned with the party. On the one hand, he stated unequivocally that he had broken with the movement and ceased all activities in it, and on the other hand, he was extraordinarily careful to avoid giving the committee the benefit of his obvious knowledge about the infiltration in one of the State's most critical public utilities, and to avoid mentioning any other party members besides himself. This is hardly an indication of disillusionment, but on the other hand, is an eloquent and emphatic indication that he was still loyal to his former comrades and to the Communist Party itself.

LOS ANGELES CITY SCHOOL SYSTEM

In 1952, the committee investigated alleged infiltration of the Los Angeles City Housing Authority. Among the other witnesses who were questioned were Frances Eisenberg and Jean Wilkinson, who were interrogated in connection with their own Communist affiliations and activities. Mrs. Eisenberg was for many years editor of the paper published by Local 430 of the Los Angeles Federation of Teachers and at the same time was a member of the board of directors of the Communist school and a teacher in the Los Angeles City School System. Mrs. Wilkinson was the wife of Frank Wilkinson, housing authority employee, and herself was an employee of the Los Angeles City School System. An analysis of the testimony given by these two witnesses together with other facts developed at the housing authority hearing tended to indicate that the Communist unit or club that comprised members of the authority also included some teachers. The committee had questioned Mrs. Eisenberg on other occasions, and had voluminous evidence which indicated the Communist nature of the union with which she was affiliated.

Following these leads, the committee quietly commenced a preliminary investigation of the infiltration of the Los Angeles City School System and soon discovered that there was, indeed, a serious problem, although the committee at that time had no information as to the depth of the penetration.

BOARD OF EDUCATION COOPERATES WITH COMMITTEE

After preliminary conferences were held with Mr. William B. Brown, Associate Superintendent in charge of personnel, and with Dr. Alexander Stoddard, Superintendent, the matter was presented to a full meeting of the Los Angeles City Board of Education on November 24, 1952. At this meeting, the committee pointed out the necessity of determining how far the infiltration had gone and of ascertaining the number of employees—both teaching and administrative—who had documentable records of serious subversive connections. The committee, accordingly, agreed to make a survey of approximately 28,000 employees of the city school system. The examination of this personnel was undertaken on December 2, 1952, and was completed on April 9, 1953.

It was realized, of course, that the academic atmosphere is peculiarly sensitive in this field of activity and that the survey which the committee undertook should be conducted unobtrusively and with scrupulous care to protect the civil rights and reputations of all concerned. To insure against an even unconscious prejudice in the process of checking these names against the committee files, we preferred to receive lists of names only; that is, without any designation of race, color, religion, nature of occupation, or even street addresses. A person in a high-salaried position with a Ph.D. degree and a residence in

Beverly Hills would immediately suggest a background of affluence and prestige, whereas a low-salaried employee who had no academic degrees, worked at trimming shrubs and lived in a less affluent neighborhood, would, of course, carry a different implication. This meant a great deal of extra work on the part of the committee, because if a common name, like James Smith, was submitted, it had to be checked against the records of every person with the same name who resided in Southern California. And in a continuous activity of some 18 years, the committee's files would ordinarily have several persons with the same common name. This meant that each individual file had to be carefully checked and all of the records included and again checked against other criteria for the purpose of identifying the individual who was, in fact, employed by the Los Angeles City School System.

The 28,000 names included all members of the Board of Education and all top administrators. After the checking had been completed, on April 9, 1953, the committee found that there was a total of 1,759 individuals who had some sort of a subversive, documentable record. To a professional educator with little experience in the counter-subversive field, this number seemed gigantic. But this was only the starting point; and in checking the files that were available to the committee (in addition to its own accumulated records) every instance of subversive affiliation or activity, however slight, was included.

EVALUATION TECHNIQUES

We must constantly bear in mind that whereas anyone with a modicum of experience can perform the mechanical function of checking records and assembling facts, an expert is required to properly evaluate the information. This is where the element of responsibility looms large, and the expert must be thoroughly versed in the history and ideology of all the subversive organizations; he must—above all—know the history, purposes and general operation of the so-called front organizations. This knowledge is indispensable since one front group may be relatively innocuous while another is virulently subversive. Furthermore, this function of evaluating personnel records should never be done by anyone who is not completely objective. He must be constantly mindful of the rights and reputations of the persons involved. Of course, these highly desirable qualities should be prerequisite in all persons who hold official positions in the counter-subversive field. It is no place for bigots, racists, reactionaries, or those who may occasionally be carried away by the cloak and dagger aspects of their work. Neither is it any place for ultra liberals, self-appointed guardians of civil liberties, or professional do-gooders.

We cannot emphasize too strongly the need to balance the public security from subversion against the rights of the individual. This requires a delicacy of balance and a solidity of perspective that can be gained only with experience, but which should be an absolute requirement in every person who assumes the grave responsibility of working in an official capacity that involves the evaluation of subversive records. It is, obviously, of paramount necessity to expose the real subversives, and to keep the Legislature constantly informed as to the extent of subversive infiltration into all phases of public life and into all of the complex operations of our State. It is also essential that this be done without making irresponsible accusations or smearing sincere liberals who may have been duped into a brief association on the fringes of a front organization.

Some front organizations are so riddled with subversive members that they are almost integral components of the Communist Party itself; others are relatively innocent. All are ingeniously designed to attract the unwary. Thus, because a person unwittingly has been affiliated with such an organization for a short period does not mean that he is necessarily indoctrinated. On the contrary, he may be more thoroughly opposed to that sort of group because he was duped, and therefore should not be summarily condemned merely by reason of the fact that he was briefly associated with such an organization. But we also find that experience in only one of the more virulent fronts very often is the medium through which a person graduates directly into the Communist Party. Since the facts and circumstances differ widely in each case, each case must be examined on its own merits before any accurate and objective conclusion can possibly be reached.

In analyzing the case histories of the 1,759 individuals originally checked, it was found that the majority of them comprised people who had a very brief association with a group of relatively innocuous fronts. Still another category comprised individuals who commenced their association with some innocuous front organization and then joined another and another until they had been affiliated with a half a dozen or more on an ascending scale of virulence and also on an ascending scale of activity. Such individuals almost invariably started as rank and file members of a front organization and soon were found enthusiastically attending a great variety of meetings and a great variety of front organizations, acting as speakers, sponsors, participants in picket line activities, spreading propaganda, and participating in drives to raise funds. Eventually, these individuals were elected to offical positions in one or more of these organizations, and in most instances their activities were continuous from the time of the first association with a front organization until the time the name was checked several years thereafter.

Another category comprised individuals who, in 1932 and in 1934, signed petitions circulated by the Communist Party for the purpose of qualifying itself for participation in the state primary elections. Almost invariably these petitions were circulated by Communist Party members who were, of course, strictly subject to party discipline. The individuals whose signatures appear on these petitions are not necessarily subversive merely because of the fact that they were persuaded to sign. On the contrary, this category of individual must be viewed against the sociological and economic conditions of that time—and the overwhelming majority of them were simply duped into signing the petitions by clever propagandists. It is, also, a well known fact that the average individual can be persuaded to sign almost any kind of petition, even without reading its contents. On the other hand, we should constantly have before us a knowledge of the real purpose for which the Communist Party circulated these petitions. It was not for the purpose of qualifying itself to participate in the primary election, but rather to get the names and addresses of the thousands of individuals who could be persuaded to sign such documents for the purpose of providing the Communist Party with thousands of individuals who might be susceptible to recruitment for the Communist Party itself. Thus, the records show that many of the people who are now party members were first attracted to the movement by the signing of one of these petitions, then by becoming affiliated with a front organization, until finally the seeds of propaganda had been sufficiently planted to swing the individual directly into party activity.

COMMUNIST PRESSURE TECHNIQUES

Investigating Communist infiltration of the Los Angeles City School System inevitably led the committee to an examination of the role played in that maneuver by the Los Angeles Federation of Teachers Local 430. This organization was expelled by the American Federation of Labor in September, 1948, because it was found to be Communist dominated. Beginning in 1952 the committee summoned many teachers who cooperated in giving the committee the benefit of their information concerning this union. It was learned that the union acted as a spearhead for pressure tactics employed by the Communist fraction of the teaching employees in every instance where it was necessary to negotiate with the Los Angeles City Board of Education. During all of the years from 1936, until 1948, when its charter was lifted, this local of the Los Angeles Federation of Teachers was constantly agitating, sending pressure groups to public meetings, propagandizing, operating picket lines, and otherwise performing a long series of disruptive activities calculated to further the Communist Party line and to intensify the class struggle.

This committee, as well as the Senate Committee on Education, had long been casting a suspicious eye in the direction of Local 430; when we started to check the names of all of the 28,000 employees of the Los Angeles City Board of Education, the testimony we had theretofore received from those teachers who had cooperated in relating their brief experiences in this Communist-saturated local, was complete corroborated. After 1948, the chapter had no connection with the American Federation of Labor from which it was expelled, but continued its disruptive and arrogant tactics as an independent organization. After the checking of all of the Board of Education employees, and the dismissal of the hard core of known agitators, the activities of the union decreased as we will explain more fully hereafter.

In addition to the tactics employed by Local 430 of the Los Angeles Federation of Teachers, the Board of Education was also harassed constantly by the dissemination of propaganda and by familiar pressure tactics from a compact, hard-hitting group of defiant teachers. After the record check was completed by this committee on April 9, 1953, and the same had been thoroughly analyzed and evaluated, it was found without question that all of the chronic agitators had impressive records of affiliation with Communist organizations.

QUALIFICATIONS OF TEACHERS

No question is raised about the propriety of boards of education examining the fitness of prospective teachers, or those currently employed, for that matter, to determine whether or not these employees have been guilty of committing criminal offenses or addicted to the use of narcotics, or sexual deviates. There seems to be complete unanimity of opinion to the effect that it is not only the right, but most assuredly a paramount duty of boards of education to make sure that prospective employees have no such records before they are placed in contact with large groups of impressionable students. This is one of the reasons the board of education exists.

No parent in his right mind would want to have his son or daughter instructed by a sex deviate, a narcotic addict, or a person with a serious criminal record. This is a normal process of determining whether or not given individuals are fit employees for teachers or administrators of an educational system. But when it comes to determining fitness to teach based on whether or not an individual has been a member of an organization that advocates the unlawful overthrow of the Government of the United States or of a front organization controlled by such a subversive group, immediately a cry of outrage is heard from an array of organizations that are self-appointed to act as guardians of the public morals and custodians of civil rights. These highly articulate organizations are silent about investigating criminal records, records of narcotic addiction or records of sexual deviation; but in spite of the fact that there is an avalanche of cold, documented evidence showing that the leadership of the Communist Party is recruited from students on all levels, and that the seeds of poisonous propaganda are sown indiscriminately in grade schools, high schools and universities, and that the parents and the public have a right that their children shall be protected from the propaganda of subversive groups as well as from criminals, sex deviates and drug addicts, a wave of protest gushes from these highly articulate left groups who protest that the civil rights of individuals with records of subversive activity are in some fashion being violated when such a check is made.

After the compendium of background information concerning the 1,759 individuals had been completed, it was taken to Los Angeles by representatives of the committee and several weeks were spent in tediously studying other criteria for the purpose of making certain that the individuals whose records have been compiled were identical with the employees by the same name who were then working for the Los Angeles City Board of Education. The next step in the process consisted of a careful evaluation of each individual record, in order that the Legislature, through its committee, could be fully informed concerning the extent of the infiltration, its effect on the school system as a whole, the various categories of subversive documentation that were considered, and whether or not remedial legislation was required for the purpose of correcting the situation and preventing its continuance.

It was determined that rather than have the committee issue subpenas for the individuals deemed to be detrimental to the interests of the school system by reason of the heavy documented subversive records, it would be better to enact suitable legislation for the purpose of allowing the board of education to handle its own problems. This was done because, realizing the peculiarly sensitive nature of an educational system, the committee wished to avoid any unnecessary disruption of morale and desired to have as few hearings on the matter as possible, and at the same time to make certain that the condition was handled properly and courageously.

After a series of conferences between the Los Angeles County Counsel, representatives of the Los Angeles City Board of Education, this committee, and the Senate Committee on Education, the so-called Dilworth Act was passed at the 1953 Regular Session of the Legislature, and amended during the Regular Session of 1955.

THE DILWORTH ACT

The preliminary portions of this legislation are the result of years of experience and investigation of subversive activities on the part of many officials and public agencies, and since the philosophy of public resistance to Communist infiltration of its school systems and other public institutions is well expressed in the first portion of this law, the committee deems it well to set forth the pertinent portions of the same, as follows:

"The Legislature of the State of California finds that:

"(a) There exists a world-wide revolutionary movement to establish a totalitarian dictatorship based upon force and power rather than upon law.

"(b) This world-wide revolutionary movement is predicated upon and it is designed and intended to carry into execution the basic precepts of Communism as expounded by Marx, Lenin, and Stalin.

"(c) Pursuant to the objectives of the world Communist movement, in numerous foreign countries the legally constituted governments have been overthrown and the totalitarian dictatorships established therein against the will of the people, and the establishment of similar dictatorships in other countries is imminently threatening. The successful establishment of totalitarian dictatorships has consistently been aided, accompanied, or accomplished by repeated acts of treachery, deceit, teaching of false doctrines, teaching untruths, together with organization confusion, insubordination, and disloyalty, fostered, directed, instigated, or employed by the Communist organizations and their members in such countries.

"(d) Within the boundaries of the State of California there are active disciplined Communist organizations presently functioning for the primary purpose of advancing the objectives of the world Communist movement, which organizations promulgate, advocate, and adhere to the precepts and the principles and doctrines of the world Communist movement. These Communist organizations are characterized by identification of their programs, policies, and objectives with those of the world Communism [sic] movement, and they regularly and consistently cooperate with and endeavor to carry into execution programs, policies, and objectives substantially identical to programs, policies, and objectives of such world Communism [sic] movement.

"(e) One of the objectives of the world Communism [sic] movement is to place its members in local government positions and in the public school system. If this objective is successful, propaganda can be disseminated by the members of these organizations among public school pupils by those members who would have the opportunity to teach them and to whom, as teachers, they would look for guidance, authority, and leadership. The members of such groups would use their positions to advocate and teach their doctrines and teach the prescribed Communist Party line group dogma or doctrine without regard to truth or free inquiry. This type of propaganda is sufficiently subtle to escape detection in the classroom.

"There is a clear and present danger, which the Legislature of the State of California finds is great and imminent, that in order to advance the program, policies and objectives of the world Communism [sic] movement, Communist organizations in the State of California and their members will engage in concerted efforts to hamper, restrict, interfere with, impede, or nullify the efforts of the governing boards of school districts to comply with and enforce Section 8275 of the Education Code of the State of California which prohibits the advocacy or teaching of Communism with the intent to indoctrinate any pupil with or inculcate a preference in the mind of any pupil for Communism for the purpose of undermining the patriotism for and the belief in the Government of the United States and of the State of California in the minds of the pupils of the Public School System.

"The Legislature specifically finds that the requirement that all persons (certificated or noncertificated) now employed by the school districts of this State, or hereafter making application for employment by any of such districts, shall declare under oath that they are not knowingly members of the Communist Party, is a reasonable measure to meet the clear and present danger hereinabove found.

"The Legislature further specifically finds that an indirect or evasive answer to a question relating to any of the matters specified in Section 12604 or 12605, or an answer which neither affirms nor denies shall, for the purposes of this act and chapter, be considered as a failure and refusal to answer, regardless of the ground or explanation given for any such answer.

"12601. No person who is knowingly a member of the Communist Party shall hereafter be employed by, or, except as provided in Section 12602, retained in the employment of, any school district. Prior to the first day of service as an employee of any school district, the applicant shall state under oath whether or not he is knowingly a member of the Communist Party. If the applicant states that he is knowingly a member of the Communist Party, he shall not become an employee of any school district.

"12602. Any employee of any school district who is now or since October 3, 1945, was knowingly a member of the Communist

Party, and who has not previously filed the statement required by this section, shall within ninety (90) days of the effective date of the amendment of this section file with the governing board of the school district employing him a verified statement that he is no longer a member of the Communist Party and that such membership has been terminated in good faith. Any such employee who fails to file such a statement within the time specified shall be guilty of insubordination and guilty of violating this section and shall be suspended and dismissed from his employment in the manner provided by law.

"12603. Any employee of any school district who hereafter knowingly becomes a member of the Communist Party shall be guilty of insubordination and guilty of violating this section and shall be suspended and dismissed from his employment in the manner provided by law.

"12604. It shall be the duty of any employee of any school district who may be subpenaed by a United States Congressional Un-American Activities Committee or a subcommittee thereof or a California Legislative Un-American Activities Committee or a subcommittee thereof or any other committee or subcommittee of the United States Congress or the California Legislature or of either house of either thereof to appear before said committee or subcommittee and specifically to answer under oath a question or questions propounded by any member or counsel of the committee or subcommittee relating to:

"(a) Present personal advocacy by the employee of the forceful or violent overthrow of the Government of the United States or of any state or political subdivision.

"(b) Present knowing membership in any organization which, to the knowledge of such employee, advocates the forceful or violent overthrow of the Government of the United States or of any state or political subdivision.

"(c) Past knowing membership at any time since October 3, 1945, in any organization which, to the knowledge of such employee, during the time of the employee's membership advocated the forceful or violent overthrow of the Government of the United States or of any state or political subdivision.

"(d) Past knowing membership of such employee in the Communist Party at any time since October 3, 1945.

"(e) Present knowing membership of such employee in the Communist Party.

"(f) Present personal advocacy by the employee of the support of a foreign government against the United States in the event of hostilities.

"Any employee who fails or refuses to answer under oath on any ground whatsoever any such question propounded by any member or counsel of any such committee or subcommittee shall be guilty of insubordination and guilty of violating this section and shall be suspended and dismissed from his employment in the manner provided by law.

"12605. It shall be the duty of any employee of any school district who is ordered to appear before the governing board of the employing school district to appear and specifically to answer under oath a question or questions propounded by a member or counsel of the governing board or by the superintendent of schools relating to any of the matters specified in Section 12604.

"Any employee who fails or refuses to appear or to answer under oath on any ground whatsoever any such question propounded by a member or counsel of the governing board or by the superintendent of schools shall be guilty of insubordination and guilty of violating this section and shall be suspended and dismissed from his employment in the manner provided by law.

"12606. It shall be sufficient cause for the suspension and dismissal, in the manner provided by law, of any employee of a school district when such employee is knowingly a member of the Communist Party.

"12607. Any certificated employee of a school district who violates any of the provisions of Sections 12601 to 12606, inclusive, of this code shall be guilty of unprofessional conduct and shall be suspended and dismissed in the manner provided by law."

The balance of this law specifies that upon the filing of a written statement charging an employee with violating any of its provisions, he may be suspended from his duties. After the elapse of 30 days following service of notice upon him of such suspension, the employee may be permanently dismissed unless he demands a hearing.

If the charges allege affiliation with the Communist Party or a refusal to answer pertinent questions concerning such affiliation within the period provided by law, the employee may, within 10 days after receiving the suspension notice, file a denial of the charges against him. The superior court then shall determine whether or not the employee may be discharged, and, pending such adjudication, the employee continues to receive his regular salary. He must, however, post an adequate bond guaranteeing refund of the salary in case the court decides against him.

Under these provisions, it will be noticed, there is no summary dismissal or suspension merely because an employee invokes the Fifth Amendment when questioned about his subversive past. On the contrary, he is afforded every legal protection—even the continued payment of his salary, but he is not permitted to continue his contact with students. Furthermore, these provisions relating to subversive affiliation are treated as they should be and are considered with other prerequisites relating to one's fitness to hold a position in our educational system.

When the first few employees were given notices of dismissal under the provisions of this act, they took the necessary steps to test the constitutionality of the law by appealing the uniformly adverse decisions handed down by the superior courts to the Supreme Court of the State. In every instance, the constitutionality of the law was upheld and the dismissals became final. After these first test cases had been disposed of, several other discharged employees began to invoke the legal machinery provided for their protection, but abandoned the appeals instead of pursuing them to their final conclusion. Thus far, all cases under the act wherein employees have elected to take their cases to the courts, have been decided in favor of the board of education.

RESULT OF PREVENTIVE MEASURES

Each of the 1,759 cases mentioned above was discussed in detail with members of the Personnel Division of the Los Angeles City School System. Thereafter, as the result of further consultations, the "Dilworth Law" was enacted, and the Board of Education then established the necessary machinery to rid itself of its subversive employees and to prevent further infiltration.

We have followed this program with intense interest, not only because the Los Angeles City School System is the second largest in the United States, but also because it has demonstrated beyond question that such a system can handle its own problem of infiltration by securing expert advice; by avoiding any semblance of irresponsible charges or sensationalism; by resorting to documentary evidence and sworn testimony in evaluating an employee's background; by giving all accused employees full opportunity to present defenses and explanations; in short, to scrupulously balance the interest of the public against the rights of the individual.

In undertaking the personnel survey in 1952, we made an extensive analysis of the techniques used by the Communist apparatus in Los Angeles to accomplish its infiltration of the public schools. For this purpose we received reliable reports from informants—teachers who had been Communists, and from other confidential and completely reliable sources.

We have since maintained a continuous check on the incidence of employees with records of subversive activities and affiliations, and we are glad to report that the incidence has steadily diminished since the Board of Education's preventive plans was developed.

We cannot say that the Los Angeles City Schools are antiseptic so far as subversive employees are concerned, but we can almost go that far. From the same confirmed sources mentioned above we have learned that the Communist Party is warning its teacher members to stay out of the Los Angeles City School System, because they will probably be exposed and forced to leave in case they succeed in obtaining employment.

We have no doubt that individuals under party discipline are still employed in the Los Angeles City Schools. Members of the "sleeper group" described earlier are doubtless still employed, but the continual vigilance of the administration has forced them to coast along in neutral gear, thereby rendering them relatively impotent.

About three hundred employees have been discharged or have resigned from the Los Angeles City School System for loyalty reasons. There are no more defiant demonstrations, no more Communist front pressure groups, no left-wing union demands and no party propaganda. The morale of the school system has not been disrupted in the slightest degree and, indeed, the school administrators tell us that an atmosphere of refreshing calm has prevailed since the subversive group has been eliminated.

We congratulate the Los Angeles City Board of Education for its diligence and fairness in handling this problem. The demonstrable success with which it has conducted this program provides a striking example of the necessity for handling subversive infiltration in the educational field with a minimum of public hearings, a maximum of sound and expert administration and with the complete cooperation between the educational institutions and official agencies that has uniformly existed between the Los Angeles City Board of Education and this committee.

INDEX

University of—Continued
  Columbia, 93
  Hamline, 16
  Minnesota, 9, 16
  Missouri, 132
  Peking, 129
  Rennes, 89
  Stanford, 3, 6, 129, 133
  Syracuse, 16
  Vienna, 89
  Washington, 8, 9, 10, 11, 12
Untermeyer, Frank, 59

V

Villion, 96
Voroshilov, 84

W

Wadsworth, Officer, 49
Wang Shu-tang, 136
Waterman, Leland R., 142-148
Weiss, Max, 80, 93, 121
Wei Ta-wei, 132
Westwood Hills Press, 28
Whang, Lola, 3, 21, 30
What I Saw Inside Red China, 126
White Case, 80
White Citizens Councils, 114, 120
White-haired Girl—An Opera in Five Acts, 136
White, Walter, 112, 121

Wilkerson, Officer, 44
Wilkins, Roy, 108, 118, 121
Wilkinson, Jean, 149
Wilkinson, Frank, 149
Williams, Franklin, 109, 110, 112, 113, 116-125
Wirin, A. L., 35, 142
Woltman, Frederick, 121
Women of China, 133
Workers Defense Guard, 87
Workers Party, 62, 92
Workers School, 143

Y

Young Communist League, 2, 21, 100
Young Democrats, 124
Y. M. C. A., 23, 71
Young Progressives of America, 30
Y. P. S. L., 47, 70, 76, 95
Young Republicans, 124
Young Socialist League, 7, 30, 31, 47, 65, 66, 67, 68, 69, 70, 71, 72, 73, 75, 76, 83, 88, 92, 95, 96, 98, 99, 101, 103, 104
Youth, The, 78
Y. W. C. A., 99

Z

Zenoviev, Gregory, 30, 85, 91

o

www.ingramcontent.com/pod-product-compliance
Lightning Source LLC
Chambersburg PA
CBHW071153050326
40689CB00011B/2100